Learn Java Fundamentals

A Primer for Java Development and Programming

Jeff Friesen

Apress®

Learn Java Fundamentals: A Primer for Java Development and Programming

Jeff Friesen
Dauphin, MB, Canada

ISBN-13 (pbk): 979-8-8688-0350-5
https://doi.org/10.1007/979-8-8688-0351-2

ISBN-13 (electronic): 979-8-8688-0351-2

Managing Director, Apress Media LLC: Welmoed Spahr
Acquisitions Editor: James Robinson-Prior
Development Editor: James Markham
Coordinating Editor: Gryffin Winkler

Cover designed by eStudioCalamar

Photo by pariwat pannium on Unsplash

Distributed to the book trade worldwide by Apress Media, LLC, 1 New York Plaza, New York, NY 10004, U.S.A. Phone 1-800-SPRINGER, fax (201) 348-4505, e-mail orders-ny@springer-sbm.com, or visit www.springeronline.com. Apress Media, LLC is a California LLC and the sole member (owner) is Springer Science + Business Media Finance Inc (SSBM Finance Inc). SSBM Finance Inc is a **Delaware** corporation.

For information on translations, please e-mail booktranslations@springernature.com; for reprint, paperback, or audio rights, please e-mail bookpermissions@springernature.com.

Apress titles may be purchased in bulk for academic, corporate, or promotional use. eBook versions and licenses are also available for most titles. For more information, reference our Print and eBook Bulk Sales web page at http://www.apress.com/bulk-sales.

Any source code or other supplementary material referenced by the author in this book is available to readers on GitHub (https://github.com/Apress). For more detailed information, please visit https://www.apress.com/gp/services/source-code.

If disposing of this product, please recycle the paper

To my Lord and Savior, Jesus Christ
and
To the memories of my parents and my older sister
and
To my younger sister and her family.

Table of Contents

About the Author

Jeff Friesen is a freelance teacher and software developer with an emphasis on Java. In addition to authoring several books on Java and Android for Apress such as *Java I/O, NIO and NIO.2* and *Java XML and JSON*, Jeff has written numerous articles on Java and other technologies for JavaWorld (now known as InfoWorld), InformIT, Java.net, SitePoint, and other websites.

About the Technical Reviewer

 **Massimo Nardone** is a seasoned cyber, information, and operational technology (OT) security professional with 28 years of experience working with companies such as IBM, HP, and Cognizant, with IT, OT, IoT, and IIoT security roles and responsibilities including CISO, BISO, IT/OT/IoT Security Architect, Security Assessor/Auditor, PCI QSA, and ICS/SCADA Expert. He is the founder of Massimo Security Services, a company providing IT-OT-IoT security consulting services, and member of ISACA, ISF, Nordic CISO Forum, and Android Global Forum and owns four international patents. He is coauthor of five Apress IT books.

Introduction

Java is a popular programming language and environment. Because it is used in the Information Technology departments of many companies, learning Java is a great way to boost your career (and earn more money in these difficult financial times).

If you have never worked with Java, this 14-chapter book is for you. Chapter 1 starts you on a gentle journey to learn Java fundamentals.

Chapters 2 through 11 focus mainly on language syntax, although a few APIs that are closely related to syntax are also presented.

Chapter 2 focuses on comments, identifiers, types, variables, and literals. These features are fundamental to many languages, and this chapter also shows you where Java differs from other languages in their implementation.

Chapter 3 focuses on expressions (and operators), and Chapter 4 focuses on statements. Again, these features are found in many languages. You will use these building blocks to construct simple Java programs and will learn where Java's implementations of expressions (and operators) and statements diverge from other languages.

Chapter 5 focuses on arrays. You will use this fundamental data structure to create programs that work with sequences of data items. For example, you might want to search a sequence of employee IDs for a specific identifier.

If this was all that Java had to offer, you would be able to create sophisticated structured programs. In a structured program, data and operations that manipulate the data are separated. However, Java goes beyond its ability to create structured programs, as revealed in Chapters 6 through 8.

Chapter 6 introduces you to classes and objects. A class is a *template* from which objects are manufactured. It provides an architecture for structuring data and associating that data with code that manipulates the data. An *object* is an instance of a class (kind of like a cookie is an instance of a cookie cutter). It stores data that can be manipulated by the code that the object receives from its class. (Don't worry if this seems complicated. After reading Chapter 6, you'll have a much better understanding.)

Java and other languages that support classes and objects are known as *object-based languages*. To go beyond object based and become an *object-oriented language*, a language must also support inheritance. Java supports inheritance, which you'll learn about in Chapter 7.

Programs can be made more efficient through polymorphism, which is based on inheritance. The idea behind polymorphism is that a single symbol can represent many different types (e.g., the + symbol can represent integer addition, floating-point addition, or string concatenation). You'll learn about polymorphism in Chapter 8.

There are a few more language features that you need to learn about before you can tour Java's many APIs. Chapter 9 begins by introducing you to static, non-static, local, and anonymous classes. These features let you logically organize your code, making it more readable and maintainable.

Packages let you organize related classes in the equivalent of a file folder. This feature helps you avoid name conflicts by organizing a library of classes under a single prefix. Check out Chapter 10 to learn about packages.

Java provides a robust exception-handling mechanism for dealing with flawed code or unexpected difficulties, such as attempting to open a nonexistent file. This mechanism is covered in Chapter 11.

The final three chapters tour some fundamental APIs that you'll use in many Java programs. Chapter 12 focuses on the `Math` class and related types, Chapter 13 focuses on `String` and `StringBuffer`, and Chapter 14 focuses on `System`. After you explore these types, you'll be able to explore additional APIs on your own to increase your Java knowledge.

Two appendixes round out this book. Appendix A provides a quick reference to Java's supported reserved words, and Appendix B provides a quick reference to Java's supported operators.

CHAPTER 1

Getting Started with Java

Welcome to Java. This technology is widely used in the business world, and you probably want to learn it quickly so you can capture a job in one of these companies as a Java programmer. Although Java is vast and constantly evolving, there are various fundamental features that are timeless and easy to understand. After you master these fundamentals, you will have an easier time writing Java programs.

This chapter launches you on a tour of Java's fundamental features. You first receive an answer to the "What is Java?" question. Next, you learn about the Java Development Kit, which is the necessary software for developing Java programs on your computer. Moving on, you are introduced to your first Java program, which outputs a simple "hello, world" message. Finally, you discover application architecture.

Note   A *program* is a sequence of instructions for a computer to execute. An *application* is a program with a single entry point of execution. (In contrast, an *applet* – an old form of Java program that is no longer widely used – has multiple entry points.) For example, a Microsoft Windows program that is stored in an `.exe` file has a single entry point. When expressed in C language *source code* (textual instructions), the entry point is defined by a *function* (a named sequence of instructions) with the name `main`.

What Is Java?

Java is like a two-sided coin. From one side, it's a computer programming language. Conversely, it's a virtual *platform* (the hardware and software context in which a program runs) for running programs written in that language.

© Jeff Friesen 2024
J. Friesen, *Learn Java Fundamentals*, https://doi.org/10.1007/979-8-8688-0351-2_1

Note   Java has an interesting history. Check out Wikipedia's "Java (programming language)" (http://en.wikipedia.org/wiki/Java_(programming_language)#History) and "Java (software platform)" (http://en.wikipedia.org/wiki/Java_ (software_platform)#History) entries to learn more.

Java Is a Programming Language

Java is a programming language with many features that are identical to those found in the C and C++ languages. This is no accident. One of Java's initial goals was to make it easy for C/C++ programmers to migrate to Java to quickly build up an initial pool of programmers that would help Java become successful.

You will discover several similarities between these languages:

- The same single-line and multiline comments for documenting source code are found in Java and C/C++.

- Various identical reserved words are found in Java and C/C++, such as if, while, for, and switch. Various other reserved words are found in Java and C++ but not in C, such as try, catch, class, and public.

- Primitive types are shared between the three languages: character and integer are examples. Furthermore, reserved words for these types are shared between these languages: char and int are examples.

- Many of the same operators are shared between Java and C/C++. Arithmetic operators (such as * and +) and relational operators (such as == and <=) are examples.

- Finally, Java and C/C++ use brace characters ({ and }) to delimit blocks of statements.

Java also differs from C/C++ in many ways. Here are a few of the many differences:

- Java supports an additional comment style for documenting source code. This comment style is known as *Javadoc*.

- Java provides reserved words that are not found in C/C++. Examples include strictfp and transient.

- Java's character type is larger than the character type in C and C++. In those languages, a character occupies one byte of memory. In contrast, Java's character type occupies two bytes.

- Java doesn't support all of C/C++'s operators. For example, you won't find the C/C++ `sizeof` operator in Java. Also, the `>>>` (unsigned right shift) operator is exclusive to Java.

- Java provides labeled `break` and `continue` statements. These variants of their C/C++ counterparts, which don't accept labels, are a safer alternative to C/C++'s `goto` statement, which Java doesn't support.

I discuss comments, reserved words, types, operators, and statements later in this book.

The Java programming language is rigorously defined by various rules that describe its *syntax* (structure) and *semantics* (meaning). These rules are used by a compiler to verify correctness when translating a program's source code into equivalent *bytecode*, which is a portable representation of the program's executable code. This bytecode is stored in one or more *class files*, which are the Java equivalent of a Windows program's executable (`.exe`) file.

Java Is a Virtual Platform

Java is a virtual platform that executes Java programs. Unlike real platforms that consist of a microprocessor (such as an Intel or AMD processor) and operating system (such as Windows 11), the Java platform consists of virtual machine and execution environment software.

A *virtual machine* is a software-based processor with its own set of instructions. The Java Virtual Machine's (JVM) associated *execution environment* consists of a huge library of prebuilt reference types (think Application Program Interfaces [APIs]) that Java programs can use to perform routine tasks (such as opening a file). The execution environment also contains "glue" code that connects the JVM to the underlying operating system via the Java Native Interface. (I don't discuss the Java Native Interface in this book because I don't consider it to be a fundamental feature.)

Note   The combination of bytecode and the virtual machine makes it possible to achieve *portability*: the same Java program runs on all platforms that support the virtual machine. It's not necessary to recompile the program's source code for each platform.

A Java program is run by a special executable, which I call the *program launcher*. Because a program consists of one or more class files, the launcher receives the name of the *main class file* (the class file where execution begins). After loading the JVM into memory, it tells the JVM to use its *class loader* component to load the main class file into memory. The JVM then verifies that the class file's bytecode is safe to run (e.g., no viruses) and runs it.

Note   The verifier and a security manager architecture make it possible to achieve *security*: a Java application will not be allowed to run when the verifier detects corrupt bytecode. Furthermore, when a security manager is installed, the application won't be able to steal sensitive information, erase files, or otherwise harm a user's computer.

During execution, a class file might refer to another class file. When this happens, the JVM uses the class loader to load the referenced class file into memory and then verifies and (if okay to run) executes that class file's bytecode.

The Java Development Kit

The Java Development Kit (JDK) provides the necessary software for creating *Java applications*, which are a category of Java programs with a single entry point of execution. They contrast with *Java applets*, another category of Java programs that run embedded in web pages. Applets are rarely used these days.

Follow these steps to download the JDK:

1. Enter `www.oracle.com/java/technologies/` in your browser. This takes you to the main page of Oracle's Java site.

2. At the time of writing, the newest download is version 21.0.1.
    Click on the **Java SE 21.0.1** link. (Java SE stands for Java Standard
    Edition. This is the foundation on which other editions are based
    and is the appropriate edition for this book. Another edition is
    Java EE, for Java Enterprise Edition. You would use this edition
    when developing complex business solutions involving web
    servers, database management systems, and client computers.)

3. In the **JDK Development Kit 21.0.1 downloads** section of the
    resulting **Java Downloads** page, you will see **Linux**, **macOS**,
    and **Windows** tabs. The JDK is available for all three operating
    systems. Choose whichever one is right for you. For example, I
    clicked the **Windows** tab because I was running Windows. I then
    had a choice between different kinds of installers. I chose the x64
    installer whose file name ends with a `.exe` file extension. I found
    this the easiest way to install the JDK.

Once you download the installer, such as `jdk-21_windows-x64_bin.exe`, run this
program and follow the onscreen prompts to install the JDK.

The JDK contains various tools for use in application development. Four of these
tools are the Java compiler (`javac.exe` in the Windows download), the Java program
launcher (`java.exe` in the Windows download), the Java documentation generator
(`javadoc.exe` in the Windows download), and the Java archiver (`jar.exe` in the
Windows download). You will only need to work with these tools in this book.

The JDK's compiler, program launcher, documentation generator, archiver, and other
tools are designed to be run from the command line within the context of a *console* (an
operating system–specific construct consisting of a window for viewing output and a
command line for obtaining command-based input). To obtain a console on Windows
operating systems, perform the following tasks:

1. Go to the **Start** menu and select **Run**.

2. In the **Run** dialog box, enter **cmd** in the text field and click the **OK**
    button. On the Windows operating system, you should observe a
    window similar to that shown in Figure 1-1.

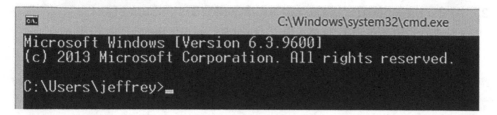

Figure 1-1. *The upper portion of a console as seen on a Windows 8.1 machine*

Figure 1-1 reveals **C:\Users\jeffrey>**, which is a prompt for entering a command on my Windows 8.1 machine. The rectangular box to the right of > is the *cursor*, which indicates the current position for entering text on the command line.

"hello, world" – Java Style

Let's create a simple application to get a taste of Java code. Traditionally, the first application does nothing but output the message hello, world on the console. Listing 1-1 presents the source code to a HelloWorld application that does just that.

Listing 1-1. HelloWorld.java

```java
class HelloWorld
{
   public static void main(String[] args)
   {
      System.out.println("hello, world");
   }
}
```

Listing 1-1 declares a HelloWorld class (I explain classes in Chapter 6) that serves as a placeholder for the main() *method* (a named sequence of instructions that executes in the context of a class).

Note   Languages such as C use functions instead of methods. A *function* is a named sequence of instructions that executes outside of any context.

The main() method serves as the entry point to the application. When the application runs, main()'s code is executed.

The main() method header (public static void main(String[] args)) exhibits some interesting features:

- The method is marked public so that the Java program launcher can locate it. If public is absent, an error message is output when attempting to run the application.

- The method is marked static so that a HelloWorld object does not need to be created in order to call main(). The launcher calls main() directly. It knows nothing of objects. If static is absent, an error message is output when attempting to run the application.

- The method is declared with a parameter list consisting of String[] args, which identifies an array of string arguments that are passed after the application's name (HelloWorld) on the command line when the application is run by the launcher. A *string is* a sequence of characters placed between double quotes (").

- The method is declared with a void return type that signifies the method returns nothing.

Don't worry if concepts such as return type and parameter list are confusing. You'll learn about these concepts later in this book.

The main() method executes System.out.println("hello, world"); to output hello, world on the console's window. I explore System.out and its System.err and System.in counterparts in Chapter 14.

INDENTATION, OPEN BRACE CHARACTER PLACEMENT, AND CODE-SEPARATION STYLES

Programmers often follow one style when indenting source code, another style when positioning a block's open brace character, and a third style when using blank lines to separate segments of source code. (I briefly discuss *blocks*, which are sequences of code surrounded by { and } characters, in Chapter 4.)

Listing 1-1 demonstrates the first two style categories. It shows my tendency to indent, by three spaces, all lines in a block. I find that doing so makes it easier to follow the organization of my source code when updating it as requirements change.

Also, Listing 1-1 shows my tendency to align the open ({) and close (}) brace characters, so I can more easily locate the start and end of a block. Many programmers prefer the following brace character alignment instead:

```java
class HelloWorld {
    public static void main(String[] args) {
        System.out.println("hello, world");
    }
}
```

Another style issue involves inserting blank lines to separate segments of code, where each segment consists of statements that work collectively on some aspect of the program. Here is a contrived example, involving a pair of classes, A and B:

```java
class A
{
    void method1()
    {
        for (int i = 0; i < 10; i++)
            System.out.println(i);

        while (true)
        {
            // ... do something here
        }
    }

    void method2()
    {
        for (int i = 0; i < 10; i++)
            System.out.println(i);

        while (true)
        {
            // ... do something here
        }
    }
}
```

```
class B
{
   void method1()
   {
      for (int i = 0; i < 10; i++)
         System.out.println(i);
      while (true)
      {
         // ... do something here
      }
   }
   void method2()
   {
      for (int i = 0; i < 10; i++)
         System.out.println(i);
      while (true)
      {
         // ... do something here
      }
   }
}
```

Each of classes A and B declares two methods: method1() and method2(). Furthermore, each of method1() and method2() declares a for statement followed by a while statement.

Don't worry about classes, methods, and statements. I cover classes and methods in Chapter 6 and cover statements in Chapter 4.

For now, pay attention to the blank line styles in each of A and B. A's style is to place a blank line between each method and between each group of related statements. B's style is to eliminate the blank line from between the methods and from between the statements.

Form your own styles for indentation, brace character placement, and code separation. Although these styles don't impact the generated code, adhering to them religiously sets you apart from other programmers and can make your source code easier to read and maintain. I tend to vary my code-separation style, which you'll discover throughout this book's code listings.

Compile the source code as follows (you must include the `.java` file extension):

```
javac HelloWorld.java
```

If everything goes well, you should observe a `HelloWorld.class` file in the current directory.

Now, execute the following command to run `HelloWorld.class` (you must not include the `.class` file extension):

```
java HelloWorld
```

If all goes well, you should observe the following output:

```
hello, world
```

Congratulations! You've just run your first Java application. You should feel proud.

Application Architecture

An application consists of at least one class, and this class must declare a `main()` entry-point method, as you saw in Listing 1-1. However, many applications will consist of multiple classes. All of these classes might be declared in a single source file, or each class might be declared in its own source file. Consider Listing 1-2.

Listing 1-2. `Classes.java`

```
class A
{
   static void a()
   {
      System.out.println("a() called");
   }
}

class B
{
   static void b()
```

```
   {
       System.out.println("b() called");
   }
}
class C
{
   public static void main(String[] args)
   {
      A.a();
      B.b();
   }
}
```

Listing 1-2 declares three classes (A, B, and C) in the same source file – Classes.java. Class C is the entry-point class because it declares the main() method.

Compile Classes.java as follows:

```
javac Classes.java
```

You should observe A.class, B.class, and C.class class files in the current directory.

Run this application as follows:

```
java C
```

You should observe the following output:

```
a() called
b() called
```

If you try to execute A (java A) or B (java B), you'll discover an error message because neither class declares the main() entry-point method.

This brings up an interesting point. You could declare main() methods in A and B and run these classes as applications. However, this could get confusing.

You might want to declare a main() method in each of A and B to test these classes, but there's probably no other good reason to do so. It's best to avoid confusion by declaring main() in the entry-point class only.

What's Next?

Now that you've had a taste of Java, it's time to build on that knowledge by exploring language features. Chapter 2 begins this process by focusing on the most basic language features: comments, identifiers (and reserved words), types, variables, and literals.

CHAPTER 2

Comments, Identifiers, Types, Variables, and Literals

When learning a new programming language, starting with the most basic of language features is best. These features are comments, identifiers (with reserved words as a subset), types, variables, and literals. This chapter introduces you to these features in a Java context.

Comments

It's important to document your source code so that you and anyone else who might maintain it in the future can understand the code's purpose. Our brains tend to forget things as we age, and we may not understand why we wrote the code the way we did. Source code should be documented when it is written. This documentation might have to be modified whenever the code is changed so that it accurately explains the new code.

Java provides *comments* for documenting source code. Whenever you compile the source code, the compiler ignores the comments – no bytecode is generated. Single-line, multiline, and Javadoc (documentation) comments are supported.

© Jeff Friesen 2024
J. Friesen, *Learn Java Fundamentals*, https://doi.org/10.1007/979-8-8688-0351-2_2

Single-Line Comments

A *single-line comment* appears on one line of source code. It begins with the `//` character sequence and continues to the end of the line. The compiler ignores everything on this line starting with the `//` characters. The following example demonstrates a single-line comment:

```
double degrees = (5.0 / 9.0) * (x - 32.0); // Convert x degrees Fahrenheit
to Celsius.
```

Single-line comments are useful for specifying short but meaningful information. They shouldn't be used to insert unhelpful information, for example, `// This is a comment`.

Multiline Comments

A *multiline comment* typically extends over multiple lines of source code although it can appear on a single line. This comment begins with `/*` and ends with `*/`. The compiler ignores everything in between (including `/*` and `*/`). The following example demonstrates a multiline comment:

```
/* Extract both components of an email address into a two-element array.
   email_parts[0] stores "xyz" and email_parts[1] stores "gmail.com". */
String[] email_parts = "xyz@gmail.com".split("@", 2); // extract
```

You cannot nest a multiline comment inside of another multiline comment. For example, the compiler generates an error when it encounters the following nested comments:

```
/*
  /*
    Nested multiline comments are illegal.
  */
*/
```

Caution   The compiler reports an error when it encounters nested multiline comments.

Javadoc Comments

A *Javadoc comment* is a variation of the multiline comment. It begins with /** (instead of /*) and (like a multiline comment) ends with */. All characters from /** through */ are ignored by the compiler. The following example presents a Javadoc comment:

```
/**
 *  Application entry point
 *
 *  @param args array of command-line arguments passed to this method
 */
public static void main(String[] args)
{
    // TODO code application logic here
}
```

This example's Javadoc comment describes an application's main() method. Sandwiched between /** and */ is a description of the method and the @param *Javadoc tag* (an @-prefixed instruction to the javadoc tool).

Here is a list of some commonly used Javadoc tags (including @param):

- @author identifies the source code's author.
- @deprecated identifies a source code entity (such as a method) that should no longer be used.
- @param identifies one of a method's parameters.
- @see provides a see-also reference.
- @since identifies the software release where the entity first originated.
- @return identifies the kind of value that the method returns.
- @throws documents an exception thrown from a method.

Listing 2-1 presents updated source code to Listing 1-1's HelloWorld application. This source code includes a pair of Javadoc comments that document the HelloWorld class and its main() entry-point method.

Listing 2-1. `HelloWorld.java`

```
/**
    A simple class for introducing Java applications.

    @author Jeff Friesen
*/

public class HelloWorld
{
    /**
        Application entry point

        @param args array of command-line arguments passed to this method
    */

    public static void main(String[] args)
    {
        System.out.println("hello, world");
    }
}
```

Apart from the Javadoc comments, Listing 2-1 differs from Listing 1-1 in that it prefixes class `HelloWorld` with the `public` keyword, which makes `HelloWorld` accessible outside of its package. (I will discuss `public` in Chapter 6 and packages in Chapter 10.)

I use the `javadoc` tool to generate HTML-based documentation for `HelloWorld.java`. This tool requires that the `public` keyword be prefixed to the `HelloWorld` class. Furthermore, the `.java` file extension is required:

```
javadoc HelloWorld.java
```

In response, `javadoc` generates the following output:

```
Loading source file HelloWorld.java...
Constructing Javadoc information...
Building index for all the packages and classes...
Standard Doclet version 20.0.1+9-29
Building tree for all the packages and classes...
Generating .\HelloWorld.html...
```

```
HelloWorld.java:7: warning: use of default constructor, which does not
provide a comment
public class HelloWorld
        ^
Generating .\package-summary.html...
Generating .\package-tree.html...
Generating .\overview-tree.html...
Building index for all classes...
Generating .\allclasses-index.html...
Generating .\allpackages-index.html...
Generating .\index-all.html...
Generating .\search.html...
Generating .\index.html...
Generating .\help-doc.html...
1 warning
```

The warning message refers to an undocumented default constructor. Constructors are used to initialize objects when they are created. I discuss constructors, objects, and the creation of objects in Chapter 6.

I've created a second version of HelloWorld.java that includes a commented constructor. You can find this file in this book's code archive. Instructions for obtaining the code archive are provided in the book's introduction.

The generated documentation includes an index file (index.html) that describes the documentation's start page. Figure 2-1 shows the start page for HelloWorld.java.

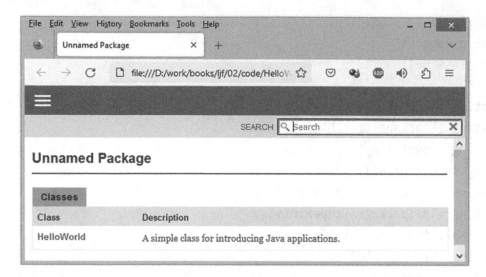

Figure 2-1. *The javadoc-generated documentation for HelloWorld.java*

The `javadoc` tool was also used to generate the documentation for JDK 21's reference type library. This documentation's start page is located at `http://docs.oracle.com/en/java/javase/21/docs/api/index.html`. Figure 2-2 shows you part of this start page.

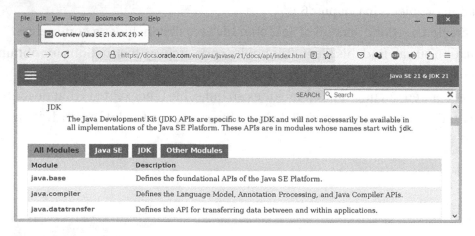

Figure 2-2. *The javadoc-generated documentation for JDK 21's reference type library*

Identifiers

Variables, statements, classes, and other language features need to be named to be referenced from elsewhere in the code. Java supports this capability through identifiers.

An *identifier* is a sequence of letters (A–Z, a–z, or equivalent uppercase/lowercase letters in other human alphabets), digits (0–9 or equivalent digits in other human alphabets), connecting punctuation characters such as the underscore, and currency symbols (e.g., the $ sign). It must begin with a letter, a currency symbol, or a connecting punctuation character. Its length cannot exceed the line in which it appears.

Note   According to page 28 of the "Java Language Specification" for JDK 21 (http://docs.oracle.com/javase/specs/jls/se21/jls21.pdf), "the dollar sign [$] should be used only in mechanically generated source code or, rarely, to access pre-existing names on legacy systems."

Examples of valid identifiers include i, grade_letter, counter10, and degreesCelsius. Examples of invalid identifiers include 6Age (starts with a digit) and last#Name (# is not a valid identifier symbol).

Note   Java is a case-sensitive language. This means that identifiers differing in case are considered different identifiers. For example, age and Age are different identifiers.

Almost any valid identifier can be used to name a language feature. However, some identifiers are reserved for special use by Java. These reserved identifiers are known as *reserved words*. Figure 2-3 reveals Java's 53 reserved words.

abstract	assert	boolean	break
byte	case	catch	char
class	const	continue	default
do	double	else	enum
extends	false	final	finally
float	for	goto	if
implements	import	instanceof	int
interface	long	native	new
null	package	private	protected
public	return	short	static
strictfp	super	switch	synchronized
this	throw	throws	transient
true	try	void	volatile
while			

Figure 2-3. *Java-reserved identifiers*

JDK 9 added a single underscore character (_) to Java's list of reserved words. It's an error to use a single underscore to name anything. However, it's okay to use multiple underscores (although you probably shouldn't).

Note   Most of Java's reserved words are also known as *keywords*. The three exceptions are `false`, `null`, and `true`. They are examples of *literals* (values expressed verbatim).

Also, `const` and `goto` are reserved by Java but are not used.

Types

Computers process different types of data: integers, characters, floating-point values, Boolean true/false values, strings of characters, and so on. Java associates a type with each data category.

A *type* identifies a set of values (and their representation in memory) and a set of operations that transform these values into other values of that set. For example, the floating-point type identifies numeric values with fractional parts and floating-point-oriented math operations, such as adding two floating-point values to produce another floating-point value that represents their sum.

Note   *Java is a strongly typed* language. Every expression, variable, and so on has a type known to the compiler. This capability helps the compiler detect type-related errors at compile time rather than having these errors manifest themselves at runtime. Expressions are discussed in Chapter 3. Variables are discussed later in this chapter.

Java supports primitive types, user-defined types, and array types. I discuss primitive and user-defined types here. I discuss array types in Chapter 5.

Primitive Types

A *primitive type* (also known as a *value type*) is a basic type from which user-defined types (discussed later in this chapter) are built. It identifies a set of values (such as integers) and operations (such as addition) that are performed on these values. These operations are built into the Java Virtual Machine (JVM).

More specifically, a primitive type consists of a reserved word that describes the memory organization of an instance of this type. The reserved word also implies the operations that can be performed on this type. For example, the Boolean primitive type consists of reserved word `boolean` and implies operations such as logical negation (!), which converts from true to false and false to true.

Java supports the Boolean, character, byte integer, short integer, integer, long integer, floating-point, and double-precision floating-point primitive types. They are described in Table 2-1.

Table 2-1. *Java's Primitive Types*

Primitive Type	Reserved Word	Size	Min Value	Max Value
Boolean	`boolean`	--	--	--
Character	`char`	16-bit	Unicode 0	Unicode $2^{16} - 1$
Byte integer	`byte`	8-bit	-128	+127
Short integer	`short`	16-bit	-32768	+32767
Integer	`int`	32-bit	-2^{31}	$+2^{31} - 1$
Long integer	`long`	64-bit	-2^{63}	$+2^{63} - 1$
Floating-point	`float`	32-bit	IEEE 754	IEEE 754
Double-precision floating-point	`double`	64-bit	IEEE 754	IEEE 754

Table 2-1 describes each primitive type in terms of its reserved word, size, minimum value, and maximum value. A -- entry indicates that the column in which it appears does not apply to the primitive type described in the entry's row.

The size column identifies the number of bits required to hold a value. Except for Boolean, whose size is JVM dependent, each type's implementation has a specific size.

The minimum and maximum size columns identify the smallest and largest values that the type represents. Besides Boolean, which has only true and false values, each type has minimum and maximum values.

The character type's minimum and maximum values refer to *Unicode*, a standard for consistently encoding, representing, and handling text expressed in most of the world's writing systems (see http://en.wikipedia.org/wiki/Unicode for more information).

Note   The character type is unsigned, which its limits suggest (the smallest value is 0). In contrast, the byte integer, short integer, integer, and long integer types are signed.

The minimum and maximum values for the four integer types reveal one more negative value than positive value (0 is usually not regarded as positive). This imbalance has to do with how integers are represented in *two's-complement* (http://en.wikipedia.org/wiki/Two's_complement) format. In contrast, the minimum and maximum values for the floating-point types are defined by the IEEE 754 (http://en.wikipedia.org/wiki/IEEE_754) specification.

User-Defined Types

A *user-defined type* is a combination of primitive types and user-defined types. For example, a user-defined type for representing the concept of man might combine a user-defined, string-based name along with a primitive integer-based age. The following code fragment shows how you would specify man as a user-defined type:

```
class Man
{
    // implementation of the structure for representing a set of Man values

    String name;
    int age;

    // implementation of the operations that are performed on these values
```

```
int getName()
{
   return name;
}

void setName(String name_)
{
   return name = name_;
}

int getAge()
{
   return age;
}

void setAge(int age_)
{
   return age = age_;
}
}
```

The class reserved word introduces Man as a user-defined type. It is conventional to begin the name of a user-defined type with a capital letter.

The class's body describes Man's implementation in terms of the structure for implementing Man values and the operations that are performed on these values.

The structure is comprised of two *fields* (variables that store a class type's values – see Chapter 6 for an introduction to fields). Man stores its values in name and age fields:

- name stores a man's name. This field's type is String, which is a special user-defined type that represents a *string* (a sequence of characters placed between double quotes ["]). JDK 21's reference type library includes the pre-created String type. (I discuss String in Chapter 13.)

- age stores a man's age. This field's type is int, which is a primitive type that represents a 32-bit integer.

The operations consist of four *methods* (functions that execute in the context of a class – see Chapter 6 for an introduction to methods). Man provides get and set operations:

- get returns a Man value by retrieving the values of its name and age fields. It provides getName() and getAge() methods for this purpose.

- set changes a Man value by changing the values of its name and age fields. It provides setName() and setAge() methods for this purpose.

User-defined types are also known as *reference types* because a variable (discussed shortly) whose type is user defined stores a *reference* (a memory address or other location identifier) to a value of that type. In contrast, a variable of a primitive type stores the type's value instead of a reference to a value.

Variables

Data items are stored in *variables*, which symbolically (via their names) identify memory locations where these items are stored. For a primitive type, the data item is stored directly in the variable. For a user-defined type, a data item is an object stored elsewhere in memory and a reference to the object is stored in the variable.

Variables must be declared before they are used. A declaration minimally consists of a type name followed by an identifier that names the variable. Here are some examples:

```
boolean first; // Determine first time through the loop.
int counter; // Count the number of times a file has been opened.
char gradeLetter; // Identify a student's end-of-year grade in a particular
subject.
double temperature; // Specify the current temperature.
String direction; // In what direction is the wind blowing?
```

The first example declares a Boolean variable named first. The second example declares an integer variable named counter. The third example declares a character variable named gradeLetter. The fourth example declares a double-precision floating-point variable named temperature. The fifth example declares a String variable named direction.

When a variable is declared and not explicitly initialized (demonstrated later in this chapter), it is implicitly initialized to a default value. A `Boolean` variable is initialized to false, variables of the four integer types are initialized to 0, a character variable is initialized to Unicode character 0, variables of the floating-point types are initialized to 0.0, and `String` variables are initialized to null.

DECLARATION VS. DEFINITION

I use the term *declaration* when introducing an identifier and associated syntax for a new variable, method, or other relevant language feature into a program's source code. (I use declaration regardless of whether or not I initialize the variable, specify a non-abstract method, and so on. [I cover methods in Chapter 6 and abstract methods in Chapter 8.] Some programmers prefer the term *definition* over declaration, which has led to confusion. If you are wondering what's the big deal, remember that being precise in terminology can minimize mistakes and clear up confusion – you'll save yourself many headaches that arise from arguments over seemingly trivial matters. However, such matters cannot be trivial if you spend time getting worked up and angry while trying to defend your position.)

According to *The C Programming Language* (http://en.wikipedia.org/wiki/The_C_Programming Language), the definitive reference book on C, which was written by Brian Kernighan and the late Dennis Ritchie (the creator of C), there is a difference. Page 76 of the 1978 edition states: "It is important to distinguish between the declaration of an external variable and its definition. A declaration announces the properties of a variable (its type, size, etc.); a definition also causes storage to be allocated."

Regarding Java, the best resource for addressing this issue is probably *The Java® Language Specification* (http://docs.oracle.com/javase/specs/jls/se21/jls21.pdf). Chapter 6 (which covers names) uses the term *declaration*. In contrast, the most popular answer to stackoverflow's "What is the difference between declaration and definition in Java" topic (http://stackoverflow.com/questions/11715485/what-is-the-difference-between-declaration-and-definition-in-java) states that declaration deals with the existence of a variable, method, and so on, whereas definition deals with "how something is implemented" – what it is. The answer goes on to state that there is little difference between declaration and definition in Java. Furthermore, the answer states that "a declaration not only includes the identifier, but also its definition."

Literals

A *literal* is a value expressed verbatim in source code. Java supports literals for its primitive types, initializing reference type variables, and a special reference type known as String (discussed in Chapter 13).

Note   Literals are also known as *simple expressions*. I discuss expressions in terms of their simple and compound variants in Chapter 3.

A Boolean literal consists of either the keyword true or the keyword false.

A character literal consists of a single Unicode character surrounded by single quotes (e.g., '6').

An integer literal consists of a sequence of digits. The type of an integer literal is int (a 32-bit value). You can change the type to long by suffixing the literal with l or L (which is easier to read).

Integer literals can be specified in the decimal, hexadecimal, octal, and binary formats:

- The decimal format is the default format, for example, 127.

- The hexadecimal format requires that the literal be prefixed with 0x or 0X and continue with hexadecimal digits (a-f and/or A-F), for example, 0x3FB2.

- The octal format requires that the literal be prefixed with 0 and continue with octal digits (0-7), for example, 0276.

- The binary format requires that the literal be prefixed with 0b or 0B and continue with 0s and 1s, for example, 0b11010110.

Starting with JDK 7, you can improve readability by inserting underscores between digits. For example, 204_555_1212 is easier to read than 2045551212. Although you can insert multiple successive underscores between digits (such as 987___235), you cannot insert a leading underscore (_4222). The compiler will report an error when you try to do so. Also, the compiler reports an error when you specify a trailing underscore, for example, 99_.

A floating-point literal consists of an integer part followed by a decimal point followed by a fractional part followed by an exponent (starting with letter E or e) followed by a type suffix (D or d for double-precision floating-point; F or f for floating-point – a floating-point literal defaults to double-precision floating-point). Most parts are optional, but you must specify enough information to distinguish the floating-point literal from an integer literal. Examples include 0.9 (double-precision floating-point), 36F (floating-point), 900D (double-precision floating-point – the D changes 32-bit integer 900 to an equivalent double-precision floating-point value), and 33.8E+22 (double-precision floating-point).

The null literal is assigned to a reference variable to indicate that the variable does not refer to an object. It signifies the absence of a meaningful value.

Caution   The compiler reports an error when you attempt to assign null to a variable that has a primitive (value) type (such as int).

It's possible to run into trouble when working with null. For example, when a user-defined variable contains the null reference instead of a reference to an object, and you attempt to access a field or *invoke* (call) a method, you will encounter the dreaded NullPointerException. (I will discuss objects, fields, and methods in Chapter 6. Also, I will discuss exceptions and mention NullPointerException in Chapter 11.)

Note   You can learn more about the concept of *nullness* (being null) and NullPointerException by reading Yoshitaka Shiotsu's excellent article "Null In Java: Understanding the Basics" (www.upwork.com/resources/what-is-null-in-java)

Finally, a string literal consists of a sequence of Unicode characters surrounded by a pair of double quotes, for example, "What is the weather like today?". It might also include *escape sequences*, which are special syntax for representing certain printable and nonprintable characters that otherwise cannot appear in a literal. For example, "The title of the book is \"Mastering Java\" and is written by John Doe." This example uses the \" escape sequence to surround Mastering Java with double quotes.

The following escape sequences are supported: \\ (backslash), \" (double quote), \' (single quote), \b (backspace), \f (form feed), \n (newline), \r (carriage return), and \t (tab).

A string literal might also contain *Unicode escape sequences*, which are a special syntax for representing Unicode characters. A Unicode escape sequence starts with \u and continues with four hexadecimal digits (0–9, A–F, or a–f) with no intervening space. For example, \u0043 represents the capital letter C, and \u20ac represents the European Union currency symbol.

The following examples use literals to initialize the previously presented variables:

```
boolean first = true;
int counter = 10;
char gradeLetter = 'A';
double temperature = 37.9;
String direction = "East";
```

Putting It All Together

Listing 2-2 presents the source code to a VarInit application that demonstrates identifiers, types, variables, and literals via the previous examples. You can modify VarInit's source code to introduce your own examples and learn more about these basic language features.

Listing 2-2. VarInit.java

```
class VarInit
{
   public static void main(String[] args)
   {
      boolean first = true;
      int counter = 10;
      char gradeLetter = 'A';
      double temperature = 37.9;
      String direction = "East";
      System.out.println(first);
      System.out.println(counter);
```

```
        System.out.println(gradeLetter);
        System.out.println(temperature);
        System.out.println(direction);
    }
}
```

Compile Listing 2-2 as follows:

```
javac VarInit.java
```

Run the application as follows:

```
java VarInit
```

You should observe the following output:

```
true
10
A
37.9
East
```

VAR

JDK 10 introduced var, a shortcut to declaring and initializing variables. To save keystrokes, you no longer have to enter a variable's type name because the compiler infers the variable's type from the literal's (or other expression's) type during initialization. For example, in var ch = 'C';, the compiler infers that variable ch has type char because the type of 'C' is char. Without var, you would specify char ch = 'C';. Although you saved one keystroke, which doesn't seem like much, you could save more keystrokes in longer syntactic contexts, such as var amount = 10.0; instead of double amount = 10.0;.

Remember two important points when working with var:

- You must always use var in an initialization and not a declaration-only context. In other words, you must always assign a literal or other expression to the variable. If you specify var and a variable name by themselves, as in var ch;, the compiler will report an error because it cannot infer a type for ch.

- The `var` identifier might seem like a reserved word (or keyword, if you like), but that is not the case. You cannot use a reserved word to name a variable. However, the following declaration is legal: `var var = 10.0;`. In this example, `var` is a double-precision floating-point variable initialized to 10.0.

I recommend not using `var` to name a variable (as in `var var`) because the result might confuse someone who is reading your source code. Also, `var` might become a reserved word someday.

What's Next?

Now that you've mastered comments, identifiers, types, variables, and literals, you're ready to explore operators and expressions. These language features let you manipulate data items to produce new data items, which is done in every kind of program, from a business payroll application to a machine-learning demo.

CHAPTER 3

Expressions

Computer programs manipulate data via expressions. This chapter introduces you to expressions in terms of simple and compound expressions.

Introducing Expressions

An *expression* is a combination of literals, variable names, method calls (discussed in Chapter 6), and operators. At runtime, the expression evaluates to a type referred to as the expression's type.

If an expression is being assigned to a variable, their types must *agree* (it must be possible to convert from one type to the other without losing information) or else the compiler will report an error.

Simple Expressions

A *simple expression* is a literal value, a variable name (containing a value), or a method call (returning a value) – I cover methods and method calls in Chapter 6. The following examples demonstrate these simple expressions being used to initialize variables:

```
int i = 2; // a literal value (2) of type int
int j = i; // a variable name (i) of type int
boolean success = open("file.txt"); // a method call that returns Boolean
true/false
```

The first example assigns literal 2 to variable i. The literal and variable have the same type: int.

The second example assigns variable i to variable j. Both variables have the same int type.

31

© Jeff Friesen 2024
J. Friesen, *Learn Java Fundamentals*, https://doi.org/10.1007/979-8-8688-0351-2_3

The third example calls an open() method, passing to this method the name of a file to open, and assigns the result to variable success. Let's assume that open()'s return type is boolean, which matches success's return type.

These examples assume that only expressions whose types match the types of the variables that they are initializing can be assigned to those variables. However, it is possible to assign a simple expression having a different type. For example, Java lets you assign various int literals to a variable of type short, as in short x = 90;, and assign a short to an int variable, as in int y = x;.

The former assignment is okay because 90 can be represented as a short integer – the largest short that can be represented is 32767, so 90 fits into a short. In contrast, the compiler would complain when encountering short x = 80000; because 80000 cannot be represented in 16-bit space, and information would be lost.

The latter assignment is acceptable because there is no loss of information when you convert from a type with a lesser set of values to a type with a greater set of values. A short's range of values can easily fit into an int's greater range of values.

Java uses widening conversion rules to support the following primitive-type conversions:

- byte to short, int, long, float, or double

- short to int, long, float, or double

- char to int, long, float, or double

- int to long, float, or double

- long to float or double

When converting a smaller integer to a longer integer, Java copies the smaller integer's sign bit into the larger integer's extra bits (on the left). If you would like to understand signed integer representation, check out Wikipedia's "Signed number representations" (http://en.wikipedia.org/wiki/Signed_number_ representations) entry.

The previous examples focus on simple expressions in a variable-declaration context. One of these simple expression categories, the method call, can also appear in a non-variable-declaration context. Here is an example:

```
success = open("file.txt");
```

This example assumes that a boolean success; declaration appeared earlier.

Compound Expressions

A *compound expression* is a sequence of simple expressions connected to each other via *operators*, which are symbolically represented sequences of instructions that transform their operands into new values. For example, -1 is a compound expression where - is an operator and int literal 1 is its operand. This expression transforms 1 into its negative equivalent: -1. Also, 4 * y is a compound expression where * is an operator and 4 and y are its operands. When this expression is evaluated, y's value is fetched and multiplied by 4. The expression's value becomes the result of the multiplication.

Note   If x's type is byte or short, the variable's value is widened to an int. However, if the type is long, double, or float, 4 is widened to the appropriate type. The addition is performed after the widening is carried out.

Java classifies its operators via the number of operands that they take:

- A *unary operator* takes a single operand. In the previous -1 example, the - (unary minus) operator takes a single operand.

- A *binary operator* takes two operands. The * (multiplication) operator in 4 * y is an example of a binary operator.

- Java supports a single *ternary operator* that takes three operands. This operator is represented by two symbols (? :) and is known as the *conditional operator*. I'll discuss this operator later.

Java also classifies its operators as prefix, postfix, and infix:

- A *prefix operator* is a unary operator that precedes its single operand (as in -1).

- A *postfix operator* is a unary operator that follows its single operand (as in x++ – increment the value in x).

- An *infix operator* is a binary operator that appears between the binary operator's two operands (as in 4 * y) or the ternary operator's three operands.

When evaluating an expression, the compiler considers each operator's precedence and associativity:

- *Precedence* determines how an expression is evaluated when it contains two or more operators with different precedences. Operators with higher precedence are evaluated first. For example, in the expression 4 + 2 * 3, subexpression 2 * 3 is evaluated first because multiplication takes precedence over addition.

- *Associativity* determines how an expression is evaluated when it contains two or more operators with the same precedence. For example, 4 + 2 + 3 would first evaluate 4 + 2 because + has left-to-right associativity. If + had right-to-left associativity, 2 + 3 would first be evaluated, and the result would be added to 4.

Table 3-1 presents all of Java's operators in terms of their symbols, descriptions, precedences, and associativity.

Table 3-1. *Java's Operators Grouped by Precedence*

Operator	Type	Precedence	Associativity
( )	Parentheses	15	Left to right
[ ]	Array index		
.	Member selection		
++	Unary post-increment	14	Right to left
--	Unary post-decrement		
++	Unary pre-increment	13	Right to left
--	Unary pre-decrement		
+	Unary plus		
-	Unary minus		
!	Unary logical negation		
~	Unary bitwise complement		
(*type*)	Unary type cast		

(continued)

Table 3-1. (*continued*)

Operator	Type	Precedence	Associativity
*	Multiplication	12	Left to right
/	Division		
%	Modulus		
+	Addition	11	Left to right
+	String concatenation		
-	Subtraction		
<<	Bitwise left shift	10	Left to right
>>	Bitwise right shift with sign extension		
>>>	Bitwise right shift with zero extension		
<	Relational less than	9	Left to right
<=	Relational less than or equal to		
>	Relational greater than		
>=	Relational greater than or equal to		
instanceof	Relational type comparison for objects		
==	Is equal to	8	Left to right
!=	Is not equal to		
&	Bitwise AND	7	Left to right
^	Bitwise exclusive OR	6	Left to right
|	Bitwise inclusive OR	5	Left to right
&&	Logical AND	4	Left to right
||	Logical OR	3	Left to right
?:	Conditional	2	Right to left

(*continued*)

Table 3-1. (*continued*)

Operator	Type	Precedence	Associativity
=	Assignment	1	Right to left
+=	Addition assignment	1	Right to left
-=	Subtraction assignment	1	Right to left
*=	Multiplication assignment	1	Right to left
/=	Division assignment	1	Right to left
%=	Modulus assignment	1	Right to left
&=	Bitwise AND assignment	1	Right to left
^=	Bitwise exclusive OR assignment	1	Right to left
|=	Bitwise inclusive OR assignment	1	Right to left
<<=	Bitwise left shift assignment	1	Right to left
>>=	Bitwise signed right shift with sign extension assignment	1	Right to left
>>>=	Bitwise unsigned right shift with zero extension assignment	1	Right to left

Each row identifies one or more operators. These operators share the same precedence. The Precedence column reveals a number ranging from 1 through 15 that specifies the precedence of all operators in the intersecting table row. The higher this number, the higher the precedence. For example, multiplication's precedence (12) is greater than addition's precedence (11) because multiplication is performed before addition.

Operator Examples

Some of Table 3-1's operators are probably familiar; others might be a mystery. The next several sections briefly describe all operators in bottom-up precedence order.

Assignment Operators

Java supports the simple assignment (=) and compound assignment (+=, -=, *=, /=, %=, &=, ^=, |=, <<=, >>=, and >>>=) operators.

Simple Assignment

The = *operator* assigns an expression's value to a variable. This operator has the following syntax:

variable '=' *expression* ';'

Note   You must specify whatever appears between the single quotes (and not also the single quotes). Also, an italicized item is a placeholder for something else that you must enter. This also applies to (*type*) in Table 3-1. (In this table, I didn't use single quotes to surround literal text that you enter verbatim because I didn't want to be confusing.)

The types of *variable* and *expression* must agree to avoid a compiler error. For example, you cannot directly assign a double to an int.

Consider the following example, which initializes self_employed to true:

```
boolean self_employed = true;
```

Compound Assignment

The +=, -=, *=, /=, %=, &=, ^=, |=, <<=, >>=, and >>>= *operators* perform their operations and then assign the results to variables. Their syntaxes are shown as follows:

variable '+=' *expression* ';'
variable '-=' *expression* ';'
variable '*=' *expression* ';'
variable '/=' *expression* ';'
variable '%=' *expression* ';'
variable '&=' *expression* ';'
variable '^=' *expression* ';'
variable '|=' *expression* ';'
variable '<<=' *expression* ';'
variable '>>=' *expression* ';'
variable '>>>=' *expression* ';'

Once again, the types of variables and expressions must agree to avoid compiler errors.

Check out these examples:

```
int x += 1; // Increment x.
int x -= 1; // Decrement x.
int x *= 2; // Multiply x by 2.
int x /= 2; // Divide x by 2.
int x %= 2; // Assign the remainder of x / 2 to x.
int x &= 0xFFFFFF00; // Turn off the rightmost eight bits in x.
int x ^= 0xFFFFFFFF; // Turn off all set bits in x.
int x |= 0xFF000000; // Turn on the leftmost eight bits in x.
int x <<= 1; // Multiply x by 2 by shifting all bits left one position.
int x >>= 1; // Divide x by 2. If x is negative, the result is negative.
int x >>>= 1; // Divide x by 2. If x is negative, the result is positive.
```

The <<= and >>= operators perform more quickly than their * and / counterparts when it comes to multiplying and dividing by powers of 2. Also, they are more intuitive when working with binary numbers.

Conditional Operator

The *?: operator* decides which of two expressions to evaluate based on a condition. It has the following syntax:

condition '?' expression1 ':' expression2

Condition is a Boolean expression. When it evaluates to true, *expression1* is evaluated and its result is returned. However, when it evaluates to false, *expression2* is evaluated and its result is returned. The types of *expression1* and *expression2* must agree to avoid a compiler error. For example, you cannot have *expression1* being of type int and *expression2* being of type double.

The following example shows how to use ?: to determine if a woman based on her age is eligible to receive a pension:

```
int age = 60;
boolean eligibleForPension = (age >= 55) ? true : false;
```

Because age is greater than 55, true is assigned to eligibleForPension.

Logical OR Operator

The || *operator* evaluates its left operand and evaluates its right operand only when its left operand is false. This is known as *short-circuiting*. It has the following syntax:

operand1 '||' *operand2*

Each of *operand1* and *operand2* must be of type boolean. This expression returns true when either or both *operand1* and *operand2* are true; otherwise, it returns false.

Consider the following example:

```
int x = 93;
boolean outOfRange = (x < 10 || x > 50);
```

The example first initializes x to 93. It then uses x with the logical OR operator to determine if x is outside the range 10 through 50. Because x is not in this range (it contains 93), true is assigned to outOfRange.

Because x equals 93, both the x < 10 and x > 50 expressions are evaluated. However, if x equalled 5, only the x < 10 expression would need to be evaluated because of short-circuiting.

Short-circuiting can help you avoid invoking a method on a null reference. Consider the following example:

```
str == null || str.isEmpty()
```

In this example, str references a String object. We want to call String's isEmpty() method on this object to determine if the string contains any characters or not. However, if str contains null, invoking isEmpty() will result in NullPointerException. We avoid this possibility by first testing str for null via the expression str == null. If str contains null, str == null is true and || does not evaluate str.isEmpty(), preventing NullPointerException. However, if str does not contain null, str == null is false and || evaluates str.isEmpty(), preventing NullPointerException. You'll learn about String, methods, and NullPointerException later in Chapters 13, 6, and 11, respectively.

Logical AND Operator

The && *operator* evaluates its left operand and evaluates its right operand only when its left operand is true. This is also known as *short-circuiting*. It has the following syntax:

operand1 '&&' *operand2*

Each of *operand1* and *operand2* must be of boolean type. This expression returns true when both *operand1* and *operand2* are true; otherwise, it returns false.

Consider the following example:

```
int x = 93;
boolean inRange = (x >= 10 && x <= 50);
```

This example is essentially the same as the example in the previous section. It simply inverts the behavior of that example.

Short-circuiting can help you avoid invoking a method on a null reference. Consider the following example:

```
str != null && !str.isEmpty()
```

This example is essentially the same as the example in the previous section. It simply inverts the behavior of that example.

Bitwise Inclusive OR Operator

The | *operator* inclusive ORs the bits of its operands together. For each bit, if either or both bits are 1, the result bit is 1; otherwise, the result bit is 0. This operator has the following syntax:

operand1 '|' *operand2*

Each of *operand1* and *operand2* must be of char, byte, short, int, or long type. This expression returns the inclusive ORed result.

Consider the following example:

```
byte status = readPort(DEVICE);
writePort(DEVICE, status | ENABLE_PRINTER);
```

This example reads a status byte from a hypothetical computer's DEVICE port. It then enables the printer by ORing the ENABLE_PRINTER value with the status field (in case the printer isn't enabled) and writes this value to the DEVICE port.

The | operator can be used like || but does not perform short-circuiting. It always evaluates its right operand. Here is an example:

```
x < 10 | x > 50
```

The right operand (x > 50) is always evaluated in this example.

Bitwise Exclusive OR Operator

The ^ *operator* exclusive ORs the bits of its operands together. For each bit, if either bit is 1 but both bits are not 1, the result bit is 1; otherwise, the result bit is 0. This operator has the following syntax:

operand1 '^' *operand2*

Each of *operand1* and *operand2* must be of char, byte, short, int, or long type. This expression returns the exclusive ORed result.

Consider the following example:

```
int i = 10;
int j = 20;
i = i ^ j; // 30
j = i ^ j; // 10
i = i ^ j; // 20
```

This example uses ^ to swap the contents of variables i and j.

Bitwise AND Operator

The & *operator* ANDs the bits of its operands together. For each bit, if both bits are 1, the result bit is 1; otherwise, the result bit is 0. This operator has the following syntax:

operand1 '&' *operand2*

Each of *operand1* and *operand2* must be of char, byte, short, int, or long type. This expression returns the exclusive ANDed result.

Consider the following example:

```
byte status = readPort(DEVICE);
writePort(DEVICE, status & ~ENABLE_PRINTER);
```

This example reads a status byte from a hypothetical computer's DEVICE port. It then disables the printer by ANDing the inverse of the ENABLE_PRINTER value with the status field (in case the printer is enabled) and writes this value to the DEVICE port.

The & operator can be used like && but does not perform short-circuiting. It always evaluates its right operand. Here is an example:

```
x >= 10 & x <= 50
```

The right operand (x <= 50) is always evaluated in this example.

Equality Operators

Java supports the is equal to (==) and is not equal to (!=) equality operators.

Is Equal To

The == *operator* compares both operands for equality. This operator has the following syntax:

operand1 '==' operand2

The == operator returns true when both operands are equal; otherwise, it returns false.

Here is an example:

```
int x = 10;
int y = 15;
boolean equal = x == y;
```

In this example, each of x and y contains an integer. The x == y expression returns false because x (10) does not equal y (15).

Is Not Equal To

The != *operator* compares both operands for inequality. This operator has the following syntax:

operand1 '!=' operand2

The != operator returns true when both operands are unequal; otherwise, it returns false.

Here is an example:

```
int x = 10;
int y = 15;
boolean equal = x != y;
```

In this example, each of x and y contains an integer. The x != y expression returns true because x (10) does not equal y (15).

For either operator, both operands must be comparable. For example, you cannot compare an integer literal with a string literal.

When it comes to objects (discussed in Chapter 6), these operators don't compare them to see if they are equal or unequal. Instead, they compare references to these objects. For example, "abc" == "abc" compares the reference to the first string literal with the reference to the second string literal. Because of something called interning (discussed in Chapter 13 where I talk about the String class), these references are the same, so the expression returns true. The expression returns false for "abc" != "abc".

Relational Operators

Java supports the less than (<), less than or equal to (<=), greater than (>), greater than or equal to (>=), and type comparison for objects (instanceof) relational operators.

Relational Less Than

The < *operator* compares both operands to discover if the left operand is less than the right operand. This operator has the following syntax:

operand1 '<' *operand2*

Each of *operand1* and *operand2* must be of char, byte, short, int, long, float, or double type. This expression returns true when *operand1* is less than *operand2*; otherwise, it returns false.

Consider the following example:

```
x < y
```

This expression evaluates to true when x is less than y; otherwise, it evaluates to false.

Relational Less Than or Equal To

The <= *operator* compares both operands to discover if the left operand is less than or equal to the right operand. This operator has the following syntax:

operand1 '<=' *operand2*

Each of *operand1* and *operand2* must be of char, byte, short, int, long, float, or double type. This expression returns true when *operand1* is less than *operand2*; otherwise, it returns false.

Consider the following example:

x <= y

This expression evaluates to true when x is less than or equal to y; otherwise, it evaluates to false.

Relational Greater Than

The > *operator* compares both operands to discover if the left operand is greater than the right operand. This operator has the following syntax:

operand1 '>' *operand2*

Each of *operand1* and *operand2* must be of char, byte, short, int, long, float, or double type. This expression returns true when *operand1* is greater than *operand2*; otherwise, it returns false.

Consider the following example:

x > y

This expression evaluates to true when x is greater than y; otherwise, it evaluates to false.

Relational Greater Than or Equal To

The >= *operator* compares both operands to discover if the left operand is greater than or equal to the right operand. This operator has the following syntax:

operand1 '>=' *operand2*

Each of *operand1* and *operand2* must be of char, byte, short, int, long, float, or double type. This expression returns true when *operand1* is greater than or equal to *operand2*; otherwise, it returns false.

Consider the following example:

```
x >= y
```

This expression evaluates to true when x is greater than or equal to y; otherwise, it evaluates to false.

Relational Type Comparison for Objects

The *instanceof operator* compares its left operand (an object) with its right operand (a reference type) to determine if the object is an instance of the reference type. This operator has the following syntax:

```
operand1 'instanceof' operand2
```

Operand1 must be an instance (object) of a reference type (such as a class – see Chapter 6 for a discussion of objects and classes). *Operand2* must be a class or other reference type. This expression returns true when *operand1* is an instance of *operand2*; otherwise, it returns false.

Consider the following example:

```
"abc" instanceof String
```

This expression evaluates to true because "abc" is an instance of the String class.

Shift Operators

Java supports the bitwise left shift (<<), bitwise right shift with sign extension (>>), and bitwise right shift with zero extension (>>>) shift operators.

Bitwise Left Shift

The << *operator* shifts the bits in its left operand to the left by the number of bits specified by its right operand. For each shift, a 0 is shifted into the rightmost bit and the leftmost bit is discarded. This operator has the following syntax:

```
operand1 '<<' operand2
```

Each of *operand1* and *operand2* must be of char, byte, short, int, or long type. This expression returns the result of *operand1* shifted *operand2* bits to the left.

Consider the following example:

```
2 << 3
```

This expression shifts 2 by 3 bits to the left. The result is 16. Essentially, we are multiplying 2 by 8. This is much faster than using the * operator. However, it is limited to multiplying by small powers of 2.

Bitwise Right Shift with Sign Extension

The >> *operator* shifts the bits in its left operand to the right by the number of bits specified by its right operand. For each shift, a copy of the leftmost bit (the *sign bit*, which indicates whether the remaining bits represent a positive or negative integer – 0 indicates a positive integer and 1 indicates a negative integer) is shifted to the right and the rightmost bit is discarded. This is known as a *signed shift*. This operator has the following syntax:

```
operand1 '>>' operand2
```

Each of *operand1* and *operand2* must be of char, byte, short, int, or long type. This expression returns the result of *operand1* shifted *operand2* bits to the left.

Consider the following example:

```
4 >> 1
-4 >> 1
```

The first expression shifts 4 by 1 bit to the right. The result is 2. The second expression shifts -4 by 1 bit to the right. The result is -2. Essentially, we are dividing 4 or -4 by 2. This is much faster than using the / operator. However, it is limited to dividing by small powers of 2.

Bitwise Right Shift with Zero Extension

The >>> *operator* shifts the bits in its left operand to the right by the number of bits specified by its right operand. For each shift, a 0 is shifted to the right and the rightmost bit is discarded. This is known as an *unsigned shift*. This operator has the following syntax:

```
operand1 '>>>' operand2
```

Each of *operand1* and *operand2* must be of char, byte, short, int, or long type. This expression returns the result of *operand1* shifted *operand2* bits to the left.

Consider the following example:

```
4 >>> 1
-4 >>> 1
```

The first expression shifts 4 by 1 bit to the right. The result is 2. The second expression shifts -4 by 1 bit to the right. The result is 2147483646 (the unsigned equivalent of -2). Essentially, we are dividing 4 or -4 by 2. This is much faster than using the / operator. However, it is limited to dividing by small powers of 2.

For each kind of shift that involves a 32-bit expression, only the five low-order bits of *operand2* are used to prevent shifting more than the number of bits in a 32-bit integer. For each kind of shift that involves a 64-bit expression, only the six low-order bits of *operand2* are used to prevent shifting more than the number of bits in a 64-bit expression.

Additive Operators

Java supports the addition/string concatenation (+) and subtraction (-) additive operators.

Addition/String Concatenation

The + *operator* adds its two numeric operands together and returns the sum. This operator has the following syntax:

operand1 '+' *operand2*

Each of *operand1* and *operand2* must be of char, byte, short, int, long, float, or double type. This expression returns the result of *operand1* plus *operand2*.

Consider the following example:

```
int x = 10;
int y = 20;
int sum = x + y;
```

This example adds the values in variables x and y, which are assigned 10 and 20, respectively. It then assigns the sum to variable sum.

The *+ operator* is also used to append a string to another string. This is known as *string concatenation*. It has the same syntax as addition.

At least one of the operands must be of String type. The other operand is converted to a string before concatenation is performed.

Consider the following example:

```
"abc" + "def"
```

The result is a new String object consisting of the sequence abcdef. (I discuss the String class in Chapter 13.)

Subtraction

The *- operator* subtracts its right numeric operand from its left numeric operand and returns the difference. This operator has the following syntax:

operand1 '-' operand2

Each of *operand1* and *operand2* must be of char, byte, short, int, long, float, or double type. This expression returns the result of *operand1* minus *operand2*.

Consider the following example:

```
int x = 10;
int y = 20;
int difference = x - y;
```

This example subtracts the value in variable y from the value in variable x, which are assigned 20 and 10, respectively. It then assigns the difference to variable difference.

Multiplicative Operators

Java supports the multiplication (*), division (/), and modulus (%) multiplicative operators.

Multiplication

The ** operator* multiplies its two numeric operands together and returns the product. This operator has the following syntax:

operand1 '*' operand2

Each of *operand1* and *operand2* must be of char, byte, short, int, long, float, or double type. This expression returns the result of *operand1* times *operand2*.

Consider the following example:

```
int x = 10;
int y = 20;
int product = x * y;
```

This example multiplies together the values in variables x and y, which are assigned 10 and 20, respectively. It then assigns the product to variable product.

Division

The */ operator* divides its left numeric operand by its right numeric operand and returns the dividend. This operator has the following syntax:

operand1 '/' *operand2*

Each of *operand1* and *operand2* must be of char, byte, short, int, long, float, or double type. This expression returns the dividend result of *operand1* divided by *operand2*.

Consider the following example:

```
int x = 10;
int y = 20;
int dividend = x / y;
```

This example divides the value in variable x by the value in variable y, which are assigned 10 and 20, respectively. It then assigns the dividend to variable dividend.

Modulus

The *% operator* divides its left numeric operand by its right numeric operand and returns the remainder. This operator has the following syntax:

operand1 '%' *operand2*

Each of *operand1* and *operand2* must be of char, byte, short, int, long, float, or double type. This expression returns the remainder result of *operand1* divided by *operand2*.

Consider the following example:

```
int x = 10;
int y = 20;
int remainder = x % y;
```

This example divides the value in variable x by the value in variable y, which are assigned 10 and 20, respectively. It then assigns the remainder to variable remainder.

Unary Operators

Java supports the pre-increment (++), pre-decrement (--), plus (+), minus (-), logical negation (-), bitwise complement (~), and type cast [(*type*)] unary operators.

Pre-increment

The *++ operator* pre-increments its operand, which must be a variable of char, byte, short, int, long, float, or double type. The result is stored in the variable. It is a fast way of adding 1 to the variable. This operator has the following syntax:

```
'++' variable
```

Consider the following example:

```
int x = 1;
int y = ++x;
```

After this example runs, each of x and y is assigned the value 2.

Pre-decrement

The *-- operator* pre-decrements its operand, which must be a variable of char, byte, short, int, long, float, or double type. The result is stored in the variable. It is a fast way of subtracting 1 from the variable. This operator has the following syntax:

```
'--' variable
```

Consider the following example:

```
int x = 1;
int y = --x;
```

After this example runs, each of x and y is assigned the value 0.

Plus

The + *operator* is a do-nothing operator (it is present for completeness). Its operand must be of char, byte, short, int, long, float, or double type. This operator has the following syntax:

'+' *operand*

Consider the following example:

```
int x = +6;
int y = +x;
```

After the example runs, y is assigned 6.

Minus

The – *operator* negates its operand, which must be of char, byte, short, int, long, float, or double type. This operator has the following syntax:

'-' *operand*

Consider the following example:

```
int x = 6;
int y = -x;
```

After the example runs, y is assigned -6.

Logical Negation

The ! *operator* logically negates its operand, which must be of boolean type. This operand has the following syntax:

'!' *operand*

Consider the following example:

```
boolean first = true;
boolean second = !first;
```

After the example runs, second contains false.

Bitwise Complement

The ~ *operator* flips all the bits in its operand, which must be of char, byte, short, int, or long type and returns the result. This operator has the following syntax:

'~' *operand*

Consider the following example:

```
int x = 20;
int y = ~x;
```

After this example runs, y is assigned -20.

Type Cast

The *(type) operator casts* (converts) the type of its operand to *type*. The operand value is changed to the equivalent value in the new type. This operator has the following syntax:

'(' *type* ')' *operand*

Consider the following example:

```
int x = (int) 1.0;
```

This example converts double value 1.0 to int value 1. This value is then assigned to int variable x. Without the cast, the compiler reports an error.

Unary Post-increment/Post-decrement Operators

Java supports the post-increment (++) and post-decrement (--) unary operators.

Post-increment

The ++ *operator* post-increments its operand, which must be a variable of char, byte, short, int, long, float, or double type. The result is stored in the variable. It is a fast way of adding 1 to the variable. This operator has the following syntax:

variable '++'

Consider the following example:

```
int x = 1;
int y = x++;
```

After this example runs, y is assigned the value 1. However, x contains 2.

Post-decrement

The -- *operator* post-decrements its operand, which must be a variable of char, byte, short, int, long, float, or double type. The result is stored in the variable. It is a fast way of subtracting 1 from the variable. This operator has the following syntax:

variable '--'

Consider the following example:

```
int x = 1;
int y = --x;
```

After this example runs, y is assigned the value 0.

Additional Operators

Java also supports the parentheses[()], array index ([ ]), and member selection (.) operators.

Parentheses

The () *operator* lets you change the precedence order of a numeric expression. For example, consider the following expression:

```
4 + 2 * 3
```

In this expression, 2 * 3 is evaluated first. Then, its product is added to 4.

You can change the evaluation order by using parentheses. Consider this expression:

```
(4 + 2) * 3
```

In this expression, 4 + 2 is evaluated first. Then, its sum is multiplied by 3.

You can nest parentheses to an arbitrary depth. Consider the following expression:

```
(4 + (5 - 3)) * 2
```

The innermost parentheses are evaluated first, so 5 - 3 is initially evaluated. Then, the result is added to 4. Finally, the result is multiplied by 2.

Array Index

The *[ ] operator* lets you extract an element from an array. I discuss arrays in Chapter 5 and will demonstrate this operator in that chapter.

Member Selection

The *. operator* lets you access a field or call a method. This operator has the following syntax:

```
operand1 '.' operand2
```

Operand1 is a reference to an object or reference type (such as a class), which is typically expressed as a variable name (including the name of an object) or a reference type name. *Operand2* is the name of a reference type's field or method. (I discuss objects, classes, fields, and methods in Chapter 6.) Consider the following example:

```
"abc".length()
```

In this expression, string literal "abc" (which is really a String object) provides a reference to this object, and length() is one of the methods in the String class. This method returns the number of characters in "abc", which happens to be 3. (I cover String and its length() method in Chapter 13.)

Playing with Expressions

Expressions can be fun to play with because you never know what you might discover. I've created an ExprDemo application and populated it with several example expressions that serve as a starting point in this exploration. Listing 3-1 presents ExprDemo's source code.

Listing 3-1. ExprDemo.java

```java
class ExprDemo
{
   public static void main(String[] args)
   {
      System.out.println("\"abc\" instanceof String: " +
                         ("abc" instanceof String));
      System.out.println("4 << 1: " + (4 << 1));
      System.out.println("-4 << 1: " + (-4 << 1));
      System.out.println("1 << 31: " + (1 << 31));
      System.out.println("1 << 32: " + (1 << 32));
      System.out.println("-1 << 31: " + (-1 << 31));
      System.out.println("-1 << 32: " + (-1 << 32));
      int x = 3;
      System.out.println("x++: " + x++);
      System.out.println("x: " + x);
      System.out.println("5 / 0: " + (5 / 0));
   }
}
```

ExprDemo focuses on the instanceof, + (string concatenation), () (parenthesis), <<
(shift left), - (negation), = (assignment), ++ (post-increment), and / (division) operators
in the context of expressions whose values are passed as arguments in System.out.
println() method calls.

The first method call's expression uses instanceof to determine if "abc" is an
instance of String, which is an example of a class. (Chapter 6 will teach you about
classes.) Recall that instanceof returns true when its left operand (a reference) is an
instance of its right operand (a reference type); otherwise, it returns false.

It turns out that the "abc" string literal is an instance of String, which makes "abc"
special. You'll learn how special string literals are in Chapter 13 (where I explore String).

The first method call's expression also uses + to concatenate two strings into a larger
string. This operator's left operand is string literal "\"abc\" instanceof String: "
(note the \" escape sequence for placing a double quote character into a string literal),
but the right operand is not a string: the parenthesized "abc" instanceof String
expression evaluates to a Boolean true/false value. What is going on?

Java's + operator adds its numeric operands and returns their sum. However, when one of the operands is a string and the other operand is not a string, + uses *string conversion* to convert the non-string to a string. If the string is an object (you'll learn about objects in Chapter 6), + uses the object's `toString()` method to obtain a string representation of the object. If the operand is a primitive type-based value (such as a Boolean true value), + converts the operand to a string without relying on `toString()`. The + operator appends the right operand string to the left operand string and returns the string that results from this concatenation.

USING THE PARENTHESIS OPERATOR WITH STRING CONCATENTATION

You might wonder why I parenthesized `"abc" instanceof String` in `"\"abc\" instanceof String: " + ("abc" instanceof String)`. I did this because I want the output to read as follows:

`"abc" instanceof String: true`

Without the parentheses, I would have observed the following output:

`true`

String concatenation (+) has higher precedence than relational type checking for objects (`instanceof`). Without parentheses, the compiler generates bytecode as if the expression was parenthesized as follows:

`("\"abc\" instanceof String: " + "abc") instanceof String`

The bytecode first evaluates `"\"abc\" instanceof String: " + "abc"`, which results in `"abcabc"`. It then evaluates `"abcabc" instanceof String`, which returns true. Finally, it executes `System.out.println()` with argument `true`, which is output.

Here is another example expression that doesn't evaluate as expected without parentheses:

`System.out.println("4 + 2: " + 4 + 2);`

This method call outputs `4 + 2: 42` instead of `4 + 2: 6`.

Recall that associativity determines how an expression is evaluated when it contains two or more operators with the same precedence. For example, expression `"4 + 2: " + 4 + 2` consists of sub-expression `"4 + 2: "`, sub-expression `4` (after the left + operator), and sub-expression `2` (after the right + operator).

Expression "4 + 2: " + 4 + 2 is evaluated as follows:

1. "4 + 2: " + 4 is evaluated. The result is string "4 + 2: 4".

2. "4 + 2: 4" + 2 is evaluated. The result is string "4 + 2: 42".

This evaluation order can be clarified by using the parenthesis operator, as follows:

(("4 + 2: " + 4) + 2)

To change this expression so that you observe 4 + 2: 6, you would wrap parentheses around 4 + 2, as follows:

"4 + 2: " + (4 + 2)

This time, (4 + 2) would be evaluated first because the parenthesis operator has the highest precedence.

The << operator shifts its left operand to the left by the number of positions indicated by its right operand. The next six method calls demonstrate this operator.

The expression in the first of these method calls shifts 4 to the left by one position. The result is 8. This is equivalent to multiplying 4 by 2 but is faster.

The second method call's expression shifts -4 to the left by one position. The result is -8. No surprise here!

The third method call's expression shifts 1 to the left by 31 positions. The result is -2147483648, which might seem surprising because 1 is positive and the result is negative. However, when you consider that a 32-bit value is being shifted left, its leftmost bit (position 31 – the rightmost bit is at position 0) is the sign bit (with 0 being positive and 1 being negative), and 31 positions are being shifted with 1 being shifted into the sign bit, it is no surprise.

Java represents integers in *two's-complement* (http://en.wikipedia.org/wiki/Two's_complement) format, which lets you "reversibly convert a positive binary number into a negative binary number with equivalent negative value" by flipping all bits to their opposite states and adding 1 to the result. For example, assuming a 4-bit integer with position 3 as the sign bit, you would represent 5 as 0101. Flipping these bits would result in 1010. Adding 1 to the result would give you 1011, which is the bit pattern for -5 (1111 is the pattern for -1, 1110 is the pattern for -2, 1101 is the pattern for -3, and 1100 is the pattern for -4). You could convert back to 5 by flipping all bits and adding 1 to the result.

The result of the 1 << 32 expression in the fourth method call might be confusing. You might expect the result to be 0 because 1 is shifted past position 31 and 0s are shifted behind it. However, the result is 1. If you recall from my earlier discussion of the shift operators, I said the following:

"For a 32-bit expression, only the five low-order bits of *operand2* are used to prevent shifting more than the number of bits in a 32-bit integer."

The right operand (*operand2*) is 32, which has 32-bit binary representation 00000000000000000000000000100000. The five low-order bits are 00000, which equates to 0. Therefore, the left operand (1) is not shifted and remains the same.

Expression -1 << 31 in the second last of the six method calls that demonstrate the << operator generates the same result as expression 1 << 31 because the rightmost bit in either case is 1 and all bits to the left are shifted out of the result. You end up with 10000000000000000000000000000000 in both cases. This results in -2147483648.

Finally, expression -1 << 32 produces a result of -1 for the same reason that 1 << 32 produces a result of 1. Only the five low-order bits of the right operand are used in the shift, and this results in an attempt to shift the left operand by zero bit positions.

Now that the << operator is out of the way, consider the - (negation) operator. Negation inverts the sign of its 4 operand in the second of the six << operator examples. It also inverts the sign of its 1 operand in each of the fifth and sixth of these examples.

We now move to the declaration of int variable x. This variable is assigned 3 via the = operator.

Next, the output of expression x++ in the System.out.println("x++: " + x++) method call is 3 because post-increment operator ++ returns the current value in its variable operand before incrementing the variable's value. Essentially, it saves the current value in another memory location, performs the increment, and returns the saved value. The same is true for the post-decrement operator (--). In contrast, pre-increment (++) and pre-decrement (--) increment and decrement, respectively, their variable's value and then return the result. To prove that the post-increment operation worked, the third-last method call outputs the value in x.

The final System.out.println() method call's expression attempts to divide by 0 so you can see what Java does in response. You'll discover that an ArithmeticException object is thrown with a "/ by zero" message that indicates an attempt to divide by 0. (I discuss exceptions in Chapter 11.)

Compile Listing 3-1 as follows:

```
javac ExprDemo.java
```

Run the resulting application as follows:

```
java ExprDemo
```

You should discover the following output:

```
"abc" instanceof String: true
4 << 1: 8
-4 << 1: -8
1 << 31: -2147483648
1 << 32: 1
-1 << 31: -2147483648
-1 << 32: -1
x++: 3
x: 4
Exception in thread "main" java.lang.ArithmeticException: / by zero
    at ExprDemo.main(ExprDemo.java:16)
```

What's Next?

Now that you've mastered expressions, you're ready to explore statements. Many statements work with expressions to help you create more interesting programs.

CHAPTER 4

Statements

Computer programs perform tasks via statements. This chapter introduces you to statements in terms of assignment statements, decision statements, loop statements, loop-branching statements, and additional statements.

Introducing Statements

A *statement* is a syntactic unit that expresses some action to be carried out. Statements are used to assign values to variables, control the flow of execution by making decisions and repeating other statements a specific number of times or indefinitely, and carry out other tasks.

Statements can be grouped together and treated as a single statement by placing them between { and } characters. The resulting compound statement is known as a *block*. Each statement except for a block must be terminated with a semicolon (;) character. Although you can terminate a block with a semicolon, doing so isn't conventional.

Assignment Statements

An *assignment statement* assigns the result of an expression to a variable. There are two forms: the simple-assignment statement and the compound-assignment statement.

Simple-Assignment Statement

The *simple-assignment statement* evaluates an expression on the right of the = operator and assigns the result to the variable on the left. It has the following syntax:

```
variable '=' expression ';'
```

61

© Jeff Friesen 2024
J. Friesen, *Learn Java Fundamentals*, https://doi.org/10.1007/979-8-8688-0351-2_4

The statement begins with a *variable* name, continues with the = operator, and concludes with an *expression* and a semicolon. Here are two examples which assume that the variables have been previously declared:

```
healthyBodyTemp = 98.6; // healthyBodyTemp is of type double
name = "John Doe"; // name is of type String
```

Note   Initializing a variable in a variable declaration is a form of the simple-assignment statement, for example, int age = 30;.

Compound-Assignment Statement

Closely related to the simple-assignment statement is the *compound-assignment statement*, which performs an operation and assigns the result to a variable in one step. This statement has the following syntax:

variable ('+=' | '-=' | '*=' | '/=' | '%=' | '&=' | '^=' | '|=' | '<=' | '>=' | '>>>=') *expression* ';'

The statement begins with a *variable* name, continues with one of the specified compound-assignment operators, and concludes with an *expression* and a semicolon. Here is an example which assumes that the variable has been previously declared:

```
counter += 1; // Add 1 to counter's value and store the resulting sum in counter.
```

Decision Statements

A *decision statement* allows a Java program to decide between two or more paths of execution. There are three kinds of decision statements: if, if-else, and switch.

If Statement

The *if statement* evaluates a Boolean expression and executes another statement when this expression is true. This statement has the following syntax:

```
'if' '(' expression ')'
    statement
```

An if statement begins with reserved word if and continues with a Boolean *expression* in parentheses. This is followed by *statement*, which is executed when *expression* is true.

The if statement is demonstrated as follows:

```
if (temperature < 70)
    turn_on_furnace();
```

If temperature's value drops below 70 degrees Fahrenheit (as determined by evaluating Boolean expression temperature < 70 and discovering true as its value), invoke method turn_on_furnace() to turn on the furnace and warm up the room. (I discuss methods in Chapter 6.)

If-Else Statement

The *if-else* statement evaluates a Boolean expression and executes either of two statements depending on whether this expression evaluates to true or false. This statement has the following syntax:

```
'if' '(' expression ')'
    statement1
'else'
    statement2
```

An if-else statement begins with reserved word if and continues with a Boolean *expression* in parentheses. This is followed by *statement1*, which is executed when *expression* is true, and (following reserved word else) *statement2*, which is executed when *expression* is false.

This statement is demonstrated as follows:

```
if (temperature < 70)
    turn_on_furnace();
else
    turn_off_furnace();
```

If temperature's value drops below 70 degrees Fahrenheit (as determined by evaluating Boolean expression temperature < 70 and discovering true as its value), invoke method turn_on_furnace() to turn on the furnace and warm up the room. Otherwise, invoke method turn_off_furnace() to turn off the furnace (the room has reached 70 degrees).

You can chain together multiple if-else statements as follows:

```
'if' '(' expression1 ')'
    statement1
'else'
'if' '(' expression2 ')'
    statement2
'else'
'if' '(' expression3 ')'
    statement3
'else'
...
    statementN
```

If *expression1* is true, *statement1* executes. However, if *expression2* is false, if '(' *expression2* ')' executes and evaluates *expression2*. If true, *statement2* executes. This process continues until one of these expressions is true and its corresponding statement executes. If none of these expressions are true, else is reached and *statementN* (the default statement) executes.

The following example demonstrates this chaining capability:

```
if (direction == "North")
    travelNorth();
else
if (direction == "East")
    travelEast();
else
if (direction == "South")
    travelSouth();
else
    travelWest();
```

DANGLING-ELSE PROBLEM

When `if` and `if-else` are used together, and the source code is not properly indented, it can be difficult to determine which `if` associates with `else`. For example:

```
if (file.isOpen())
if (file.isReadable())
file.read();
else
file.open();
```

Did the developer intend for `else` to match the inner `if` but improperly formatted the code to make it appear otherwise? For example:

```
if (file.isOpen())
   if (file.isReadable())
      file.read();
   else
      file.open();
```

If `file.isOpen()` and `file.isReadable()` each return true, `file.read();` executes. If `file.isOpen()` returns true and `file.isReadable()` returns false, `file.open();` executes. Attempting to open an open file makes no sense.

The developer must have wanted `else` to match the outer `if` but forgot that `else` matches the nearest `if`. This problem can be fixed by surrounding the inner `if` with braces, as follows:

```
if (file.isOpen())
{
   if (file.isReadable())
      file.read();
}
else
   file.open();
```

When `file.isOpen()` returns true, the block that follows executes. When this method returns false, `file.open();` executes, which makes sense.

Forgetting that `else` matches the nearest `if` and using poor indentation to obscure this fact is known as the *dangling-else problem*.

Switch Statement

The *switch statement* lets you select one of multiple execution paths more efficiently than with equivalent chained `if-else` statements. This statement has the following syntax:

```
'switch' '(' selector expression ')'
'{'
    'case' value1 ':' statement1 ['break' ';']
    'case' value2 ':' statement2 ['break' ';']
    ...
    'case' valueN ':' statementN ['break' ';']
    ['default' ':' statement]
'}'
```

The `switch` statement begins with reserved word `switch`, followed by a *selector expression* in parentheses and a body of cases. The *selector expression* is any expression that evaluates to an integer, character, or string.

Each `case` begins with reserved word `case`, continues with a literal value and a colon (`:`) character, continues with a statement to execute, and optionally concludes with a `break` statement (discussed later in this chapter). The `break` statement causes execution to continue after the `switch` statement.

After evaluating *selector_expression*, `switch` compares this value with each `case`'s value until it finds a match. If there is a match, the `case`'s statement is executed. For example, if *selector_expression*'s value matches *value1*, *statement1* executes.

The optional `break` statement (anything in square brackets is optional), which consists of reserved word `break` followed by a semicolon (`;`), prevents the flow of execution from continuing with the next `case`'s statement. Instead, execution continues with the first statement following `switch`.

BREAK STATEMENT PLACEMENT AND A HARD-TO-FIND BUG

You will usually place a `break` statement after a `case`'s statement. Forgetting to include `break` can lead to a hard-to-find bug in which execution flows from the end of a `case` and to the beginning of the following `case`, instead of leaving the `switch` statement immediately after the first `case` finishes. However, there are situations where you want to group several cases together and have them execute common code. For example, you have written code that prompts the user to enter character Y (for Yes) or character y (for yes) to continue a program, and you want to execute the same code regardless of which character has been entered. In such a situation, you would omit the break statement from the participating cases except for the last case in the group.Consider the following example:

```
System.out.print("Enter Y or y to end program:");
// Code to input Y or y and store this character in char variable ch.
switch (ch)
{
   case 'Y':
   case 'y': System.out.println("Y or y has been entered.");
           break;
}
```

If none of the cases' values match the *selector_expression*'s value, and if a default case (signified by the default reserved word followed by a colon) is present, the default case's statement is executed. The following example demonstrates this statement:

```
String direction = "East";
switch (direction)
{
   case "North": travelNorth(); break;
   case "East": travelEast(); break;
   case "South": travelSouth(); break;
   default: travelWest();
}
```

After declaring variable direction and initializing this variable to "East", the example enters the switch statement. This statement reads direction's string and then compares this value with each case's string in top-down order until a match is found.

It first compares "East" with "North". Because they don't match, switch proceeds to the next case, whose string value is "East". Because they match, switch calls a method (I discuss methods in Chapter 6) named travelEast(). When this method returns, switch executes the break statement, which causes execution to proceed to the first statement following switch.

Suppose that `direction` had been initialized to `"SouthWest"`. Because none of the cases' strings would have matched, `switch` would have executed the `default` case: its `travelWest()` method would have been invoked.

Loop Statements

A *loop statement* allows a Java program to repeatedly execute other statements. There are three kinds of loop statements: `for`, `while`, and `do-while`.

Note   Each occurrence of a repeated execution is known as a *loop*. Furthermore, each loop execution is known as an *iteration*.

For Statement

The *for statement* iterates over another statement a specific number of times or indefinitely. This statement has the following syntax:

```
'for' '(' [initialize] ';' [test] ';' [update] ')'
   statement
```

The `for` statement begins with reserved word `for`, followed by a header in parentheses, followed by *statement*. The header begins with an optional *initialize* section followed by a non-optional semicolon character. It continues with an optional *test* section followed by a semicolon character. It concludes with an optional *update* section.

The *initialize* section consists of a comma (`,`)-separated list of variable declarations or variable assignments. Some or all of these variables are typically used to control the loop's duration and are known as *loop-control variables*.

The *test* section consists of a Boolean expression that determines the length of the loop. The loop continues for as long as this expression is true.

The *update* section consists of a comma-separated list of expressions that typically modify the loop-control variables.

The for statement first executes the *initialize* section. It then executes the *test* section to determine if the loop should continue. The *test* section consists of a Boolean expression that returns true to continue or false not to continue. After *statement* executes, the *update* section is executed, followed by *test*, *statement*, *update*, *test*, *statement*, *update*, and so on.

The following example demonstrates the for statement:

```
for (int i = 0; i < 10; i++)
{
    for (int j = 0; j < i; j++)
        System.out.print("*");
    System.out.println();
}
```

The outer for statement begins with an initialization section consisting of int i = 0;. This compound-assignment statement declares an int variable named i and initializes it to 0. After executing this section, for turns its attention to the testing section, which consists of i < 10.

The i < 10 Boolean expression compares the value in i with 10. As long as i's value is less than 10, the for statement will continue to iterate over its *statement*.

Continuing, this example enters the block that follows the for statement's header.

The block initially executes the inner for statement, whose initialization section introduces another int variable, j, which is initialized to 0. Furthermore, its testing section evaluates j < i, which compares the current values in j and i. For as long as j's value is less than i's value, this Boolean expression will evaluate to true and this other for statement will continue to iterate.

Assuming that the expression is true, execution passes to System.out.print("*");, which outputs an asterisk (*) without subsequently advancing to the next output line. Following the output, the inner for statement's updating section executes j++, which increments the value stored in j.

The inner for statement begins another iteration by evaluating j < i. Once j's value exceeds i's value, execution will leave the inner for statement and System.out.println(); will execute, causing subsequent output to begin at the start of the next output line.

This example draws the following pattern:

```
*
**
***
****
*****
******
*******
********
*********
```

While Statement

The *while statement* repeatedly executes a statement while its Boolean expression is true. This statement has the following syntax:

```
'while' '(' expression ')'
   statement
```

The while statement consists of reserved word while, followed by a parenthesized Boolean *expression*, followed by *statement*, which is executed repeatedly.

The while statement first evaluates *expression*. If it returns true, the program executes *statement*. It then evaluates *expression*. If it is still true, *statement* is once again executed. This behavior continues until *expression* evaluates to false, at which time execution proceeds to the first statement following *statement*.

The following example demonstrates the while statement:

```
long fact = 1;
int i = 1;
while (i <= 4)
    fact *= i++;
System.out.println(fact);
```

This example calculates 4! (factorial). A *factorial* is the product of integers starting at 1 and ranging to the integer whose factorial is desired. For example, 4! = 1 x 2 x 3 x 4 (or 24). (Note that 0! evaluates to 1.)

After declaring variables fact (to hold the factorial) and i (a loop counter that records the current loop iteration), the example enters a while loop. This loop first verifies that i has not exceeded four iterations by evaluating i <= 4. As long as this Boolean expression evaluates to true, the while loop will continue.

Each iteration executes fact *= i++;. This compound-assignment statement accomplishes several things:

1. It retrieves i's value and stores it in a memory location before incrementing this value and storing the resulting sum in i.

2. It retrieves fact's value along with the stored value read from i and multiplies these values together.

3. It stores the value resulting from the multiplication in fact.

When the while loop finishes, System.out.println(fact); is executed. The value stored in fact is retrieved and then output to the console.

Note the presence of the post-increment operator ++. This operator increments variable i, allowing the loop to end eventually. If it weren't present, the loop would never end because i would never advance and always contain 1, which is less than 4.

Note   A never-ending loop is known as an *infinite loop*.

This example produces the following output:

24

A for statement can be easily coded via an equivalent while statement, as the following example (which sums the integers from 1 through 10) demonstrates:

```
int sum = 0;
for (int i = 1; i < 10; i++)
   sum += i;
```

After declaring variable sum, the example enters the for statement, which first declares variable i and initializes it to 1. It then evaluates Boolean expression i < 10. As long as i's value is less than 10, the for statement will keep looping over the sum += i; statement that follows.

This latter expression statement uses += (one of the compound-assignment operators) to add the value in i to the value in sum. Following this update, the for statement executes i++ to increment i. Next, it evaluates i < 10 and re-executes sum += i; for as long as i's value is less than 10.

The equivalent while statement appears as follows:

```
int sum = 0;
int i = 1;
while (i < 10)
{
   sum += i;
   i++;
}
```

Do-While Statement

The *do-while statement* repeatedly executes a statement while its Boolean expression is true. Unlike the while statement, which evaluates the Boolean expression at the top of the loop, do-while evaluates the Boolean expression at the bottom of the loop. This statement has the following syntax:

```
'do'
  statement
'while' '(' expression ')' ';'
```

The do-while statement consists of reserved word do, followed by *statement*, which it executes repeatedly, followed by reserved word while, followed by a parenthesized Boolean expression, followed by a semicolon.

The do-while statement first executes *statement*. It then evaluates *expression*. If it is true, do-while executes *statement*. Again, the Boolean expression is evaluated. If it is still true, do-while re-executes *statement*. This cyclic pattern continues until *expression* is false.

The following example demonstrates the do-while statement:

```
long fact = 1;
int i = 1;
```

```
do
    fact *= i++;
while (i <= 4)
System.out.println(fact);
```

This example is functionally identical to the example in the previous section. The only difference is the location of the test expression.

Tip Use a while statement when the loop must execute zero or more times. Use a do-while statement when the loop must execute one or more times.

Loop-Branching Statements

Computer programs often need to terminate a loop or skip the current iteration of a loop. They perform these tasks by executing a break or continue *loop-branching statement*.

Break Statement

The *break statement* lets you terminate a switch statement, which you've already seen. However, the *break statement* also lets you terminate a loop. This is necessary when the loop is infinite, as in a for (;;), while (true), or do ... while(true) loop. It can also be necessary in a finite loop context.

The break statement has the following syntax:

```
'break' ';'
```

The following example shows how to break out of an infinite loop:

```
while (true)
{
    System.out.println("Press x to exit the loop.");
    // The following method call reads a character from the keyboard
    and assigns
    // its int value to ch. I will have more to say about System.in.read()
    in Chapter 14.
    int ch = System.in.read();
```

73

```
    if (ch == 'x')
        break;
}
```

When ch == 'x' is true, the if statement executes break, which transfers execution to the first statement following the while loop.

The following example shows how to break out of a finite loop:

```
for (int i = 0; i < 100000; i++)
    if (i > 500)
        break;
    else
        System.out.println(i);
```

This example breaks out of the loop when the value in i exceeds 500.

Labeled Break

The break statement can be specified with a *label* (an identifier followed by a colon), which lets you break out of *nested loops* (loops inside of other loops). This variation of the break statement lets you transfer execution to the first statement following the loop that's prefixed by the label and has the following syntax:

```
'break' label ';'
```

The following example demonstrates labeled break:

```
outer:
for (int a = 0; a < 5; a++)
{
    for (int b = 0; b < 5; b++)
    {
        System.out.println("a = " + a + ", b = " + b);
        if (b == 3)
            break outer;
    }
    System.out.println();
}
System.out.println("Both loops have finished");
```

This example presents a pair of for loops. The outer loop potentially executes five times. For each of these iterations, the inner loop potentially executes five times. However, when b == 3 evaluates to true, the flow of execution leaves both the inner and outer loops and continues with the first statement following the outer:-labeled for loop.

The following output is generated:

```
a = 0, b = 0
a = 0, b = 1
a = 0, b = 2
a = 0, b = 3
Both loops have finished
```

Continue Statement

The *continue statement* lets you skip the current iteration of a loop. This is necessary when a certain condition is met earlier in the iteration and you don't want to continue with the rest of the iteration.

The continue statement has the following syntax:

```
'continue' ';'
```

The following example shows how to cancel the rest of an iteration:

```
int count = 0;
String s = "To be or not to be, that is the question.";
for (int i = 0; i < s.length(); i++)
{
   if (s.charAt(i) != 'e')
      continue;
   count++;
}
System.out.println("Number of 'e' characters = " + count);
```

This example counts the number of letter 'e's in a string. After initializing a count variable to record the number of 'e's and an s variable to refer to a sample string, it enters a for loop, which iterates over the length of the string. Expression s.length() invokes String's length() method on variable s, which holds a reference to the string being processed, to return this string's length. (I explore String and its length() method in Chapter 13.)

For each loop iteration, an `if-else` statement is executed. This statement invokes `String`'s `charAt()` method to return the next character from the string. (I explore `charAt()` in Chapter 13.) If this character doesn't equal e, the `continue` statement is executed to skip the rest of the loop iteration so that `count++` isn't executed. However, if this character equals e, `continue` isn't executed but `count++` is executed to increase the tally of 'e's seen. Once the entire string has been examined, the loop ends, and the count of 'e's is output.

Labeled Continue

The `continue` statement can be specified with a label, which lets you skip the rest of the current iteration of nested loops. This variation of the `continue` statement lets you transfer execution to the Boolean expression of the loop statement that's prefixed by the label and has the following syntax:

```
'continue' label ';'
```

The following example demonstrates labeled `continue`:

```
outer:
for (int a = 0; a < 5; a++)
{
   for (int b = 0; b < 5; b++)
   {
      System.out.println("a = " + a + ", b = " + b);
      if (b == 3)
         continue outer;
   }
   System.out.println();
}
System.out.println("Both loops have finished");
```

This example is similar to the earlier example when I discussed labeled `break`. However, the output is somewhat different:

```
a = 0, b = 0
a = 0, b = 1
a = 0, b = 2
```

```
a = 0, b = 3
a = 1, b = 0
a = 1, b = 1
a = 1, b = 2
a = 1, b = 3
a = 2, b = 0
a = 2, b = 1
a = 2, b = 2
a = 2, b = 3
a = 3, b = 0
a = 3, b = 1
a = 3, b = 2
a = 3, b = 3
a = 4, b = 0
a = 4, b = 1
a = 4, b = 2
a = 4, b = 3
Both loops have finished
```

Previously, the output stopped after a = 0, b = 3. Now, it continues for each value of a from 0 through 4. However, you still won't see b = 4 in the output because the inner loop is skipped over when b equals 3.

Additional Statements

Java supports additional statements that deserve mention: the `assert` statement, the empty statement, the `import` statement, the method-call statement, the `package` statement, the `return` statement, the `try` statement, and the `try-with-resources` statement.

Assert Statement

The *assert statement* lets you express an assumption of program correctness via a Boolean expression. I don't discuss this statement in this book.

Empty Statement

The *empty statement* is a single semicolon (;) character. It's occasionally convenient to have a for statement repeatedly execute this statement because the actual work is performed in for's header. Consider the following example:

```
for (String line; (line = readLine()) != null; System.out.println(line));
```

This example uses a for loop to read and print out all lines (possibly from a file) until there are no more lines to read. We are copying lines from a source to a destination.

A line is read by calling a readLine() method (which you would specify elsewhere). The line is printed via the System.out.println() method call. Note the semicolon at the end of the line. This semicolon is the empty statement.

Caution   The empty statement can introduce subtle bugs into your code. For example, the following loop should output Java is great! on 15 lines. Instead, only one instance of this message appears because it's the empty statement that's executed 15 times.

```
for (int i = 0; i < 15; i++);
    System.out.println("Java is great!");
```

Import Statement

The *import statement* imports a type from a package. I fully discuss import in Chapter 10.

Method-Call Statement

The *method-call statement* calls a method, which may or may not return a result. If the method's return type is void, the method doesn't return a value. For example, the various println() methods in System.out.println() method-call contexts have void return types – this reserved word indicates that each println() method doesn't return a value. I fully discuss the method-call statement in Chapter 6.

Package Statement

The *package statement* places one or more reference types in a package. I fully discuss package in Chapter 10.

Return Statement

The *return statement* returns execution from a method to the code that called that method. It optionally returns a value whose type matches the method's return type. I fully discuss return in Chapter 6.

Try Statement

The *try statement* provides a way to detect a thrown *exception* (a divergence from the normal flow of execution) from a block of code and then pass it to another block of code to handle the exception. I fully discuss try in Chapter 11.

Try-with-resources Statement

The *try-with-resources statement* is a try statement that declares one or more *resources* (objects that must be closed when not needed). It closes each resource. I fully discuss try-with-resources in Chapter 11.

Playing with Statements

Statements can be fun to play with because you never know what you might discover. I've created a StmtDemo application and populated it with several example statements that serve as a starting point in this exploration. Listing 4-1 presents StmtDemo's source code.

Listing 4-1. StmtDemo.java

```java
class StmtDemo
{
   public static void main(String[] args)
   {
      if (args.length != 1)
```

```java
        {
            System.out.println("usage: java StmtDemo ([-h] | [-v] | " +
            "[positive integer count])");
            return;
        }

        switch (args[0])
        {
            case "-H":
            case "-h": System.out.println("help");
                       return;

            case "-V":
            case "-v": System.out.println("version 1.0");
                       return;

            default  : int count = 0;
                       for (int i = 0; i < args[0].length(); i++)
                       {
                           char digit = args[0].charAt(i);
                           if (digit < '0' || digit > '9')
                           {
                               System.out.println("invalid character detected: "
                               + digit);
                               return;
                           }
                           count *= 10;
                           count += digit - '0';
                       }
                       for (int i = 0; i < count; i++)
                           System.out.print("*");
                       System.out.println();
        }
    }
}
```

StmtDemo focuses on the if, method-call, return, switch, simple-assignment, for, and compound-assignment statements.

The main() method's first example statement uses if to ensure that a single command-line argument has been specified. It evaluates Boolean expression args. length != 1 and then executes a block when this isn't the case (the Boolean expression evaluates to true because zero arguments were specified or more than one argument was specified).

The second example statement uses the System.out.println() method call to output a usage message. System.out.println() is the first statement of the block.

The third example statement uses return to exit the main() method and terminate the program. This is the second statement of the block.

The fourth example statement uses switch to identify the first and only command-line argument passed to the program. The command-line argument is stored in args[0], which is the first location in the args array. (I cover arrays in Chapter 5.)

The switch statement presents additional statements via its cases.

The first two cases compare args[0] with "-H" and "-h", respectively. Notice that case "-H" is empty: it doesn't specify any statements, not even a break statement. Because there is no break statement, execution falls through to case "-h"'s statements when -H is specified on the command line.

The first of case "-h"'s statements is a System.out.println() method call that outputs a brief help message. Presumably, -h results in useful help information on program usage. In this example, I've provided a simple message to give you a sense of what could appear.

The second of case "-h"'s statements is a return statement, which transfers execution out of the switch statement and the main() method, terminating the program.

The next two cases compare args[0] with "-V" and "-v", respectively. They are functionally identical to the first two cases but output a brief version number message instead.

Note   Many programs have version numbers. For example, 1.0 typically indicates the first version of a program. The number before the period (.) is often referred to as the major component, and the number after the period is often referred to as the minor component. In this example, "1" is the major component and "0" is the minor component.

The major component indicates a major change to a program. The minor component indicates a minor change to a program. Check out Wikipedia's "Software versioning" entry (`http://en.wikipedia.org/wiki/Software_versioning`) to learn more about version numbers.

The `default` case is executed when something other than -H, -h, -V, or –v is specified on the command line.

The first statement executed by `default` is a variation of the simple-assignment statement that declares and initializes, to 0, a `count` variable.

The next statement to execute is a `for` statement that iterates over the command-line argument's characters.

The `for` statement declares an `int` variable named `i` and initializes this variable to 0 in its initialization section. It then compares this variable with `args[0].length()`, which returns the number of characters that make up the command-line argument.

The `args[0].length()` expression consists of two operands separated by the member-selection operator (`.`). The `args[0]` operand uses the array index operator (`[]`) to return the first command-line argument from the array, which is expressed as a string. The `length()` operand is a `String` method that returns the number of characters in the string.

The block that `for` executes begins with `char digit = args[0].charAt(i);`, which extracts the next character (which is expected to be a digit) from the `args[0]` string and assigns it to `char` variable `digit`. `String` provides a `charAt()` method that returns the character at the index specified by its single argument, which must be an `int`.

The block next executes an `if` statement whose Boolean expression compares `digit`'s stored character with `'0'` and also with `'9'`. If this character is numerically less than `'0'`'s Unicode number or greater than `'9'`'s Unicode number, a block is invoked.

Note   When creating a Java program that is to be used in countries with digit characters other than 0 through 9 (see `http://en.wikipedia.org/wiki/Tamil_numerals` for an example), it is not a good idea to hard-code expressions such as `digit < '0' || digit > '9'`. Instead, you would invoke the `Character` class's `boolean isDigit(char ch)` method to determine whether a character represents a digit or not. (`Character` is a member of Java's reference type library.)

The block first executes a System.out.println() method call to output an error message along with the offending character. (Note the + operator's use in concatenating two strings into a third string.)

The block then executes a return statement, which causes execution to leave main() and terminate the program.

If the character stored in the digit variable is, in fact, a digit, execution proceeds to a pair of compound-assignment statements:

```
count *= 10;
count += digit - '0';
```

The first compound-assignment statement reads count's value, multiplies it by 10, and stores the result in count. The second compound statement reads count's value, adds the Unicode number in digit to this value, and then subtracts the Unicode number for '0'. The result is stored in count.

The main() method's last two example statements consist of a for statement to output count asterisks (*) and a System.out.println(); method call statement to cause subsequent output to begin at the start of the next output line.

Compile Listing 4-1 as follows:

```
javac StmtDemo.java
```

Run the resulting application as follows:

```
java StmtDemo
```

You should observe the following output:

```
usage: java StmtDemo ([-h] | [-v] | [positive integer count])
```

Now, run the application with the –h (or -H) command-line option:

```
java StmtDemo -h
```

The application responds by outputting the following message:

```
help
```

Continuing, run the application with the -v (or -V) command-line option:

```
java StmtDemo -v
```

You should observe the following output:

```
version 1.0
```

Finally, run the application with argument 10:

```
java StmtDemo 10
```

You should now observe ten asterisks on the output line:

```
**********
```

What's Next?

Now that you've mastered statements, you can start to create interesting programs. The next chapter introduces the array, which lets you associate multiple values with a single variable. Arrays let you create programs that are more interesting than what you've seen so far in this book.

CHAPTER 5

Arrays

Java supports arrays, one of the oldest and most widely used data structures ("a data organization, management, and storage format that is usually chosen for efficient access to data" – see http://en.wikipedia.org/wiki/Data_structure for more information). This chapter introduces you to this support in terms of one-dimensional arrays and two-dimensional arrays. It demonstrates one-dimensional arrays in terms of searching and sorting and two-dimensional arrays in terms of matrix multiplication.

Introducing Arrays

An *array* is a *data structure* consisting of a sequence of *elements* (values stored in an array) with the same memory size, where each element is associated with at least one *index* (a non-negative integer that uniquely identifies an element). The number of indexes associated with an element is known as the array's *dimension*.

In Java, arrays have fixed sizes. You cannot expand or contract an array. Instead, you need to create a new array of the desired size and copy the elements from the current array to the new array before destroying the current array.

One-Dimensional Arrays

A *one-dimensional array* (1D array – also known as a *vector*) is an array that associates each element with one index. It's used to store a list of values. The array is stored with an array variable, whose syntax appears as follows:

type '[' ']' *identifier*

　or

type identifier '[' ']'

© Jeff Friesen 2024
J. Friesen, *Learn Java Fundamentals*, https://doi.org/10.1007/979-8-8688-0351-2_5

The square brackets may appear after the *type* name (the preferred approach) or after the *identifier* that names the variable (an approach introduced to smooth the transition of C and C++ programmers to Java). They signify that *identifier* refers to a 1D array whose elements have the specified *type*. The type of the array is *type*[].

Creating a 1D Array

There are three approaches to creating a 1D array: use only an initializer, use only keyword new, and use keyword new with an initializer.

Use Only an Initializer

The initializer-only approach adheres to the following syntax:

```
'{' [expr (',' expr)*]  '}'
```

This syntax reveals that a 1D array is an optional comma-separated list of expressions appearing between open and close brace characters. Furthermore, the types of all expressions must be compatible. For example, one expression cannot be a string while another expression is an integer.

Note   The preceding syntax uses special notation to provide a compact representation. Furthermore, a value that a programmer must supply is placed between quotes, single (') or double ("). Everything between [and] is optional. Everything between (and) is treated as a single unit. The * means repeat everything between (and) zero or more times. A + would mean repeat everything between (and) one or more times. I've presented some of this syntax in previous chapters and will continue to use the syntax in later chapters.

The following example demonstrates the initializer approach to creating a 1D array:

```
String[] directions = {"North", "South", "East", "West"};
```

The example creates a 1D array of four strings and assigns the 1D array's reference to directions. Figure 5-1 presents a conceptual view of this array.

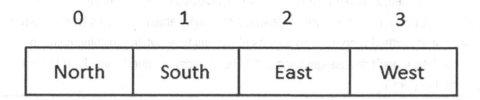

Figure 5-1. *A conceptual view of the array assigned to directions*

North is located at index 0, South is located at index 1, East is located at index 2, and West is located at index 3.

Use Only Keyword new

The keyword new-only approach adheres to the following syntax:

```
'new' type '[' int_expr ']'
```

Keyword new allocates memory for the array. The number of elements is specified by *int_expr* (a non-negative integer that's typically greater than 0), and the size of each element is implied by *type*. All elements are zeroed (and interpreted as 0, 0L, 0.0F, 0.0, false, null, or '\u0000').

PREALLOCATING AN ARRAY WITH A ZERO SIZE

Sometimes, 0 is specified for *int_expr*. A zero is specified when the programmer writes a method to preallocate an array, and the method needs to know the array's element type — the method doesn't care about the array's size. For example, you might specify the following:

```
ArrayList list = new ArrayList(100);
int[] copy = list.toArray(new int[0]);
```

This example first creates an array list and assigns its reference to a list variable of type ArrayList. It then invokes ArrayList's toArray() method (see Chapter 6 for a discussion of methods) to convert the array list to an array. Expression new int[0] is passed to toArray() so that the method will preallocate an int[] array that can hold all of the elements in the list. (We'll assume that each element has type int.) Furthermore, toArray() returns the array. However, if you specified the following:

```
double[] copy = list.toArray(new double[0]);
```

the `toArray()` method would return an array of type `double[]`. The ability for `toArray()` to change its return type is a feature of *generics*, an enhancement to Java's type system that allows a type or method to operate on objects of various types while providing compile-time type safety. (I don't discuss generics in this book because I don't consider it to be a fundamental feature.)

The previous example (minus the element values) could be expressed as follows:

```
String[] directions = new String[4];
```

Values would be filled in later.

Use Keyword new with an Initializer

The final approach to creating an array is to use keyword new with an initializer. This approach has the following syntax:

```
'new' type '[' ']' '{' [expr (',' expr)*] '}'
```

This syntax blends the previous two syntaxes. Because the number of elements can be determined from the comma-separated list of expressions, it isn't necessary (or allowed) to provide an *int_expr* between the square brackets.

The following example demonstrates the keyword new with initializer approach to creating a 1D array:

```
String[] directions = new String[] {"North", "South", "East", "West"};
```

The initializer-only approach's syntax serves as *syntactic sugar* (syntax that makes the language sweeter to use) for the third approach. You would use the array index operator to index into this array and access an element.

Accessing 1D Array Elements

A 1D array variable is associated with a `.length` property that returns the length of the associated 1D array as a positive `int`; for example, `directions.length` returns 4. This value is important when accessing a 1D array's elements.

Given a 1D array variable, you can access any element by specifying an expression that agrees with the following syntax:

array_var '[' *index* ']'

Here, *index* is a positive int that ranges from zero (Java arrays are zero based) to one less than the value returned from the .length property.

Consider the previous directions array. The following example references the first element:

```
directions[0]
```

You can print out this element as follows:

```
System.out.println(directions[0]);
```

You could use a for loop to print out all elements as follows:

```
for (int i = 0; i < directions.length; i++)
   System.out.println(directions[i]);
```

You could modify the third element as follows:

```
directions[2] = "EAST"; // Because Java arrays are 0-based, directions[2]
                        // accesses the third element.
```

If you specify a negative index or an index greater than or equal to the array's length, Java will create and throw an ArrayIndexOutOfBoundsException object. I'll have more to say about this topic when I discuss exceptions in Chapter 11.

Searching and Sorting

Programmers often write code to search a 1D array for a specific element and to sort a 1D array's elements into ascending or descending order of value. Two commonly used search algorithms are *Linear Search* and *Binary Search*. *Bubble Sort* is a simple algorithm for sorting, but one that isn't efficient for large arrays.

Linear Search

Linear Search searches a 1D array of *n* elements for a specific element by comparing elements from the lowest to the highest index until it finds the element or there are no more elements to compare.

I've created an LSearch application that demonstrates Linear Search. Listing 5-1 presents this application's source code.

Listing 5-1. LSearch.java

```java
class LSearch
{
   public static void main(String[] args)
   {
      int[] grades = { 86, 92, 68, 75, 79, 81 };

      int gradeToSearch = 68;
      int i;
      for (i = 0; i < grades.length; i++)
         if (grades[i] == gradeToSearch)
         {
            System.out.println("Found " + gradeToSearch + " at
            position " + i);
            break;
         }
      if (i == grades.length)
         System.out.println("Could not find " + gradeToSearch);

      gradeToSearch = 74;
      for (i = 0; i < grades.length; i++)
         if (grades[i] == gradeToSearch)
         {
            System.out.println("Found " + gradeToSearch + " at
            position " + i);
            break;
         }
```

```
    if (i == grades.length)
        System.out.println("Could not find " + gradeToSearch);
  }
}
```

LSearch first searches a grades array for element 68. It finds this element and outputs a success message. It then searches grades for element 74. Because this element is not present, LSearch outputs a failure message.

Assuming that you've copied Listing 5-1 to a file named LSearch.java, compile Listing 5-1 as follows:

```
javac LSearch.java
```

If compilation succeeds, you should observe an LSearch.class file in the current directory. Run this application as follows:

```
java LSearch
```

You should observe the following output:

```
Found 68 at position 2
Could not find 74
```

Binary Search

Linear Search is a simple algorithm to implement. However, it is quite slow to accomplish its task for very long arrays. In the worst case, it might have to examine all elements when the desired element is in the last array slot. On average, it has to search about half the array. Fortunately, there exists a faster algorithm for searching 1D arrays.

Binary Search searches a 1D array of *n* elements for a specific element by adhering to the following steps:

1. Set low and high index variables to the indexes of the array's first and last elements, respectively.

2. Terminate when the low index is greater than the high index. The searched-for element is not in the array.

3. Calculate the middle index by summing the low and high indexes and dividing the sum by 2.

4.   Compare the searched-for element with the middle-indexed data item. Terminate when they are the same. The searched-for element has been found.

5.   If the searched-for element is greater than the middle-indexed element, set the low index to the middle index plus one and transfer execution to step 2. Binary Search repeats the search in the upper half of the array.

6.   The searched-for element must be smaller than the middle-indexed element, so set the high index to the middle index minus one and transfer execution to step 2. Binary Search repeats the search in the lower half of the array.

Although not as intuitive to understand as Linear Search, Binary Search is much faster. For example, when confronted with a 1D array with 4294967296 elements, Linear Search must perform an average of 2147483648 comparisons. In contrast, Binary Search performs a maximum of 32 comparisons.

I've created a BSearch application that demonstrates Binary Search. Listing 5-2 presents this application's source code.

Listing 5-2. BSearch.java

```java
class BSearch
{
   public static void main(String[] args)
   {
      int[] nums = { 4, 5, 8, 11, 19, 33, 42, 51, 67, 69, 83, 84, 86, 91,
      93, 98 };

      int high = nums.length - 1, low = 0, mid;
      int srchint = 83;
      while (low <= high)
      {
         mid = (low + high) / 2;
         if (srchint > nums[mid])
            low = mid + 1;
```

```
        else
        if (srchint < nums[mid])
            high = mid - 1;
        else
        {
            System.out.println("Found " + srchint);
            break;
        }
    }
    if (low > high)
        System.out.println("Could not find " + srchint);

    high = nums.length - 1;
    low = 0;
    srchint = 27;
    while (low <= high)
    {
        mid = (low + high) / 2;
        if (srchint > nums[mid])
            low = mid + 1;
        else
        if (srchint < nums[mid])
            high = mid - 1;
        else
        {
            System.out.println("Found " + srchint);
            break;
        }
    }
    System.out.println("Could not find " + srchint);
    }
}
```

BSearch first searches a nums array for element 83. It finds this element and outputs a success message. It then searches grades for element 27. Because this element is not present, BSearch outputs a failure message.

Assuming that you've copied Listing 5-2 to a file named `BSearch.java`, compile Listing 5-2 as follows:

```
javac BSearch.java
```

If compilation succeeds, you should observe a `BSearch.class` file in the current directory. Run this application as follows:

```
java BSearch
```

You should observe the following output:

```
Found 83
Could not find 27
```

Bubble Sort

Unlike Linear Search, Binary Search requires the 1D array to be sorted. A simple but not very efficient algorithm for this task is Bubble Sort.

Bubble Sort sorts a 1D array of *n* elements into ascending or descending order. An outer loop makes *n* - 1 passes over the array. Each pass invokes an inner loop to exchange elements such that the next smallest (ascending sort) or largest (descending sort) element "bubbles" toward the beginning of the array.

Each inner loop iteration compares the pass-numbered element with each successive element. If a successor element is smaller (ascending sort) or larger (descending sort) than the pass-numbered element, the successor element is exchanged with the pass-numbered element.

I've created a `BSort` application to demonstrate Bubble Sort. Listing 5-3 presents this application's source code.

Listing 5-3. `BSort.java`

```
class BSort
{
   public static void main(String[] args)
   {
      int[] grades = { 86, 92, 68, 75, 79, 81 };

      for (int pass = 0; pass < grades.length - 1; pass++)
```

```
        for (int i = grades.length - 1; i > pass; i--)
            if (grades[i] < grades[pass])
            {
                // Swap grades[i] with grades[pass].
                int temp = grades[i];
                grades[i] = grades[pass];
                grades[pass] = temp;
            }

        for (int i = 0; i < grades.length; i++)
            System.out.println(grades[i]);
    }
}
```

BSort sorts an array of grades into ascending order. It makes `grades.length - 1` passes over the `grades` array. Each pass swaps elements until the next smallest element is placed into the proper position.

Assuming that you've copied Listing 5-3 to a file named `BSort.java`, compile Listing 5-3 as follows:

```
javac BSort.java
```

If compilation succeeds, you should observe a `BSort.java` file in the current directory. Run this application as follows:

```
java BSort
```

You should observe the following output:

```
68
75
79
81
86
92
```

Two-Dimensional Arrays

A *two-dimensional array* (2D array – also known as a *table* or *matrix*) is an array that associates each element with two indexes. It's used to store a table of values. The array is stored with an array variable, whose syntax appears as follows:

type '[' ']' '[' ']' *identifier*

   or

type *identifier* '[' ']' '[' ']'

The two pairs of square brackets may appear after the *type* name or after the *identifier* that names the variable. They signify that *identifier* refers to a 2D array whose elements have the specified *type*. The type of the array is *type*[ ][ ].

Creating a 2D Array

There are three approaches to creating a 2D array: use only an initializer, use only keyword new, and use keyword new with an initializer.

Use Only an Initializer

The initializer-only approach adheres to the following syntax:

'{' [*rowInitializer* (',' *rowInitializer*)*] '}'

   where *rowInitializer* has the following syntax:

'{' [*expr* (',' *expr*)*] '}'

This syntax reveals that a 2D array is an optional comma-separated list of row initializers appearing between open and close brace characters. Furthermore, each row initializer is an optional comma-separated list of expressions between open and close brace characters. As with 1D arrays, all expressions must evaluate to compatible types.

The following example demonstrates the initializer approach to creating a 2D array:

```
int[][] tempsForNextThreeDays = { {30, 25, 26}, {14, 16, 13} };
```

The example creates a 2D array of high (row 0) and low (row 1) temperatures over the next three days and assigns the 2D array's reference to tempsForNextThreeDays. Figure 5-2 presents a conceptual view of this array.

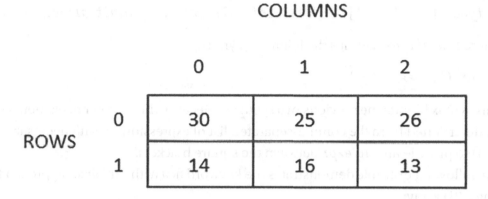

Figure 5-2. *A conceptual view of the array assigned to tempsForNextThreeDays*

Value 30 is located at row 0 and column 0, 25 is located at row 0 and column 1, and 26 is located at row 0 and column 2. Value 14 is located at row 1 and column 0, 16 is located at row 1 and column 1, and 13 is located at row 2 and column 2.

Use Only Keyword new

The keyword new-only approach adheres to the following syntax:

```
'new' type '[' int_expr1 ']' '[' int_expr2 ']'
```

Keyword new allocates memory for the array. The number of row elements is specified by *int_expr1* (a non-negative integer typically greater than 0), the number of column elements is specified by *int_expr2*, and the size of each element is implied by *type*. All elements share the same type and are zeroed (and interpreted as 0, 0L, 0.0F, 0.0, false, null, or '\u0000').

The previous example (minus the element values) could be expressed as follows:

```
int[][] tempsForNextThreeDays = new int[3][3];
```

Values would be filled in later.

Use Keyword new with an Initializer

There is one more way to create an array: use keyword new with an initializer. You'll need to adhere to the following syntax:

`'new' type '[' ']' [' ']' '{' [rowInitializer (',' rowInitializer)*] '}'`

where *rowInitializer* has the following syntax:

`'{' [expr (',' expr)*] '}'`

This syntax blends the previous two syntaxes. Because the number of elements can be determined from the comma-separated list of expressions, it isn't necessary (or allowed) to provide an *int_expr* between the square brackets.

The following example demonstrates the keyword new with initializer approach to creating a 2D array:

`int[][] tempsForNextThreeDays = new int[][] { {30, 25, 26}, {14, 16, 13} };`

The first syntax is syntactic sugar for the third approach.

Accessing 2D Array Elements

Java implements a 2D array as a 1D row array of 1D column arrays. Each element in the row array references the column array.

A 2D array variable is associated with a .length property for its 1D row array that returns the length of this array as a positive int; for example, tempsForNextThreeDays. length returns 2 (there are two rows). This value is important when accessing a 1D array's elements.

Given a 2D array variable, you can access any element in the row array by specifying an expression that agrees with the following syntax:

`array_var '[' index ']'`

Here, *index* is a positive int that ranges from zero (Java arrays are zero based) to one less than the value returned from the .length property.

Consider the previous tempsForNextThreeDays array. The following example references the first row element:

`tempsForNextThreeDays[0]`

You can print out this element as follows:

```
System.out.println(tempsForNextThreeDays[0]);
```

In response, you would see something very strange that looks similar to the following:

```
[I@372f7a8d
```

This is a special code indicating that tempsForNextThreeDays[0] references an array.

To print out the very first element (in row 0 and column 0), you would execute the following code:

```
System.out.println(tempsForNextThreeDays[0][0]); // Output 30
```

You could use a for loop to print out all elements as follows:

```
int[][] tempsForNextThreeDays = new int[][] { {30, 25, 26}, {14, 16, 13} };
for (int row = 0; row < tempsForNextThreeDays.length; row++)
{
    for (int col = 0; col < tempsForNextThreeDays[row].length; col++)
        System.out.print(tempsForNextThreeDays[row][col] + " ");
    System.out.println();
}
```

Note System.out.print() outputs text without outputting a newline character after this text. As a result, further printing outputs to the same line. System.out.println() without anything between (and) outputs only a newline character so that further output appears on the next line. The combination of these two method calls behaves like the System.out.println() method calls that take an argument and that you've previously seen in this book.

You could modify the third element in the second row as follows:

```
tempsForNextThreeDays[1][2] = 15;
```

For either the row array or one of the column arrays, if you specify a negative index or an index that is greater than or equal to the array's length, Java will create and throw an `ArrayIndexOutOfBoundsException` object. I'll have more to say about this topic when I discuss exceptions in Chapter 11.

Ragged Arrays

Java supports the creation of 2D arrays where each row has a different number of columns. The result is known as a *ragged array*. Figure 5-3 presents an example.

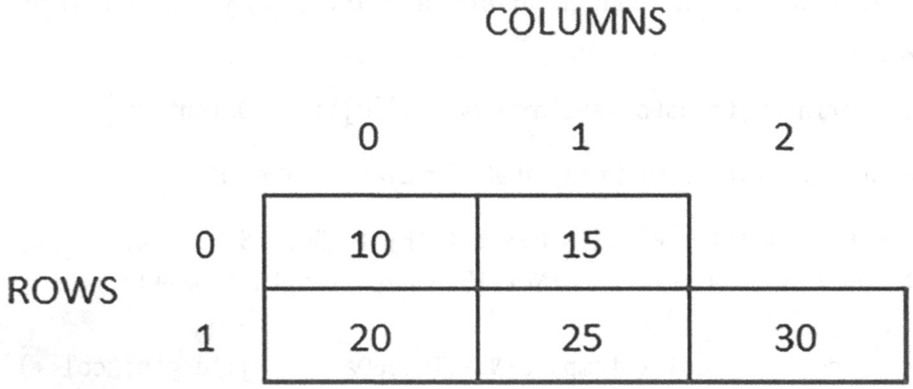

Figure 5-3. *A 2D array where each row has a different number of columns*

In this example, row 0 has two columns, and row 1 has three columns.

You can create this ragged array in three ways:

```
int[][] table1 = { { 10, 15 }, { 20, 25, 30 } };
int[][] table2 = new int[2][];
int[][] table3 = new int[][] { { 10, 15 }, { 20, 25, 30 } };
```

The first and third examples create a 2D array where the first row contains two columns and the second row contains three columns. The second example creates an array with two rows and an unspecified number of columns.

After creating `table2`'s row array, its elements must be populated with references to new column arrays. The following example demonstrates assigning two columns to the first row and three columns to the second row and populating these columns with the elements shown in Figure 5-3:

```
table2[0] = new int[2];
table2[0][0] = 10;
table2[0][1] = 15;
table2[1] = new int[3];
table2[1][0] = 20;
table2[1][1] = 25;
table2[1][2] = 30;
```

You can then iterate over a ragged array (such as `table1`) and print out its elements as follows:

```
for (int i = 0; i < table1.length; i++)
{
   for (int j = 0; j < table1[i].length; j++)
      System.out.print(table1[i][j] + " ");
   System.out.println();
}
```

You would observe the same output as shown in Figure 5-3.

These code fragments are excerpts from the `RagArray` application accompanying this book's code archive.

Why would you want to use a ragged array? They save memory when a *square table* (a table with the same number of rows and columns) mirrors its elements across the diagonal. Check out Figure 5-4.

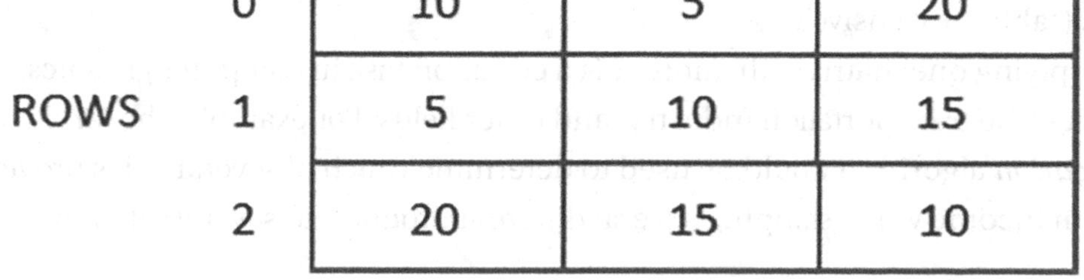

COLUMNS

		0	1	2
	0	10	5	20
ROWS	1	5	10	15
	2	20	15	10

Figure 5-4. *A 2D array that mirrors its elements across the diagonal*

Each diagonal element is 10. Notice that row 0, column 1 (5) is the same as row 1, column 0 (5); row 0, column 2 (20) is the same as row 2, column 0 (20); and row 1, column 2 (15) is the same as row 2, column 1 (15). Because the elements are the same, there is no point in storing the elements above and to the right of the diagonal. This leads us to Figure 5-5.

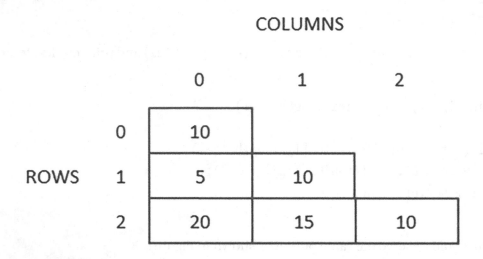

Figure 5-5. *A ragged array that reduces the number of elements by 3*

Ragged arrays are useful in linear algebra when working with very large *diagonal matrixes* (the elements outside the main diagonals are all zeroes – see `http://en.wikipedia.org/wiki/Diagonal_matrix`). Because diagonal matrixes are square, you can save a lot of memory by not storing the 0 elements above the main diagonal.

Matrix Multiplication

Linear algebra is a branch of mathematics that involves *linear* (line) equations. It uses *matrixes* (tables) extensively.

Multiplying one matrix with another is a common task in computer graphics, economics, the transportation industry, and other fields. For example, the *Matrix Multiplication* algorithm would be used to determine which of several cities provides maximum income when shipping several different products to several different cities.

Matrix Multiplication works as follows. Let A represent a matrix with m rows and p columns. Let B represent a matrix with p rows and n columns. Multiply A by B to produce matrix C, with m rows and n columns. Each C_{ij} entry in C is obtained by multiplying all entries in A's ith row by corresponding entries in B's jth column and adding the results. Figure 5-6 shows you these operations.

$$\begin{bmatrix} A_{11} & A_{12} & ... & A_{1p} \\ A_{21} & A_{22} & ... & A_{2p} \\ ... & ... & ... & ... \\ A_{m1} & A_{m2} & ... & A_{mp} \end{bmatrix} \times \begin{bmatrix} B_{11} & B_{12} & ... & B_{1n} \\ B_{21} & B_{22} & ... & B_{2n} \\ ... & ... & ... & ... \\ B_{p1} & B_{p2} & ... & B_{pn} \end{bmatrix} = \begin{bmatrix} C_{11} & C_{12} & ... & C_{1n} \\ C_{21} & C_{22} & ... & C_{2n} \\ ... & ... & ... & ... \\ C_{m1} & C_{m2} & ... & C_{mn} \end{bmatrix}$$

$$C_{11} = a_{11}b_{11} + a_{12}b_{21} + ... + a_{1p}b_{p1}$$

Figure 5-6. A look at each row in A being multiplied and added with the corresponding column in B to produce an entry in C

Note Matrix Multiplication requires that the number of columns (p) in the left matrix (A) equal the number of rows (p) in the right matrix (B). Otherwise, this algorithm won't work.

I've created a MatMult application to demonstrate Matrix Multiplication. Listing 5-4 presents this application's source code.

Listing 5-4. MatMult.java

```java
class MatMult
{
   public static void main(String[] args)
   {
      // Allocate two matrixes to be multiplied together.
      // m1 is a 2 row-by-2 column matrix.
      // m2 is a 2 row-by-1 column matrix.
```

```java
int[][] m1 = {{ 80, 60 }, { 59, 32 }};
int[][] m2 = {{ 4 }, { 19 }};

// Print out m1.

for (int i = 0; i < m1.length; i++)
{
   for (int j = 0; j < m1[0].length; j++)
      System.out.print(m1[i][j] + " ");
   System.out.println();
}
System.out.println();

// Print out m2.

for (int i = 0; i < m2.length; i++)
{
   for (int j = 0; j < m2[0].length; j++)
      System.out.print(m2[i][j] + " ");
   System.out.println();
}
System.out.println();

// Allocate result 2-by-1 matrix.

int[][] m3 = new int[m1.length][m2[0].length];

// Multiply m1 by m2 and add results to m3.

for (int i = 0; i < m1.length; i++)
   for (int j = 0; j < m2[0].length; j++)
      for (int k = 0; k < m1[0].length; k++) // or k < m2.length
         m3[i][j] += m1[i][k] * m2[k][j];

// Print out m3.

for (int i = 0; i < m3.length; i++)
{
   for (int j = 0; j < m3[0].length; j++)
      System.out.print(m3[i][j] + " ");
```

```
        System.out.println();
      }
   }
}
```

MatMult first declares a pair of matrixes m1 and m2 and prints out their contents. It then allocates space for a result matrix m3, holding the multiplication result. The multiplication is performed, and the contents of m3 are printed.

Assuming that you've copied Listing 5-4 to a file named MatMult.java, compile Listing 5-4 as follows:

```
javac MatMult.java
```

If compilation succeeds, you should observe a MatMult.java file in the current directory. Run this application as follows:

```
java MatMult
```

You should observe the following output:

```
80 60
59 32

4
19

1460
844
```

What's Next?

Arrays are objects that are created from array types, which are similar to classes. I focus on classes and objects in Chapter 6.

CHAPTER 6

Classes and Objects

This chapter introduces you to classes and objects. It then focuses on ten additional topics that you need to know when working with these language features.

Introducing Classes

Classes are templates for creating your own user-defined types. You use classes to describe virtual entities such as an account or physical entities such as a vehicle.

In this section, you first learn how to declare classes. You then learn how to populate classes with fields, methods, and constructors.

Declaring Classes

You declare a class by specifying keyword `class` followed by an identifier that is not a reserved word and that names the class. A pair of matching open (`{`) and close (`}`) brace characters follows and delimits the class's body. This syntax is presented as follows:

```
'class' identifier
'{'
   // body
'}'
```

It's conventional to uppercase the first letter of the class's name. Subsequent letters are specified in lowercase. When a name consists of multiple words, you uppercase the first letter of each word (e.g., `ChequingAccount` – the British spelling that has been adopted by Canada, whereas `CheckingAccount` is the preferred spelling in the United States). This is known as *camel casing*.

© Jeff Friesen 2024
J. Friesen, *Learn Java Fundamentals*, https://doi.org/10.1007/979-8-8688-0351-2_6

The following example declares a class named `Vehicle`:

```
class Vehicle
{
    // body
}
```

Following its declaration, you populate `Vehicle`'s (or any other class's) body with fields, methods, and constructors.

Describing State via Fields

A class models an abstract or physical entity in terms of its attributes, collectively known as *state*. For example, an account (an abstract entity) has a balance. Also, a vehicle (a physical entity) has a make, a model, and a year of manufacture. This state is stored in variables that are known as *fields*.

A field declaration has the following minimal syntax:

type identifier ';'

A field declaration consists of a `type` followed by an `identifier` that is not a reserved word. A semicolon terminates the declaration.

A field is implicitly initialized to a default value that is interpreted as null for a reference field, 0 for an integer field, 0.0 for a floating-point field, and false for a Boolean field.

The following example declares three fields in `Vehicle`:

```
class Vehicle
{
    String make;
    String model;
    int year;
}
```

These three fields are an example of *instance fields* (also known as *object fields* or *non-static fields*) because each `Vehicle` instance (object) will have its own copy of these non-static fields.

Describing Behaviors via Methods

A class also models an abstract or physical entity's behaviors. For example, an account supports deposits, and a vehicle supports movement. These behaviors are implemented by named blocks of code that are known as *methods*. Another definition: a *method* is a function that executes in the context of a class.

A method declaration has the following minimal syntax:

```
returnType identifier '(' [parameterList] ')'
'{'
   // method body
'}'
```

A method declaration begins with a `returnType` that is followed by a non-reserved identifier that names the method. A parentheses-delimited `parameterList` follows this name. A brace-delimited body of code (a *block*) completes the declaration.

The `returnType` identifies the type of values that the method returns via the `return` statement, which I'll discuss later. For example, if a method returns 32-bit integers, its return type would be `int`. When a method doesn't return a value, its return type is `void`.

The `parameterList` is a comma-separated list of parameter declarations: each declaration is a type followed by a non-reserved identifier that names the parameter.

A *parameter* is a variable that receives an argument when a method or constructor is called. (An *argument* is an expression value whose type is compatible with its corresponding parameter.)

A parameter is local to its method or constructor. It is created when the method or constructor is called and dies when the method or constructor returns to its caller. In other words, its *lifetime* is the method execution. Any code can access a parameter within the method. In other words, its *scope* is the entire method.

The following example declares six methods (along with the previous three fields) in the `Vehicle` class:

```
class Vehicle
{
   String make;
   String model;
   int year;
```

109

```
    String getMake()
    {
        return make;
    }
    String getModel()
    {
        return model;
    }

    int getYear()
    {
        return year;
    }
    void setMake(String _make)
    {
        make = _make;
    }
    void setModel(String _model)
    {
        model = _model;
    }
    void setYear(int _year)
    {
        year = _year;
    }
}
```

The getMake(), getModel(), and getYear() methods use the return statement to return the values of their respective fields to the caller. This statement has the following syntax:

```
'return' [expression] ';'
```

An expression followed by a semicolon optionally follows reserved word return. The type of return's expression must agree with the method's returnType.

Note   You specify `return` by itself, as in `return;`, when prematurely exiting a method whose return type is `void`, or a constructor, which doesn't have a return type. Perhaps some condition has been met, and you need to exit immediately. For example, you have a `copy()` method that copies the contents of one file to another in the context of a `while` loop. Its return type is `void`, and you only want to copy until the end-of-file is reached. You test for this possibility via an `if` statement (which assumes that a Boolean `eof` variable has been declared earlier in the code): `if (eof) return;`.

The `setMake()`, `setModel()`, and `setYear()` methods set the values of the `make`, `model`, and `year` fields. Their return types are set to keyword `void` to indicate that they don't return values to their callers.

These three methods are an example of *instance methods* (also known as *object methods* or *non-static methods*) because they can use keyword `this` to access a Vehicle instance's (object's) non-static fields (I show how later).

Note   The "`set`" prefix on each of `setMake()`, `setModel()`, and `setYear()` identifies these methods as *setter methods*. Similarly, the "`get`" prefix on each of `getMake()`, `getModel()`, and `getYear()` identifies these methods as *getter methods*.

Local Variables

You can declare additional variables within a method as part of the method's implementation. These variables are known as *local variables* because they are local to the method – they cannot be accessed from outside the method. Furthermore, they only exist while the method is executing. In both cases, the same is true of parameters.

Consider the following example, which calculates *n*! (factorial):

```
long factorial(int n)
{
   if (n < 0)
      return -1;
```

```
  if (n == 0 || n == 1)
    return 1;
  long result = 1;
  for (int i = n; i > 1; i--)
    result *= i;
  return result;
}
```

This method computes the *factorial* (the product of all positive integers less than or equal to some number *n*, as in $n \times (n - 1) \times (n - 2) \times \ldots \times 3 \times 2 \times 1$ of the argument passed to parameter n.

The `factorial()` method first tests parameter n's value to ensure that it is positive. If the value is less than 0, `factorial()` returns -1 to signify that a negative argument has been passed. By definition, a factorial cannot include negative integers in its product.

Note   Chapter 11 presents a better technique for dealing with unexpected arguments, such as a negative integer being passed to `factorial()`'s parameter n.

The method next tests parameter n's value for 0 or 1. If either value has been passed, `factorial()` returns 1. According to the convention for an empty product (`http://en.wikipedia.org/wiki/Empty_product`), the value of 0! is 1.

Continuing, `factorial()` declares a local variable named `result` and initializes this variable to 1.

Caution   Local variables must be initialized. The compiler reports an error when it discovers an attempt to read a local variable that has not been initialized.

This method then enters a `for` loop to calculate the factorial. The `for` statement's test section consists of `i > 1` instead of `i >= 1` because any integer multiplied by 1 is itself; assigning 1 to `result` takes care of this multiplication.

Each loop iteration uses the `*=` compound assignment operator to multiply `result`'s value by `i`'s value and store the product in `result`.

Finally, `result`'s value is returned to the caller.

Along with `result`, `factorial()` declares a second local variable: `i`. Although both variables exist only during this method's execution, they have different scopes. The `result` variable is accessible throughout the whole method. However, `i` is accessible only in the `for` loop and its `result *= i;` compound-assignment statement. It cannot be accessed before or after the `for` loop statement in which it is declared.

More specifically, a local variable's lifetime and scope are limited to the block in which it has been declared and to subblocks. This is why `i` is inaccessible outside of the `for` loop whose header is followed by a single-statement block. The following example should clarify this fact:

```
{
    int j; // j comes into existence at this point
    {
        j = 5; // okay: j still exists
    }
}
j = 10; // error: j no longer exists
```

Method Overloading

You can declare methods with the same name but with different parameter lists in the same class, a feature known as *method overloading*. When the compiler encounters a method-call expression, it compares the called method's comma-separated list of arguments with each overloaded method's parameter list as it looks for the correct method to call.

Two same-named methods are overloaded when their parameter lists differ in number or order of parameters. Alternatively, two same-named methods are overloaded when at least one parameter differs in type. For example, consider the following three `add()` methods, which add two or three values together – the first adds two double-precision floating-point values, the second adds two integers, and the third adds three integers:

```
double add(double a, double b)
{
    return a + b;
}
```

```
int add(int a, int b)
{
   return a + b;
}

int add(int a, int b, int c)
{
   return a + b + c;
}
```

You cannot overload a method by changing only its return type. For example, you could not specify int add(int a, int b) and double add(int a, int b) because the compiler doesn't have enough information to distinguish between these methods when encountering add(4, 5);. The compiler would report a "redefinition" error.

Describing Initialization via Constructors

A class can declare one or more blocks of code to initialize an object when it is created. This code block is known as a *constructor*. Its declaration consists of a header followed by a brace-delimited body. The header begins with the name of the class in which the constructor is declared because a constructor doesn't have its own name. An optional parameter list between parentheses follows:

```
className '(' [parameterList] ')'
'{'
   // constructor body
'}'
```

The className must match the name of the class in which the constructor is declared. The parameterList is a comma-separated list of parameters. A brace-delimited body containing code to execute when the constructor is called follows. Unlike a method, a constructor doesn't have a return type because it doesn't return a value.

Note   When a class doesn't declare any constructors, the compiler generates a default and empty no-argument constructor.

The following example declares a constructor in the Vehicle class. The constructor initializes a Vehicle's make, model, and year fields to the arguments that are passed to the constructor's _make, _model, and _year parameters:

```
class Vehicle
{
   // ...
   Vehicle(String _make, String _model, int _year)
   {
      make = _make;
      model = _model;
      year = _year;
   }
   // ...
}
```

For brevity, I haven't included everything in the Vehicle class. The first //... is a shortcut for specifying the field declarations. The second //... is a shortcut for specifying the various method declarations.

The parameter names have leading underscores to prevent a problem with the assignments. For example, if you renamed _make to make and specified make = make;, you accomplish nothing because you assign the parameter's value to itself. You can also avoid this problem by prefixing the field names with this.:

```
Vehicle(String make, String model, int year)
{
   this.make = make;
   this.model = model;
   this.year = year;
}
```

Reserved word this refers to the current object. By prefixing a field name with this., you are indicating that you are referring to the current object's copy of the field.

While you are refactoring the constructor, you might also want to refactor the setMake(), setModel(), and setYear() methods. For example, you could change setMake() from

```
void setMake(String _make)
{
    make = _make;
}
```

to

```
void setMake(String make)
{
    this.make = make;
}
```

to take advantage of the this. prefix.

A parameter (or local variable) name that's identical to an instance field name *shadows* (hides or masks) the field. The keyword this represents the current object's reference. Prepending this. to the field name removes the shadowing by accessing the field name instead of the same-named parameter.

Although you can initialize fields such as make through the assignment shown in the constructor, it's preferable to perform the assignments via setter methods such as the previously shown setMake(), which I demonstrate as follows:

```
Vehicle(String make, String model, int year)
{
    setMake(make);
    setModel(model);
    setYear(year);
}
```

Because future versions of setMake(), setModel(), and setYear() might perform additional initialization tasks, why duplicate this code in the constructor?

Calling Constructors

Classes can declare multiple constructors. For example, consider a Vehicle constructor that accepts make and model arguments only – it sets the year to -1 to indicate that the vehicle's year of manufacture is unknown. This constructor is shown as follows:

```java
Vehicle(String make, String model)
{
   setMake(make);
   setModel(model);
   setYear(-1);
}
```

The problem with this new constructor is that it duplicates code located in the original constructor: setMake(make); followed by setModel(model);. Duplicate code adds unnecessary bulk to the class. Java lets you avoid this duplication by offering this() syntax for having one constructor call another constructor:

```java
Vehicle(String make, String model)
{
   this(make, model, -1);
}
```

The this() call passes its arguments to the Vehicle(String make, String model, int year) constructor. The compiler knows to call this constructor because it matches the constructor's number of parameters and parameter types with the this() call's number of arguments and argument types.

Caution   The compiler will report an error when you place any code before a constructor's this() call. For example, make = "{" + make + "}"; this(make, model, -1); is erroneous because the assignment statement precedes the this() call.

Putting It All Together

I've created a Vehicle class that contains the various enhancements presented earlier. Listing 6-1 presents Vehicle's source code.

Listing 6-1. Vehicle.java

```java
class Vehicle
{
    String make;
    String model;
    int year;

    Vehicle(String make, String model)
    {
        setMake(make);
        setModel(model);
        setYear(-1);
    }

    Vehicle(String make, String model, int year)
    {
        setMake(make);
        setModel(model);
        setYear(year);
    }

    String getMake()
    {
        return make;
    }

    String getModel()
    {
        return model;
    }

    int getYear()
    {
        return year;
    }
```

```
    void setMake(String make)
    {
        this.make = make;
    }

    void setModel(String model)
    {
        this.model = model;
    }

    void setYear(int year)
    {
        this.year = year;
    }
}
```

Compile Listing 6-1 as follows:

```
javac Vehicle.java
```

Because the resulting Vehicle.class file is not an application, you cannot run it. We will access it from a class with a main() method similar to the one shown in Chapter 1 later in this chapter. The pair of classes will collectively describe our application.

Introducing Objects

Objects are instances of classes. They represent specific abstract entities, such as your savings account, or specific physical entities, such as the comic book you are reading or the truck you are driving.

In this section, you first learn how to construct objects. You then learn how to access their fields and call their methods.

Constructing Objects

After declaring a class, you can construct objects from it. You construct an object by using the new operator in conjunction with a constructor. For example, you can construct one or more Vehicle objects by specifying the new operator followed by a Vehicle constructor, as follows:

```
Vehicle v = new Vehicle("Ford", "F150", 2023);
```

The new operator causes memory to be assigned to a Vehicle object and then calls its three-parameter constructor with arguments "Ford", "F150", and 2023. Vehicle's make, model, and year fields are initialized to these values. When done, new returns a reference to the newly created Vehicle object. This reference is then assigned to variable v.

Note   If you've wondered why a constructor does not have a return type, the reason is that there is no way that new can return a constructor value while it is also returning a reference to the newly constructed object.

Accessing Fields

Now that you've constructed an object, you can use the member-selection operator (.) with an object reference to access the object's fields. For example, access the previously created Vehicle object's fields as follows:

```
System.out.println(v.make); // Ford
System.out.println(v.model); // F150
System.out.println(v.year); // 2023
```

It's usually not a good idea to access fields directly. Instead, you invoke a getter method to access the field. Although this might seem redundant, it prevents the code that accesses the field from breaking should you need to remove or rename the field. You will learn more about this topic when I discuss information hiding later in this chapter.

Calling Methods

Use the . operator with an object reference to call the object's methods. For example, call the previously created Vehicle object's methods as follows:

```
v.setMake("Dodge");
v.setModel("Durango");
v.setYear(2023);
```

Later, you can call the counterpart "get" methods to return these values:

```
System.out.println(v.getMake()); // Dodge
System.out.println(v.getModel()); // Durango
System.out.println(v.getYear()); // 2023
```

A method (or constructor) call includes zero or more arguments that are passed to the method's (or constructor's) parameters. Java passes arguments via *pass-by-value*, which passes the value of a variable or the value of another expression. In contrast, the C++ language also supports *pass-by-reference*, which passes the address of the argument to a method so that the argument (which cannot be a value) is modified.

A method call requires a method-call stack to keep track of the statement to which execution must return when a called method finishes. (A *stack* is a data structure for remembering things such as the previous locations that have been visited when navigating out of a maze.)

A *method-call stack* is a stack of method calls that lets the Java Virtual Machine (JVM) remember what statement to return to when a `return` statement is executed or when execution leaves a method without `return`. Furthermore, the method-call stack keeps track of parameters and local variables on a per-method-call basis.

Note   Think of the method-call stack as a pile of clean trays in a cafeteria – you *pop* a clean tray from the top of the pile and the dishwasher will *push* the next clean tray onto the top of the pile. Conversely, you could think of this stack as a pile of dirty trays – you push a dirty tray onto the top of the pile and the dishwasher will pop the next dirty tray from the pile's top.

When a method is called, the JVM pushes the address of the next statement to execute after the called method returns onto the method-call stack, along with the called method's arguments. The JVM also allocates stack space for the method's parameters and/or local variables. When the method returns, the JVM removes the parameter/local variable space, pops the address and arguments off of the stack, and transfers execution to the statement at the given address.

Putting It All Together

I've created a Vehicles class that contains the various enhancements presented earlier. Listing 6-2 presents Vehicles's source code.

Listing 6-2. `Vehicles.java`

```java
class Vehicles
{
   public static void main(String[] args)
   {
      Vehicle v = new Vehicle("Ford", "F150", 2023);

      System.out.println(v.make);
      System.out.println(v.model);
      System.out.println(v.year);

      v.setMake("Dodge");
      v.setModel("Durango");
      v.setYear(2023);

      System.out.println(v.getMake());
      System.out.println(v.getModel());
      System.out.println(v.getYear());
   }
}
```

Assuming that Vehicles.java is in the same directory as Vehicle.java and the previously created Vehicle.class, compile Listing 6-2 as follows:

```
javac Vehicles.java
```

Assuming that Vehicles.class is successfully created, run the application as follows:

```
java Vehicles
```

You should observe the following output:

```
Ford
F150
2023
Dodge
Durango
2023
```

Additional Topics

There is more to learn about classes and objects. This section introduces you to information hiding, object initialization, another use for classes, class initialization, field-access rules, method-call rules, constants, method-call chaining, recursion, and varargs.

Information Hiding

A class's body is composed of interface and implementation. The *interface* is that part of the class that is accessible to code located outside of the class. The *implementation* is that part of the class that exists to support the interface. Implementation should be hidden from external code so that it can be changed to meet evolving requirements.

Developers strive to develop classes that provide unchangeable interfaces while hiding the implementation so that it can evolve without impacting external code. The task of hiding the implementation is known as *information hiding*, which is related to *encapsulation*, combining fields, methods, and constructors into classes.

Note   Encapsulation lets us program at a higher level of abstraction (classes and objects) rather than focusing separately on data structures and functionality.

Consider the Vehicle class. Constructor and method headers form this class's interface. The code within the constructors and methods and the various fields are part of the implementation. There is no need to access these fields because they can be read or written via the getter and setter methods.

Because no precautions have been taken, directly accessing these fields is possible. Using the previous v reference variable, you could specify v.make, v.model, and v.year, and that would be okay with the compiler. You need to take advantage of access levels to prevent access to these fields (or at least determine who can access them).

An *access level* indicates who can access a field, method, or constructor. Java supports four access levels: private, public, protected, and package private (the default) – I discuss packages in Chapter 10. Java provides three keywords that correspond to the first three access levels:

- private: Only code in the same class as the field, method, or constructor can access the member.

- public: Any code in any class in any package can access the member.

- protected: Any code in the same class or its subclasses (discussed in Chapter 7) can access the member.

If there is no keyword, then package private access is implied. Package private access is similar to public access in that code outside the class can access the member. However, unlike public access, the code must be located in a class that belongs to the same package as the class containing the member to be accessed – see Chapter 10.

You can prevent external code from accessing Vehicle's make, model, and year fields so that any attempt to access these fields from beyond Vehicle will result in a compiler error message. Accomplish this task by prepending private to their declarations, as demonstrated here:

```java
class Vehicle
{
   private String make;
   private String model;
   private int year;

   // ...
}
```

To give you a better example of why you should get into the habit of hiding at least most of your class's implementation, consider the following abbreviated Employee class:

```
class Employee
{
   private String firstName;
   private String lastName;

   String getFullName()
   {
      return firstName + " " + lastName;
   }
}
```

The getFullName() method returns an employee's full name. It hides the fact that there is no fullName field. If firstName and lastName were exposed, they would be part of the class's interface. That interface would break when the developer decided to replace firstName and lastName with a single fullName field.

Object Initialization

Objects are typically initialized via their constructors. However, there are a couple of other ways to perform at least some of this initialization.

Note   When an object is constructed, the new operator zeroes the object's non-static fields.

Explicit Field Initialization via an Instance Field Initializer

An *instance field initializer* (also known as an *object field initializer* or a *non-static field initializer*) is an assignment operator followed by an expression that is type compatible with an instance field's type and that assigns the expression's value to the instance field. For example, consider the following Database class:

```
class Database
{
   private Driver driver = DEFAULT_DRIVER;

   Database(/* ... */)
```

```
   {
      // ...
      driver = loadDriver();
      if (driver == null)
         System.out.println("unable to load driver ... using default
         instead");
   }

   Driver loadDriver()
   {
      // ...
   }

   // ...
}
```

Database presents a driver field initialized to a default device driver via an instance field initializer. The constructor attempts to load a nondefault more capable driver. If the driver cannot be loaded, a message is output, and a Database object will have to work with the default driver instead.

Instance Initialization Block

An *instance initialization block* (also known as an *object initialization block* or a *non-static initialization block*) is a block of statements introduced into a class body instead of a method body. For example, consider the following change to the Vehicle class:

```
class Vehicle
{
   private String make;
   private String model;
   private int year;

   // The following instance initialization block initializes the make,
   // model, and year fields to the specified values.
```

```
   {
      make = "Ford";
      model = "F150";
      year = 2023;
   }
}
```

Because you can initialize an object in a constructor, the only good use for an instance initialization block is in the context of an *anonymous class* (a class without a name), which doesn't have a constructor and which I discuss in Chapter 9.

Note   For each constructor, the compiler generates a special `<init>()` method in the class file. (Because of the `<` and `>` characters, which are illegal in an identifier, there is no way that such a method can exist in source code, so there is no way a programmer could create a same-named method and cause a conflict.)

The `<init>()` method contains the bytecode for all object initialization that takes place. The compiler works its way from the top of the class to the bottom, placing bytecode first for each encountered instance field initializer and instance initialization block, and then the constructor's initialization code into this method. The JVM invokes `<init>()` at runtime when constructing an object.

Utility Classes

Classes are used mainly to create objects. However, there is another use for them: utility classes. A *utility class* consists of class fields and/or class methods.

Class Fields

A *class field* (also known as a *static field*) is declared by prepending reserved word `static` to the declaration, as in the following syntax:

```
'static' type ['=' expression] ';'
```

Unlike an instance field in which each object has its own copy, a class field is shared by all objects. When the field is updated, all objects see the change.

An object must be created to access an instance field. In contrast, no objects need to be created to access a class field.

Consider the following example of a simple `Counter` utility class:

```
class Counter
{
   static int count;
}
```

We are creating a `Counter` class to hold a `count` field that code in multiple classes can access. Each code block increments this field to track some activity, and other code blocks can read `count`'s current value to decide on the course of action they want.

A code block would typically access `count` by specifying the following expression, which consists of the class name followed by the `.` operator followed by the field name:

```
Counter.count
```

You could specify `Counter.count = 1;` to initialize `count` to 1. You could specify `System.out.println(Counter.count)` to read `count`'s value, which is then output.

Class Methods

A *class method* (also known as a *static method*) is declared by prepending reserved word `static` to the declaration, as in the following syntax:

```
'static' returnType identifier '(' [parameterList] ')'
'{'
   // method body
'}'
```

Unlike an instance method, which can access its copy of an instance field, a class method cannot access any instance fields. However, it can access class fields.

Consider Listing 6-3's example of a `Temperature` utility class.

Listing 6-3. Temperature.java

```java
class Temperature
{
   static double c2f(double degrees)
   {
      return degrees * 9.0 / 5.0 + 32.0;
   }
}
```

Temperature declares a single utility method: c2f(). This method converts the argument passed to parameter degrees from Celsius to Fahrenheit and returns the result.

I've created a UseTemperature class that demonstrates Temperature. Listing 6-4 presents its source code.

Listing 6-4. UseTemperature.java

```java
class UseTemperature
{
   public static void main(String[] args)
   {
      System.out.println(Temperature.c2f(37));
   }
}
```

Assuming that Temperature.java and UseTemperature.java are located in the same directory, you can compile both source files by using the following handy trick:

```
javac *.java
```

The * (asterisk) character serves as a wildcard that matches all *Java source files* (files with the .java file extension) in the current directory.

Assuming that nothing goes wrong, you should observe Temperature.class and UseTemperature.class files in the current directory.

Run the resulting application as follows:

```
java UseTemperature
```

You should observe the following output:

98.6

Note that 37 degrees Celsius is equivalent to 98.6 degrees Fahrenheit (the normal body temperature).

Look carefully at Listing 6-4: you'll notice something interesting. The `main()` method is marked `static`. This method serves as a utility method for defining an application's entry point – every application class is a utility class. When you run the application via the `java` tool, this tool loads the JVM, and `main()` gets executed.

Class Initialization

Classes are initialized through class field initializers and class initialization blocks, which are equivalent to instance field initializers and instance initialization blocks.

Note   When a class is loaded into memory, the JVM zeroes the class's static fields.

Explicit Field Initialization via a Class Field Initializer

A *class field initializer* (also known as a *static field initializer*) is an assignment operator followed by an expression that is type compatible with a class field's type and that assigns the expression's value to the class field. For example, consider the following `Product` class:

```
class Product
{
   static int productID = 1;

   void manufacture(String name)
   {
      // ...
      System.out.println("Manufacturing product " + productID++);
   }

   // ...
}
```

Product represents some kind of manufactured product. The productID field is marked static because it describes a product identification number. This number starts at 1 thanks to the class field initializer that assigns 1 to productID and is incremented in manufacture() after a product has been manufactured.

Class Initialization Block

A *class initialization block* (also known as a *static initialization block*) is a static-prefixed block of statements introduced into a class body. For example, consider the following Graphics class, which is part of a simple graphics package:

```
class Graphics
{
   static double[] sines, cosines;
   static
   {
      sines = new double[360];
      cosines = new double[360];
      for (int i = 0; i < sines.length; i++)
      {
         sines[i] = sin(toRadians(i));
         cosines[i] = cos(toRadians(i));
      }
   }
   // ...
}
```

Graphics declares sines and cosines array variables. It also declares a class initialization block that creates 360-element arrays of doubles whose references are assigned to sines and cosines. It then uses a for loop to initialize these array elements to the appropriate sine and cosine values by calling sin() and cos() methods. The loop index in i represents a degree unit from 0 to 360 degrees. This argument is passed to toRadians() in each of the calls to sin() and cos() to convert the degree value to radians.

Tip   Performance is important to graphics applications, and it's faster to access an array element than to call a method. As a result, developers resort to performance tricks such as creating and initializing arrays of sines and cosines.

Note   For each class, the compiler generates a `<clinit>()` method that contains the bytecode for all class initialization that takes place. The compiler works its way from the top of the class to the bottom, placing bytecode for each encountered class field initializer and class initialization block into this method. The JVM invokes `<clinit>()` at runtime after loading its class file into memory.

Field-Access Rules

Fields are accessed in different ways depending on the kind of field (object or class) and context (from within a class or from code external to the class). These four rules will help you avoid mistakes when accessing different kinds of fields in different contexts:

- Specify an instance field name without a prefix when accessing this field from another instance field, constructor, or instance method in the same class. Example: `make`.

- Specify a class field name without a prefix when accessing this field from another instance or class field, constructor, or instance or class method in the same class. Example: `count`.

- Specify an object reference followed by the `.` operator followed by the instance field name when accessing this field (provided that it is accessible) from outside of its class or from a class method in the same class. Example: `v.make`.

- Specify a class name followed by the `.` operator followed by the class field name when accessing this field (provided that it is accessible) from outside of its class. Example: `Counter.count`.

Don't forget that, in some cases, shadowing is an issue. You can resolve it by prepending this followed by the . operator to an instance field name or the class name followed by the . operator to a class field name. For example, if you had to assign a parameter value to a same-named instance field, you would also prepend this and the . operator to the field name.

Method-Call Rules

Methods are called in different ways depending on the kind of method (object or class) and context (from within a class or from code external to the class). Here are four rules for calling different kinds of methods in various contexts:

- Specify an instance method name without a prefix when calling the method from another instance method or constructor in the same class. Example: getMake().

- Specify a class method name without a prefix when calling it from another object, class method, or a constructor in the same class. Example: c2f(37).

- Specify an object reference followed by the . operator followed by the instance method name when calling a method from outside its class or from a class method in the same class (provided that it is accessible). Example: v.getMake().

- Specify a class name followed by the . operator followed by the class method name when calling a method from outside its class (provided that it is accessible). Example: Temperature.c2f(37).

Don't forget to ensure that the number of arguments passed to a method – along with the order in which they are passed and the types of these arguments – agrees with their parameter counterparts in the method being called. Otherwise, the compiler will report an error.

Final Fields

A *final field* is a field whose declaration is prefixed with keyword final. There are two kinds of final fields: class final fields and instance final fields.

Class Final Fields

A *class final field* is a final field that's declared with the static keyword. The final field is associated with a class when the class is loaded and initialized.

Class final fields are also known as *constants* because the field's value never changes. You often declare constants in utility classes.

The following example declares a constant named PI:

```
final static double PI = 3.14159;
```

According to Oracle's (the current maintainer of Java) "Code Conventions for the Java Language" (www.oracle.com/java/technologies/javase/codeconventions-contents.html) document, constants should be all uppercase with words separated by underscores (_).

It's a good idea to get into the habit of using constants instead of "magic numbers" in your code. For example, consider the following code fragment:

```
radius = 10;
area = 3.14159 * radius * radius;
circumference = 3.14159 * radius * 2;
```

This code fragment calculates the area and circumference of a circle whose radius is 10 units. Notice that 3.14159 appears twice in the code.

It's not a good idea to code a magic number like this because you would have to change all instances of the number when it needs to change. If you forget to modify an instance, you risk introducing a bug into your code. The following code fragment overcomes this problem by replacing 3.14159 with PI:

```
radius = 10;
area = PI * radius * radius;
circumference = PI * radius * 2;
```

Instance Final Fields

An *instance final field* is a final field that's declared without the static keyword. The final field is associated with an object when the object is created.

Some developers believe that instance final fields are constants because an instance final field never changes while the object to which it is associated exists. Other developers believe that instance final fields are not constants because they haven't been assigned values at compile time and don't have to follow the same naming convention as is followed by class final fields.

Unlike constants, which must be initialized when declared (see the previous PI example), instance final fields don't have to be initialized when declared. Instead, initialization can be deferred to a constructor. When this happens, an instance final field is known as a *blank final*.

Consider the following examples:

```
class Counter
{
    final int Count1 = 10; // instance final field that will remain the same
                           // for each constructed object
    final int Count2;      // blank final that is initialized in constructor

    Counter(int initialCount) // each blank final can receive a different
                              value that
    {                         // remains unchanged throughout the life of
                              the object
        Count2 = initialCount;
    }
}
```

It's difficult to think of a valid use for instance final fields. For some insight into what they might be used for, check out stackoverflow's "Exposing instance constants with non-static public final variables" article (http://stackoverflow.com/questions/12248635/exposing-instance-constants-with-non-static-public-final-variables).

Method-Call Chaining

Two or more instance method calls can be chained together via the . operator, which results in more compact code. To accomplish instance method-call chaining, you need to re-architect your instance methods. The key is to design your methods to return a reference to the current object, which is indicated via the this keyword.

I've refactored Vehicle.java and Vehicles.java to demonstrate method-call chaining. Listing 6-5 reveals Vehicle.java's contents.

Listing 6-5. Vehicle.java

```java
class Vehicle
{
   private String make;
   private String model;
   private int year;

   Vehicle(String make, String model)
   {
      setMake(make).setModel(model).setYear(-1);
   }

   Vehicle(String make, String model, int year)
   {
      setMake(make).setModel(model).setYear(year);
   }

   String getMake()
   {
      return make;
   }

   String getModel()
   {
      return model;
   }

   int getYear()
   {
      return year;
   }
```

```java
Vehicle setMake(String make)
{
   this.make = make;
   return this;
}

Vehicle setModel(String model)
{
   this.model = model;
   return this;
}

Vehicle setYear(int year)
{
   this.year = year;
   return this;
}
}
```

Note that the return type for setMake(), setModel(), and setYear() has been changed from void to Vehicle and that each method now ends with a return this; statement to return a reference to the current Vehicle object. Also, note the setMake(make).setModel(model).setYear(-1); and setMake(make).setModel(model).setYear(year); calls in the constructors.

Listing 6-6 reveals Vehicles.java's contents.

Listing 6-6. Vehicles.java

```java
class Vehicles
{
   public static void main(String[] args)
   {
      Vehicle v = new Vehicle("Ford", "F150", 2023);

      System.out.println(v.getMake());
      System.out.println(v.getModel());
      System.out.println(v.getYear());

      v.setMake("Dodge").setModel("Durango").setYear(2023);
```

```
        System.out.println(v.getMake());
        System.out.println(v.getModel());
        System.out.println(v.getYear());
    }
}
```

Note the `v.setMake("Dodge").setModel("Durango").setYear(2023);` chained method calls, which demonstrate method-call chaining.

Compile and run `Vehicles.java` and `Vehicle.java` in the same way as I demonstrated following Listing 6-2 and you should observe the same output.

Recursion

A method normally executes statements that may include calls to other methods. However, it's often useful to have a method call itself. This programming technique is known as *recursion*.

For example, suppose you need to write a method that returns a *factorial*, which is the product of all the positive integers up to and including a specific integer. Knowing that ! is the mathematical symbol for factorial, you can guess that 4! equals 4x3x2x1, or 24. Also, 1! is 1 and 0! is 1. A first approach to writing this method could consist of the code presented earlier in this chapter.

The previously presented `factorial()` code accomplishes its task via iteration. However, this method could be written more compactly by adopting a recursive style:

```
long factorial(int n)
{
   if (n < 0)
      return -1;
   if (n == 0 || n == 1)
      return 1; // base problem
   else
      return n * factorial(n - 1);
}
```

The recursive approach expresses a problem in simpler terms of itself. According to this example, the simplest problem, which is also known as the *base problem*, is 0! (1) or 1! (1).

When an argument greater than 1 is passed to `factorial()`, this method divides the problem into a simpler problem by calling itself with the next smaller argument value. Eventually, the base problem will be reached. For example, calling `factorial(4)` results in the following stack of expressions:

```
4 * factorial(3)
3 * factorial(2)
2 * factorial(1)
```

This last expression is at the top of the stack. When `factorial(1)` returns 1, these expressions are evaluated as the stack begins to unwind, in the following order:

> 2 * `factorial(1)` now becomes 2*1 (2)
>
> 3 * `factorial(2)` now becomes 3*2 (6)
>
> 4 * `factorial(3)` now becomes 4*6 (24)

Recursion provides an elegant way to express many problems. Additional examples include searching tree-based data structures for specific values and, in a hierarchical file system, finding and outputting the names of all files that contain specific text.

Caution   Recursion consumes stack space, so make sure that your recursion eventually ends in a base problem; otherwise, you will run out of stack space and your application will be forced to terminate.

Varargs

JDK 5 introduced a feature that simplifies the syntax for passing a variable number of arguments to methods and constructors. This feature is known as *varargs*.

Specify three consecutive periods after the type name of the rightmost parameter when declaring a method or constructor that takes a variable number of arguments. Consider the following instance method example, which returns the minimum integer in a list of integers:

```
int min(int... values)
```

This method header declares a min() method that declares a variable number of arguments. You might call this method as follows:

```
min(-8, 55, 0, -12, 14);
```

Before JDK 5, you would have to declare the method with an array type:

```
int min(int[] values)
```

This method would be called in the following manner:

```
min(new int[] {-8, 55, 0, -12, 14});
```

The varargs feature is an example of *syntactic sugar* (syntax that makes code sweeter to write). During compilation, the compiler converts from the older and more cumbersome int[] {} syntax to the more modern ... version of this feature.

Listing 6-7 presents the source code to a VarargsDemo application class that demonstrates varargs in the context of two versions of the min() method.

Listing 6-7. VarargsDemo.java

```
class VarargsDemo
{
   public static void main(String[] args)
   {
      System.out.println(min(-8, 55, 0, -12, 14));
      System.out.println(min(new int[] {-8, 55, 0, -12, 14}));
      System.out.println(min2(new int[] {-8, 55, 0, -12, 14}));
//    System.out.println(min2(-8, 55, 0, -12, 14));
   }

   static int min(int... values)
   {
      int smallest = 0;
      for (int i = 0; i < values.length; i++)
         if (values[i] < smallest)
            smallest = values[i];
      return smallest;
   }
```

```
static int min2(int[] values)
{
   int smallest = 0;
   for (int i = 0; i < values.length; i++)
      if (values[i] < smallest)
         smallest = values[i];
   return smallest;
}
}
```

VarargsDemo declares main(), min(), and min2() methods. The main() method runs the application. The min() and min2() methods use the newer varargs and older array features, respectively, to receive a variable number of arguments.

Although these methods have different headers, they have identical bodies, which proves that varargs is implemented in terms of one-dimensional arrays.

Each method's body consists of code to locate and return the smallest integer from the values array. The array's length is specified by values.length.

Perhaps you are wondering why I didn't try to overload min() by specifying min(int[] values) instead of min(int... values). If I tried to do this, the compiler would report an error about not being able to declare min(int... values) and min(int[] values). Behind the scenes, min(int... values) is transformed into min(int[] values).

Compile Listing 6-7 as follows:

```
javac VarargsDemo.java
```

Run the resulting VarargsDemo.class class file as follows:

```
java VarargsDemo
```

You should observe the following output:

```
-12
-12
-12
```

What's Next?

Vehicle is too generalized to represent a specific kind of vehicle such as a truck or a car. It could also represent a skateboard or a bicycle. To accommodate more specific kinds of vehicles, we need to specialize through class extension, which is the subject of Chapter 7.

Reusing Classes via Inheritance and Composition

Chapter 6 introduced you to classes, which *encapsulate* (combine) fields (that store state), methods (that implement behaviors), and constructors (that instantiate objects). This arrangement is known as *object-based programming*.

Java provides an inheritance mechanism for deriving a class from another class. The idea is to reuse this other class in a more specialized manner. This arrangement is known as *object-oriented programming*.

Java also provides a composition mechanism for defining a class as the sum of its parts. In other words, the class's fields are implemented by other classes. Composition offers another way to reuse other classes.

This chapter first introduces you to inheritance. It then introduces you to composition.

Inheritance

Inheritance is a programming technique for class reuse in which you derive a class from another class. It lets you create more specialized classes from more generalized classes.

Consider Chapter 6's `Vehicle` class. `Vehicle` generalizes what it means to be a vehicle. A vehicle has a make, a model, and a year. Also, a vehicle can be driven.

Suppose you want to model a truck. You could derive a `Truck` class from `Vehicle` that would inherit `Vehicle`'s make, `model`, and `year` fields along with the capability to be driven via `Vehicle`'s `drive()` method. You could then add whatever fields and methods are required to differentiate `Truck` from `Vehicle`.

You could model a bicycle, a motorcycle, a boat, or a skateboard in a similar way.

© Jeff Friesen 2024
J. Friesen, *Learn Java Fundamentals*, https://doi.org/10.1007/979-8-8688-0351-2_7

In each of these examples, inheritance is used to form an *is-a relationship* between a pair of classes. A `Truck` is a `Vehicle`. The same is true for `Bicycle`, `Motorcycle`, `Boat`, and `SkateBoard`.

This section first shows you how to form an is-a relationship by using Java's class extension feature. It then discusses method overriding and tours the ultimate ancestor of all classes.

Class Extension

Java's class extension feature consists of the `extends` keyword. When present, extends specifies a parent-child relationship between two classes. This relationship is described by the following syntax:

```
'class' child 'extends' parent
'{'
   // class body
'}'
```

Given this syntax, the *child* class extends the *parent* class, inheriting *parent*'s accessible members.

Note   It's impossible to specify multiple class names after `extends` because Java doesn't support class-based multiple inheritance.

For example, I'll use `extends` to establish a relationship between classes `Vehicle` and `Truck` and then between classes `Account` and `CheckingAccount`:

```
class Vehicle
{
   // member declarations
}

class Truck extends Vehicle
{
   // inherit accessible members from Vehicle
   // provide own member declarations
}
```

```
class Account
{
   // member declarations
}

class CheckingAccount extends Account
{
   // inherit accessible members from Account
   // provide own member declarations
}
```

These examples codify is-a relationships. Truck is a specialized Vehicle, and CheckingAccount is a specialized Account. Vehicle and Account are known as *base classes, parent classes,* or *superclasses*. Truck and CheckingAccount are known as *derived classes, child classes,* or *subclasses*.

Note   You might declare a class that should not be extended for security or another reason. Java provides the final keyword to prevent the class from being extended. Simply prefix a class header with final, as in final class Password. Given this declaration, the compiler will report an error when someone attempts to extend Password.

Child classes inherit accessible fields and methods from their parent classes and other ancestor classes. They never inherit constructors. Instead, child classes declare their own constructors. Furthermore, they can declare their own fields and methods to differentiate them from their parents. Consider Listing 7-1.

Listing 7-1. Account.java

```
class Account
{
   private String name;
   private long amount;
```

```java
Account(String name, long amount)
{
    this.name = name;
    setAmount(amount);
}

void deposit(long amount)
{
    this.amount += amount;
}

String getName()
{
    return name;
}

long getAmount()
{
    return amount;
}

void setAmount(long amount)
{
    this.amount = amount;
}
}
```

Listing 7-1 describes a generic bank account class with a name and an initial amount, which are both set in the constructor. Also, it lets users make deposits. (You can withdraw by depositing negative amounts of money, but we'll ignore this possibility.) Note that the account name must be set when an account is created.

Note   I chose to represent a monetary value as a `long`, where the value is stored as a count of pennies. You might prefer to use a `double` or a `float` to store a dollars and cents value, but doing that can lead to inaccuracies. Chapter 12 presents a better alternative.

Listing 7-2 presents a CheckingAccount subclass that extends its Account superclass.

Listing 7-2. CheckingAccount.java

```java
class CheckingAccount extends Account
{
   CheckingAccount(long amount)
   {
      super("checking", amount);
   }

   void withdraw(long amount)
   {
      setAmount(getAmount() - amount);
   }
}
```

The CheckingAccount class subclasses Account and provides a constructor that initializes the amount and name fields in its superclass by passing "checking" and amount to the superclass constructor.

The constructor uses the super reserved word to pass these values to its equivalent superclass constructor. It uses super in a call context via super("checking", amount);. This is analogous to a this() call context to pass arguments to another constructor in the same class.

Caution   Just as this() must be the first element in a constructor that calls another constructor in the same class, super() must be the first element in a constructor that calls a constructor in its superclass. If you break this rule, the compiler will report an error. The compiler will also report an error when it detects a super() call in a method; only ever call super() in a constructor.

CheckingAccount also provides a withdraw() method that reduces the account balance by the amount to be withdrawn. Because Account's amount field is private, CheckingAccount cannot directly access it. Instead, it invokes the setAmount() and getAmount() methods that it inherits from Account, subtracting its amount parameter value from getAmount()'s return value and passing the difference to setAmount().

Listing 7-3 presents a SavingsAccount subclass that extends its Account superclass.

Listing 7-3. SavingsAccount.java

```
class SavingsAccount extends Account
{
   SavingsAccount(long amount)
   {
      super("savings", amount);
   }
}
```

The SavingsAccount class is trivial because it doesn't need to declare additional fields or methods. It does, however, declare a constructor that initializes the fields in its Account superclass. Initialization happens when Account's constructor is called via Java's super keyword, followed by a parenthesized arguments list.

Caution   If super() is not specified in a subclass constructor, and if the superclass doesn't declare a no-argument constructor, then the compiler will report an error. This is because the subclass constructor must call a no-argument superclass constructor when super() isn't present.

I've created an AccountDemo application class demonstrating the Account superclass and its CheckingAccount and SavingsAccount subclasses. Listing 7-4 presents AccountDemo's source code.

Listing 7-4. AccountDemo.java

```
class AccountDemo
{
   public static void main(String[] args)
   {
      SavingsAccount sa = new SavingsAccount(40000);
      System.out.println("account name: " + sa.getName());
      System.out.println("initial amount: " + sa.getAmount());
      sa.deposit(3500);
      System.out.println("new amount after deposit: " + sa.getAmount());
```

```
CheckingAccount ca = new CheckingAccount(2000);
System.out.println("account name: " + ca.getName());
System.out.println("initial amount: " + ca.getAmount());
ca.deposit(6000);
System.out.println("new amount after deposit: " + ca.getAmount());
ca.withdraw(1500);
System.out.println("new amount after withdrawal: " + ca.getAmount());
    }
}
```

Assuming that Account.java, CheckingAccount.java, SavingsAccount.java, and AccountDemo.java are located in the same directory, execute the following command to compile all four source files:

```
javac *.java
```

Execute the following command to run the application:

```
java AccountDemo
```

You should observe the following output:

```
account name: savings
initial amount: 40000
new amount after deposit: 43500
account name: checking
initial amount: 2000
new amount after deposit: 8000
new amount after withdrawal: 6500
```

Method Overriding

A subclass can *override* (replace) an inherited method so that the subclass's version of the method is called instead. An overriding method must specify the same name, parameter list, and return type as the method being overridden. I've declared an info() method in Listing 7-5's Vehicle class to demonstrate.

Listing 7-5. Vehicle.java

```java
class Vehicle
{
    private String make;
    private String model;
    private int year;
    Vehicle(String make, String model, int year)
    {
        this.make = make;
        this.model = model;
        this.year = year;
    }

    String getMake()
    {
        return make;
    }

    String getModel()
    {
        return model;
    }

    int getYear()
    {
        return year;
    }

    void info()
    {
        System.out.println("Make: " + make + ", Model: " + model +
        ", Year: " + year);
    }
}
```

Next, I override `info()` in Listing 7-6's Truck class.

Listing 7-6. `Truck.java`

```java
class Truck extends Vehicle
{
    private boolean isExtendedCab;

    Truck(String make, String model, int year, boolean isExtendedCab)
    {
        super(make, model, year);
        this.isExtendedCab = isExtendedCab;
    }

    boolean isExtendedCab()
    {
        return isExtendedCab;
    }

    void info()
    {
        super.info();
        System.out.println("Is extended cab: " + isExtendedCab);
    }
}
```

Truck's `info()` method has the same name, return type, and parameter list as Vehicle's `info()` method. Note, too, that Truck's `info()` method first calls Vehicle's `info()` method by prefixing `super` followed by the member-selection operator (`.`) to the method name. It's often a good idea to execute the superclass logic first and then execute the subclass logic.

Note   To call a superclass method from the overriding subclass method, prefix the method's name with `super` and the `.` operator. Otherwise, you end up calling the subclass's overriding method recursively. In some cases, a subclass will mask non-`private` superclass fields by declaring same-named fields. You can use `super` and `.` to access the non-`private` superclass fields.

Listing 7-7 completes this example by presenting the source code to a VehicleDemo application class.

Listing 7-7. VehicleDemo.java

```java
class VehicleDemo
{
   public static void main(String[] args)
   {
      Truck truck = new Truck("Ford", "F150", 2023, true);
      System.out.println("Make = " + truck.getMake());
      System.out.println("Model = " + truck.getModel());
      System.out.println("Year = " + truck.getYear());
      System.out.println("Is extended cab = " + truck.isExtendedCab());
      truck.info();
   }
}
```

Compile Listing 7-7 and the other source files as follows:

```
javac VehicleDemo.java
```

or

```
javac *.java
```

Assuming no compilation errors, run the VehicleDemo application as follows:

```
java VehicleDemo
```

You should observe the following output:

```
Make = Ford
Model = F150
Year = 2023
Is extended cab = true
Make: Ford, Model: F150, Year: 2023
Is extended cab: true
```

The final two output lines are the result of the `truck.info()` call. The first line, `Make: Ford, Model: F150, Year: 2023`, results from Truck's `info()` method invoking its Vehicle superclass's `info()` method via `super.info()`. The second line executes `System.out.println("Is extended cab: " + isExtendedCab);` to output whether or not the truck is an extended cab.

Note   You might declare a method that should not be overridden for security or another reason. Java provides the `final` keyword to prevent the method from being overridden. Simply prefix a method header with `final`, as in `final String getMake()`. Given this declaration, the compiler will report an error when someone attempts to override `getMake()`.

Method Overloading Instead of Overriding

Assume that you replace Listing 7-6's `info()` method with the following `info()` method that lets you also output a license number:

```
void info(String licenseNumber)
{
    System.out.print("License number: " + licenseNumber);
    super.info();
}
```

The modified Truck class now has two `info()` methods: the preceding explicitly declared method and the method inherited from Vehicle.

The `void info(String licenseNumber)` method doesn't override Vehicle's `info()` method. Instead, it *overloads* (supplies a different method with the same name) the `info()` method.

The `truck.info()` call will not invoke `void info(String licenseNumber)`.

You can detect an attempt to overload instead of override a method at compile time by prefixing a subclass's method header with the `@Override` *annotation* (additional information that is attached to a method). The following `info()` method demonstrates:

```
@Override
void info(String licenseNumber)
{
    System.out.print("License number: " + licenseNumber);
    super.info();
}
```

Specifying @Override tells the compiler that the method overrides another method. If someone attempted to overload the method instead, the compiler would report an error. Without this annotation, the compiler would not report an error because method overloading is legal. (I don't discuss annotations further in this book because I don't consider them to be a fundamental Java language feature.)

Tip   Get into the habit of prefixing overriding methods with @Override. This habit will help you detect overloading mistakes much sooner.

Method Overriding and Protected Methods

Java provides the protected keyword for use in a method-overriding context. You can also use protected for fields. This keyword is commonly used to identify methods that are designed to be overridden, given that not all accessible methods should be overridden.

When you declare a method or field protected, the method or field becomes accessible to all of the code within any class that has been declared in the same package. It is also accessible to subclasses regardless of their packages. (I discuss packages in Chapter 10.)

The Ultimate Ancestor of All Classes

Java provides a huge library of classes and other reference types that lets programmers work with files and databases, collections of objects, concurrency, and more. This library includes the Object class, which serves as the ultimate ancestor of all classes. Think of Object as the ultimate superclass.

Every class directly or indirectly extends the Object class. For example, class Employee extends Object and class Vehicle both extend Object. Employee directly extends Object, and Vehicle indirectly extends Object. It is optional to extend Object (and typically not done by convention) because Java doesn't support multiple inheritance.

Note *Multiple inheritance* involves extending multiple classes. This isn't done in Java because problems can arise. For example, two classes might provide the same method with different implementations. If a class extended both classes, which method would it inherit? If allowed, multiple inheritance in a class context would be called *multiple implementation inheritance.*

Multiple inheritance is supported by interfaces, another kind of reference type that I explore in Chapter 8. Because interfaces don't support code bodies for methods, there is no conflict when a class implements two or more interfaces that identify the same method. Multiple inheritance in an interface context is called *multiple interface inheritance.*

Object declares the following methods:

- protected Object clone()
- boolean equals(Object obj)
- protected void finalize()
- final Class<?> getClass()
- int hashCode()
- final void notify()
- final void notifyAll()
- String toString()
- final void wait()
- final void wait(long timeout)
- final void wait(long timeout, int nanos)

These methods perform tasks that are common to all classes. For example, clone() lets you create and return a copy of the object on which this method is invoked.

I introduce most of these methods in the following sections. I don't cover the notify(), notifyAll(), and overloaded wait() methods because they are covered in my *Java Threads and the Concurrency Utilities* book (www.amazon.ca/Java-Threads-Concurrency-Utilities-FRIESEN/dp/1484216997/).

Cloning Objects

The clone() method creates and returns a copy of the object on which it's called. There are two forms of cloning: shallow cloning and deep cloning. After discussing these forms, this section explores array cloning.

Shallow Cloning

Shallow cloning (also known as *shallow copying*) duplicates an object's fields without duplicating the objects referenced from those fields. Listing 7-8 presents a CloneDemo application's source code that shows you how to accomplish shallow cloning.

Listing 7-8. CloneDemo.java

```java
class Date
{
   private int year, month, day;

   Date(int year, int month, int day)
   {
      this.year = year;
      this.month = month;
      this.day = day;
   }

   int getDay()
   {
      return day;
   }
```

```java
    int getMonth()
    {
        return month;
    }

    int getYear()
    {
        return year;
    }
}

class Employee implements Cloneable
{
    private String name;
    private int age;
    private Date hireDate;

    Employee(String name, int age, Date hireDate)
    {
        this.name = name;
        this.age = age;
        this.hireDate = hireDate;
    }

    String getName()
    {
        return name;
    }

    int getAge()
    {
        return age;
    }

    Date getHireDate()
    {
        return hireDate;
    }
```

```
  @Override
  public Object clone() throws CloneNotSupportedException
  {
    return super.clone();
  }
}

class CloneDemo
{
  public static void main(String[] args) throws CloneNotSupportedException
  {
    Employee john = new Employee("John Doe", 37, new Date(1999, 10, 8));
    System.out.println("Name: " + john.getName() +
                       ", Age: " + john.getAge() +
                       ", Hire Date: " + john.getHireDate());

    Employee john2 = (Employee) john.clone();
    System.out.println("Name: " + john2.getName() +
                       ", Age: " + john2.getAge() +
                       ", Hire Date: " + john2.getHireDate());
  }
}
```

Listing 7-8 first declares a simple Date class that describes a date in terms of year, month, and day integer fields. The constructor updates these fields, and getter methods return their values.

Listing 7-8 next declares an Employee class whose objects are to be cloned. This class must implement the empty Cloneable interface to inform clone() that it's legal for that method to make a field-for-field copy of Employee objects. (I introduce interfaces in Chapter 8.) When Cloneable isn't implemented, clone() throws CloneNotSupportedException. (I discuss exceptions in Chapter 11.)

Because clone() is marked protected, it must be overridden in Employee. Note the presence of the @Override annotation, which I briefly mentioned earlier in this chapter.

You must specify the public access specifier when overriding clone(). When you don't specify an access specifier (you are indicating package private access), the compiler reports an attempt to assign weaker access privileges.

When you specify `private`, the compiler reports that `clone()` has private access in `Employee`, in addition to an attempt to assign weaker access privileges. When you specify `protected`, the source code compiles, but a `CloneNotSupportedException` object is thrown at runtime.

`Employee`'s `clone()` method executes `super.clone()` to invoke `Object`'s `clone()` method, which performs a field-for-field copy of the class that implements `Cloneable`. In this case, `Object`'s `clone()` method copies the invoking `Employee` object's name, age, and `hireDate` fields.

The `main()` method's `Employee john2 = (Employee) john.clone();` statement demonstrates the clone operation. It casts `john.clone()`'s return type to `Employee` because `clone()`'s return type is `Object`.

Compile Listing 7-8 as follows:

```
javac CloneDemo.java
```

Run the resulting application as follows:

```
java CloneDemo
```

You should observe the following output (the hexadecimal number after the @ symbol might be different):

```
Name: John Doe, Age: 37, Hire Date: Date@28a418fc
Name: John Doe, Age: 37, Hire Date: Date@28a418fc
```

You might be expecting to see the employee's hiring date in terms of year, month, and day components. Instead, you see a default string representation of the `Date` object. This representation consists of the `Date` class name, the @ symbol, and a hexadecimal value (which represents a hash code, discussed later in this chapter). This default string representation is a visual way of noting an object's reference.

You can see that the original `Employee` object and its clone refer to the same `Date` object because the default string representation is the same for each object. This is an example of shallow cloning.

To be a true clone, the `Employee` clone should reference a new `Date` object that records the hire date. In other words, the `Employee` object should be deeply cloned.

Deep Cloning

Deep cloning (also known as *deep copying*) performs shallow cloning and also recursively duplicates objects referenced from an object's fields along with objects referenced in those objects fields, and so on. Listing 7-9 presents the source code to a second version of the CloneDemo application's source code that shows you how to accomplish deep cloning.

Listing 7-9. CloneDemo.java (version 2)

```
class Date implements Cloneable
{
    private int year, month, day;

    Date(int year, int month, int day)
    {
        this.year = year;
        this.month = month;
        this.day = day;
    }

    int getDay()
    {
        return day;
    }

    int getMonth()
    {
        return month;
    }

    int getYear()
    {
        return year;
    }
```

```java
    @Override
    public Object clone() throws CloneNotSupportedException
    {
        return super.clone();
    }
}

class Employee implements Cloneable
{
    private String name;
    private int age;
    private Date hireDate;

    Employee(String name, int age, Date hireDate)
    {
        this.name = name;
        this.age = age;
        this.hireDate = hireDate;
    }

    String getName()
    {
        return name;
    }

    int getAge()
    {
        return age;
    }

    Date getHireDate()
    {
        return hireDate;
    }
```

```java
    @Override
    public Object clone() throws CloneNotSupportedException
    {
        Date hire_Date = (Date) hireDate.clone();
        Employee emp = new Employee(name, age, hire_Date);
        return emp;
    }
}

class CloneDemo
{
    public static void main(String[] args) throws CloneNotSupportedException
    {
        Employee john = new Employee("John Doe", 37, new Date(1999, 10, 8));
        System.out.println("Name: " + john.getName() +
                            ", Age: " + john.getAge() +
                            ", Hire Date: " + john.getHireDate());

        Employee john2 = (Employee) john.clone();
        System.out.println("Name: " + john2.getName() +
                            ", Age: " + john2.getAge() +
                            ", Hire Date: " + john2.getHireDate());
    }
}
```

Listing 7-9 updates the Date class to shallowly clone itself. It does so by implementing Cloneable and overriding the clone() method to invoke super.clone(), which invokes Object's clone() method to perform the actual cloning. This is the same as what the previous listing accomplished for Employee, which shallowly cloned itself.

However, Employee's overriding clone() method has been changed. It first clones Employee's hireDate field that returns a new Date object whose reference is assigned to hire_Date. As part of the deep copy, a new Employee object is created and populated with the name, age, and hire_Date values. The Employee object's reference is returned.

Perhaps you are wondering why the name field wasn't cloned. This field is of type String and cannot be cloned because String objects are *immutable* (unchangeable). Immutability is necessary to implement a feature known as *interning* so that String objects can be compared via the equality operators (== and !=), which greatly improves performance. I won't say anything more about this now, but you can learn about it in Chapter 13.

Compile Listing 7-9 as follows:

```
javac CloneDemo.java
```

Run the resulting application:

```
java CloneDemo
```

You should observe the following output (the hexadecimal numbers after the @ symbols might be different from what you see):

```
Name: John Doe, Age: 37, Hire Date: Date@28a418fc
Name: John Doe, Age: 37, Hire Date: Date@eed1f14
```

Array Cloning

Array types have access to the clone() method, which lets you shallowly clone an array. When used in an array context, you don't have to cast clone()'s return value to the array type. Listing 7-10 demonstrates array cloning.

Listing 7-10. CloneDemo.java (version 3)

```java
class Date
{
    private int year, month, day;

    Date(int year, int month, int day)
    {
        this.year = year;
        this.month = month;
        this.day = day;
    }

    int getYear()
    {
        return year;
    }
}
```

```java
    int getMonth()
    {
        return month;
    }

    int getDay()
    {
        return day;
    }
}

class CloneDemo
{
    public static void main(String[] args)
    {
        int[] populations = { 100000000, 50000000, 10000 };
        for (int i = 0; i < populations.length; i++)
            System.out.print(populations[i] + " ");
        System.out.println();

        int[] populations2 = populations.clone();
        for (int i = 0; i < populations.length; i++)
            System.out.print(populations[i] + " ");
        System.out.println();

        System.out.println();

        Date[] dates = { new Date(1983, 10, 15), new Date(2022, 5, 6) };
        for (int i = 0; i < dates.length; i++)
            System.out.print(dates[i] + " ");
        System.out.println();

        Date[] dates2 = dates.clone();
        for (int i = 0; i < dates.length; i++)
            System.out.print(dates[i] + " ");
        System.out.println();
    }
}
```

Listing 7-10 declares a Date class that records a date in terms of its year, month, and day components. It also declares a CloneDemo class whose main() method demonstrates array cloning.

main() first declares an array of integers that denote populations. After outputting this array's values, it clones the array – note the absence of a cast operator. Next, it outputs the clone's identical population values.

Note   A cast operator is not required when cloning an array because of *covariant return types*, a feature that JDK 5 introduced and which I discuss in Chapter 8. The stackoverflow article "Why can clone array without type cast?" (http://stackoverflow.com/questions/15501032/why-can-clone-array-without-type-cast) explains why a cast operator isn't needed.

Continuing, main() creates an array of Date objects, outputs the dates, clones this array, and outputs the cloned array's dates. As a proof that shallow cloning was used, the output will show identical string representations for the Date objects in the corresponding positions of their respective arrays.

Compile Listing 7-10 as follows:

```
javac CloneDemo.java
```

Run the resulting application as follows:

```
java CloneDemo
```

You should observe output that is similar to the following (the hash codes will probably differ but will be identical for the first pair of Date objects and will be identical [but differ] for the second pair of Date objects):

```
100000000 50000000 10000
100000000 50000000 10000

Date@33c7353a Date@3af49f1c
Date@33c7353a Date@3af49f1c
```

Determining Object Equality

In Chapter 3, you learned that the equality operators don't compare objects but compare their references, which is much faster than comparing individual fields (shallow and deep cloning) and objects referenced from any reference fields (deep cloning only). However, it's often necessary to compare objects in terms of their fields. One example is storing objects in container objects, such as an array list or a linked list.

Object provides the equals() method to let you compare objects in terms of their content. However, the default implementation that all other classes inherit compares objects in terms of their references. If you want to compare a class's objects in terms of their content, you must override equals() in that class.

There are rules that must be followed when overriding equals():

- Be reflexive: For any non-null reference value x, x.equals(x) should return true.

- Be symmetric: For any non-null reference values x and y, x.equals(y) should return true if and only if y.equals(x) returns true.

- Be transitive: For any non-null reference values x, y, and z, if x.equals(y) returns true and y.equals(z) returns true, then x.equals(z) should return true.

- Be consistent: For any non-null reference values x and y, multiple invocations of x.equals(y) consistently return true or consistently return false, provided no information used in equals comparisons on the objects is modified.

- Additionally, for any non-null reference value x, x.equals(null) should return false.

Listing 7-11 presents an EqualsDemo application's source code that shows you how to properly override equals() to satisfy these rules.

Listing 7-11. EqualsDemo.java

```java
class Employee
{
   private String name;
   private int age;
```

```java
   Employee(String name, int age)
   {
      this.name = name;
      this.age = age;
   }

   String getName()
   {
      return name;
   }

   int getAge()
   {
      return age;
   }

   @Override
   public boolean equals(Object obj)
   {
      if (!(obj instanceof Employee))
         return false;
      Employee emp = (Employee) obj;
      return emp.getName().equals(name) && emp.getAge() == age;
   }
}

class EqualsDemo
{
   public static void main(String[] args)
   {
      Employee john = new Employee("John Doe", 29);
      System.out.println("Name: " + john.getName() +
                     ", Age: " + john.getAge());

      Employee jane = new Employee("Jane Doe", 33);
      System.out.println("Name: " + jane.getName() +
                     ", Age: " + jane.getAge());
```

```java
Employee john2 = new Employee("John Doe", 27 + 2);
System.out.println("Name: " + john2.getName() +
                   ", Age: " + john2.getAge());

Employee john3 = new Employee("John Doe", 30 - 1);
System.out.println("Name: " + john3.getName() +
                   ", Age: " + john3.getAge());

System.out.println();

// Demonstrate reflexivity.

System.out.println("Demonstrating reflexivity...");
System.out.println();
System.out.println("john.equals(john): " + john.equals(john));
System.out.println();

// Demonstrate symmetry.

System.out.println("Demonstrating symmetry...");
System.out.println();
System.out.println("john.equals(jane): " + john.equals(jane));
System.out.println("jane.equals(john): " + jane.equals(john));
System.out.println("john.equals(john2): " + john.equals(john2));
System.out.println("john2.equals(john): " + john2.equals(john));
System.out.println("jane.equals(john2): " + jane.equals(john2));
System.out.println("john2.equals(jane): " + john2.equals(jane));
System.out.println();

// Demonstrate transitivity.

System.out.println("Demonstrating transitivity...");
System.out.println();
System.out.println("john.equals(john2): " + john.equals(john2));
System.out.println("john2.equals(john3): " + john2.equals(john3));
System.out.println("john.equals(john3): " + john.equals(john3));
System.out.println();

// Demonstrate consistency.
```

```
    System.out.println("Demonstrating consistency...");
    System.out.println();
    for (int i = 0; i < 5; i++)
    {
        System.out.println("john.equals(jane): " + john.equals(jane));
        System.out.println("john.equals(john2): " + john.equals(john2));
    }
    System.out.println();

    // Demonstrate the null check.

    System.out.println("Demonstrating null check...");
    System.out.println();
    System.out.println("john.equals(null): " + john.equals(null));
    }
}
```

Employee's overriding equals() method first verifies that an Employee object has been passed. If not, it returns false. This check relies on the instanceof operator, which also evaluates to false when null is passed as an argument. This satisfies the final rule mentioned previously: "for any non-null reference value *x*, *x*.equals(null) should return false."

Note   You need to override equals() and hashCode() when planning to store your class's objects in a container object. Otherwise, you'll probably have trouble when working with hash-based containers. I'll discuss hashCode() later in this chapter.

Continuing, the object argument is cast to Employee. You don't have to worry about a possible ClassCastException because the previous instanceof test guarantees that the argument's type is Employee. Following the cast, both name fields are compared, which relies on String's equals() method (I discuss String in Chapter 13), and the two age fields are compared.

Compile Listing 7-11 as follows:

```
javac EqualsDemo.java
```

Run the resulting application as follows:

```
java EqualsDemo
```

You should observe the following output:

```
Name: John Doe, Age: 29
Name: Jane Doe, Age: 33
Name: John Doe, Age: 29
Name: John Doe, Age: 29

Demonstrating reflexivity...

john.equals(john): true

Demonstrating symmetry...

john.equals(jane): false
jane.equals(john): false
john.equals(john2): true
john2.equals(john): true
jane.equals(john2): false
john2.equals(jane): false

Demonstrating transitivity...

john.equals(john2): true
john2.equals(john3): true
john.equals(john3): true

Demonstrating consistency...

john.equals(jane): false
john.equals(john2): true
john.equals(jane): false
john.equals(john2): true
john.equals(jane): false
john.equals(john2): true
john.equals(jane): false
john.equals(john2): true
```

```
john.equals(jane): false
john.equals(john2): true
```

Demonstrating null check...

```
john.equals(null): false
```

Note   You can call equals() on an array reference, which is demonstrated here:

```
int[] grades = { 89, 90, 73 };
```

```
int[] grades2 = { 89, 90, 73 };
```

```
System.out.println(grades.equals(grades2));
```

Don't do this. This capability isn't useful because in an array context, equals() compares array references and not array elements. Because grades and grades2 are assigned different references, System.out.println(grades. equals(grades2)); outputs false instead of true.

Finalization

The finalize() method *finalizes* (cleans up) the current object. Java's garbage collector (introduced shortly) calls this method when it determines that there are no more references to the object. A subclass overrides finalize() to close open files, dispose of system resources, and to perform other cleanup tasks.

Note   A *garbage collector* is that part of a programming language's runtime system or runtime environment (such as the Java Virtual Machine, or JVM) that automatically manages memory. It does so by facilitating the allocation of memory (typically for objects) and the reclamation of memory (formerly occupied by objects) that is no longer *reachable* (accessible to a program).

By automatically handling memory allocation and deallocation, a garbage collector saves programmers from having to perform these tasks. Instead, they can focus on writing code and being more productive.

The Object class's version of finalize() does nothing; it is overridden to provide needed cleanup code. Because the JVM might not call finalize() before an application ends, you should provide a cleanup method that is called to perform cleanup. Also, have finalize() call this method in case the method is not called.

Caution   The finalize() method has been deprecated and will be removed in a future JDK release. Because finalize() can cause security, performance, and reliability problems, I won't discuss it further, apart from providing a brief example while discussing garbage collection in Chapter 14.

Getting the Class Object

The getClass() method returns the runtime class of the object on which this method is called. The runtime class is represented by a Class object.

Class is the entry point into the Java Reflection API. A Java application uses Class and the rest of the Java Reflection API to learn about its own structure. (I don't discuss Class and the rest of the Java Reflection API in this book because I don't consider them a fundamental part of Java.)

Hash Codes

The hashCode() method returns a 32-bit integer that identifies the current object's *hash code*, a small value that results from applying a mathematical function to a potentially large amount of data. The calculation of this value is known as *hashing*.

Hash Maps

Hash codes are used when working with *hash maps* (also known as *hash tables*), which are data structures that serve as hash code–based map implementations.

Note   A *map* is an association between keys (also known as names) and values. A *key* is an identifier that uniquely identifies a name-value entry in a map. A *value* is the desired information to be recorded in the map and is always associated with a key/name.

A map could be implemented via a hash map, a tree, or another kind of data structure.

A hash map uses *hashing* (a scrambling operation) to convert (a typically string-based) key into a positive integer that starts at 0. This positive integer, which is known as a hash code, is provided by the hashCode() method.

The hash code indexes into an array of *buckets* (array slots). Ideally, each key would be mapped to its own bucket, which would store the value associated with the key. However, for a very large number of keys, there may not be enough memory to store their values.

Note   Imagine implementing a spreadsheet, which potentially consists of millions of cells. Most of the cells will not be in use so you wouldn't want to waste memory by creating a bucket for each cell row/column number combination.

Because of limited memory, it's often necessary to reduce the number of buckets so that the number of keys greatly exceeds the bucket count. As a result, there is the possibility of *collisions* where multiple keys hash to the same bucket. You cannot store a value in a bucket because each key might be associated with a different value.

The solution is to use the bucket to store a reference to a linked list of nodes that store (key, value) pairs. All nodes in the linked list share the same hash code. For example, suppose you create a hash map to store English words and their definitions. The implementation could use 26 buckets where each bucket represents all words starting with a single letter of the English alphabet (a–z).

During storage or lookup of a value, the key is hashed, and the resulting hash code identifies the bucket that points to the first node in its linked list. The linked list is then searched for a node whose key matches the key that was hashed. If not found, either a new node is created, populated with a key-value pair, and attached to the list (for a storage operation); or null is returned (for a lookup operation). The act of searching a linked list is known as *linear probing*.

173

Figure 7-1 shows the organization of a hash map.

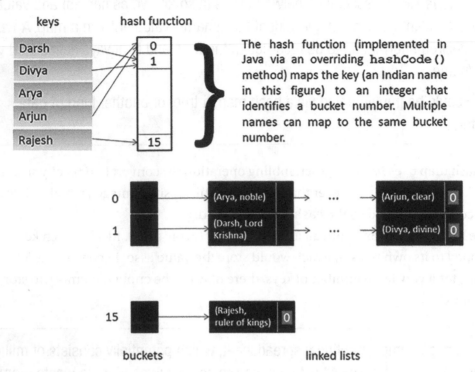

Figure 7-1. *The organization of a hash map*

I've created an implementation of a hash map in order to demonstrate hashCode().
This implementation consists of Node and HashMap classes. Listing 7-12 presents the
implementation of Node.

Listing 7-12. Node.java

```java
class Node
{
    Node next;

    Object key;
    Object value;

    Node(Object key, Object value)
    {
```

```
      this.key = key;
      this.value = value;
   }
}
```

Node represents a node in a linked list and declares key and value, which store the key-value pair, and next, which points to the next node in the list. These fields are initialized by the constructor.

Listing 7-13 presents the implementation of HashMap.

Listing 7-13. HashMap.java

```java
class HashMap
{
   private static final int SIZE = 16;
   private Node[] buckets;

   public HashMap()
   {
      buckets = ncw Node[SIZE];
   }

   public void put(Object key, Object value)
   {
      int index = Math.abs(key.hashCode()) % SIZE;
      Node node = buckets[index];

      while (node != null)
      {
         if (node.key.equals(key))
         {
            node.value = value;
            return;
         }
         node = node.next;
      }
```

```
        Node newNode = new Node(key, value);
        newNode.next = buckets[index];
        buckets[index] = newNode;
    }

    public Object get(Object key)
    {
        int index = Math.abs(key.hashCode()) % SIZE;
        Node node = buckets[index];

        while (node != null)
        {
            if (node.key.equals(key))
                return node.value;
            node = node.next;
        }

        return null;
    }

    public void remove(Object key)
    {
        int hashCode = key.hashCode();
        int index = hashCode % SIZE;

        Node node = buckets[index];
        Node prev = null;

        while (node != null)
        {
            if (node.key.equals(key))
            {
                if (prev != null)
                    prev.next = node.next;
                else
                    buckets[index] = node.next;
                return;
            }
```

```
        prev = node;
        node = node.next;
    }
  }
}
```

Listing 7-13's HashMap class implements a hash map as described earlier. It first declares a SIZE constant that presents the initial size of the buckets array.

HashMap next declares buckets. Each slot stores a reference to a linked list of key-value pairs whose keys all hash to the same bucket index.

HashMap's constructor initializes the buckets array with a new array of Node objects. The number of elements in this array is specified by constant SIZE.

Continuing, HashMap declares a void put(Object key, Object value) method. This method inserts a key-value pair into the hash map.

The put() method first computes the hash code of the key using key.hashCode(). It then takes the absolute value of the hash code and uses the modulus operator (%) to determine the index where the key-value pair will be stored in the buckets array.

Continuing, put() iterates through the linked list at that index. If a node with the same key is found, this method updates the value and returns. If not, put() creates a new node and adds it to the linked list.

HashMap now declares an Object get(Object key) method. This method is used to retrieve the value associated with a given key.

The get() method computes the index in a similar way to the put() method. It then iterates through the linked list at that index. If a node with the matching key is found, it returns the associated value.

HashMap finally declares a void remove(Object key) method. This method removes a key-value pair from the hash map.

The remove() method first computes the index based on the key's hash code. It then iterates through the linked list at that index. If a node with the matching key is found, it removes that node from the linked list. (If there are multiple nodes with the same key, remove() only removes the first node that it encounters.)

Demonstrating the Hash Map

I've created a simple application that demonstrates HashMap (and Node). Listing 7-14 presents the source code.

Listing 7-14. HashCodeDemo.java

```java
class HashCodeDemo
{
   public static void main(String[] args)
   {
      HashMap westernProvinceCapitals = new HashMap();
      westernProvinceCapitals.put("British Columbia", "Victoria");
      westernProvinceCapitals.put("Alberta", "Edmonton");
      westernProvinceCapitals.put("Saskatchewan", "Regina");
      westernProvinceCapitals.put("Manitoba", "Winnipeg");

      System.out.println(westernProvinceCapitals.get("Manitoba"));
      System.out.println(westernProvinceCapitals.get("Saskatchewan"));
      System.out.println(westernProvinceCapitals.get("British Columbia"));
      System.out.println(westernProvinceCapitals.get("Alberta"));
      System.out.println(westernProvinceCapitals.get("Quebec"));
   }
}
```

HashCodeDemo's main() method first instantiates HashMap and assigns its reference to the westernProvinceCapitals local variable. It then populates the hash map with province keys and capital city values by calling HashMap's put() method via this reference.

The main() method then invokes get() on various province names to retrieve their values, which are then output via System.out.println() method calls. I included a get() call with Quebec as the key in order to show get() returning null when it cannot find a key in the map.

Compile Listing 7-14 as follows:

```
javac HashCodeDemo.java
```

Run the resulting application as follows:

```
java HashCodeDemo
```

You should observe the following output:

```
Winnipeg
Regina
Victoria
Edmonton
null
```

Overriding hashCode() and equals() Together

You must override hashCode() when overriding equals(), and in accordance with the following contract, which is specified in hashCode()'s Java documentation:

- Whenever hashCode() is invoked on the same object more than once during an execution of a Java application, hashCode() must consistently return the same integer, provided no information used in equals() comparisons on the object is modified. However, this integer doesn't need to remain consistent from one execution of an application to another. For example, hashCode() might return 5000 each time it is called for one execution and return 8700 each time it is called for another execution.

- When two objects are equal according to the overriding equals() method, calling hashCode() on each of the two objects must produce the same integer result.

- When two objects are unequal according to the overriding equals() method, the integers returned from calling hashCode() on these objects can be identical. However, having hashCode() return distinct values for unequal objects may improve hash table performance.

Fail to obey this contract and your class's instances will not work properly with the aforementioned HashMap class.

If you override equals() but not hashCode(), you most importantly violate the second item in the contract: The hash codes of equal objects must also be equal. This violation can lead to serious consequences, as demonstrated in Listings 7-15 and 7-16.

Listing 7-15. `Point.java`

```java
class Point
{
    int x, y;

    Point(int x, int y)
    {
        this.x = x; this.y = y;
    }

    int getX()
    {
        return x;
    }

    int getY()
    {
        return y;
    }

    @Override
    public boolean equals(Object o)
    {
        if (!(o instanceof Point))
            return false;
        Point p = (Point) o;
        return p.x == x && p.y == y;
    }
}
```

The Point class describes a point via a pair of int-based x and y fields. It declares a Point(x, y) constructor that initializes these fields along with getX() and getY() methods that return their values. It also overrides the equals() method to determine whether two Point objects are the same (based on identical x and y values).

Listing 7-16. HashCodeDemo.java (version 2)

```java
class HashCodeDemo
{
   public static void main(String[] args)
   {
      HashMap map = new HashMap();
      Point p = new Point(10, 20);
      map.put(p, "some point");
      System.out.println(map.get(p));
      System.out.println(map.get(new Point(10, 20)));
   }
}
```

HashMapDemo's main() method first instantiates HashMap and assigns its reference to the map local variable. It then instantiates Point and assigns its reference to local variable p, and initializes the object to 10 (x) and 20 (y).

The subsequent map.put() call stores p's reference and a reference to the "some point" String object in the hash map.

Next, HashMapDemo invokes get(p) to return the "some point" value associated with the Point object key. This value is then output via System.out.println().

A second System.out.println() call outputs the value associated with the key described by new Point(10, 20).

Compile Listing 7-16 as follows:

```
javac HashCodeDemo.java
```

Run the resulting application as follows:

```
java HashCodeDemo
```

You should observe the following output:

```
some point
null
```

You might expect some point to be output because new Point(10, 20) and the Point(10, 20) object assigned to p logically describe the same key. However, this isn't the case: null outputs instead.

Although the Point object referenced by p and the object described by new Point(10, 20) are logically equivalent, these objects have different hash codes, resulting in each object referring to a different entry in the hash map. If an object is not stored (via put()) in that entry, get() returns the null reference.

Correcting this problem requires that hashCode() be overridden to return the same integer value for logically equivalent objects. This is what the String class does, which is why you won't encounter a problem when storing String-based keys.

Let's fix this problem. Consider Listing 7-17's upgraded Point class.

Listing 7-17. Point.java (version 3)

```java
class Point
{
   int x, y;

   Point(int x, int y)
   {
      this.x = x; this.y = y;
   }

   int getX()
   {
      return x;
   }

   int getY()
   {
      return y;
   }

   @Override
   public boolean equals(Object o)
   {
      if (!(o instanceof Point))
         return false;
      Point p = (Point) o;
      return p.x == x && p.y == y;
   }
```

182

```
@Override
public int hashCode()
{
    int result = 17; // A prime number to start with
    result = 31 * result + x; // Combine with x
    result = 31 * result + y; // Combine with y
    return result;
}
}
```

The only difference between this version of Point and the previous version is the presence of a hashCode() method. This method works as follows:

1. The first line, int result = 17;, initializes local variable result to 17. This starting value is arbitrary and is chosen to be a prime number. A prime number helps reduce the likelihood of collisions.

2. The second line, result = 31 * result + x;, combines result's current value with Point's x field value. Multiplying result's value by 31 is commonly done because 31 is an odd prime number, which helps to create a more unique result. This line mixes x's value into the hash code.

3. The third line, result = 31 * result + y;, similarly combines result's current value with Point's y field value, which mixes y's value into the hash code.

4. The final line, return result;, returns the resulting hash code to this method's caller.

To summarize, this hashCode() method implementation creates a unique hash code for each Point object. This unique hash code is based on combining Point's x and y field values, which specify the point's coordinates. Using prime numbers (17 and 31) in the calculation helps distribute the hash codes more evenly, reducing the possibility of collisions.

Note that this implementation is suitable for most cases. However, depending on your application, you might have to tune the implementation further. You need to ensure that objects that are considered equal (according to the equals() method) produce the same hash code.

183

Compile Listing 7-17 as follows:

```
javac HashCodeDemo.java
```

Run the resulting application as follows:

```
java HashCodeDemo
```

You should observe the following output:

```
some point
some point
```

String Representation and Debugging

The toString() method returns a string representation of the object on which it is called. The returned string is useful for debugging. Consider Listings 7-18 through 7-20.

Listing 7-18. Vehicle.java

```
class Vehicle
{
    private String make;
    private String model;
    private int year;

    Vehicle(String make, String model, int year)
    {
        this.make = make;
        this.model = model;
        this.year = year;
    }
    String getMake()
    {
        return make;
    }
```

```java
    String getModel()
    {
        return model;
    }

    int getYear()
    {
        return year;
    }

    @Override
    public String toString()
    {
        return "Make: " + make + ", Model: " + model + ", Year: " + year;
    }
}
```

Listing 7-19. Truck.java

```java
class Truck extends Vehicle
{
    private boolean isExtendedCab;

    Truck(String make, String model, int year, boolean isExtendedCab)
    {
        super(make, model, year);
        this.isExtendedCab = isExtendedCab;
    }

    boolean isExtendedCab()
    {
        return isExtendedCab;
    }

    @Override
    public String toString()
    {
        return super.toString() + "\n" + "Is extended cab: " + isExtendedCab;
    }
}
```

Listing 7-20. `VehicleDemo.java`

```java
class VehicleDemo
{
    public static void main(String[] args)
    {
        Truck truck = new Truck("Ford", "F150", 2023, true);
        System.out.println("Make = " + truck.getMake());
        System.out.println("Model = " + truck.getModel());
        System.out.println("Year = " + truck.getYear());
        System.out.println("Is extended cab = " + truck.isExtendedCab());
        System.out.println(truck.toString());
    }
}
```

Listing 7-18 presents the `Vehicle` class. Notice that it removes the `info()` method and overrides `toString()`, which it indirectly inherits from `Object`.

Listing 7-19 presents the `Truck` class. It also removes the `info()` method and overrides `toString()`, which it directly inherits from `Vehicle`.

Listing 7-20 presents the `VehicleDemo` class. Its `main()` method calls `truck. toString()` to return a string representation of `truck`, which gets output via `System. out.println()`.

Note   I could have specified `System.out.println(truck);` instead of `System.out.println(truck.toString());`. The former method invokes the `System.out.println(Object o)` overloaded `println()` method, and the latter method invokes the `System.out.println(String s)` overloaded `println()` method.

Compile these three source files via `javac *.java` or `javac VehicleDemo. java`. Run the resulting application via `java VehicleDemo`. You should observe the following output:

```
Make = Ford
Model = F150
Year = 2023
```

```
Is extended cab = true
Make: Ford, Model: F150, Year: 2023
Is extended cab: true
```

Note   When the toString() method is not overridden, Object's version of toString() is called. It returns a string in the format *class name@hexadecimal hashcode*. For example, if neither toString() in Truck nor toString() in Vehicle were present, you would observe output such as Truck@3af49f1c. You don't see this default output because of the presence of both overriding toString() methods. Furthermore, you wouldn't see this default output if you removed only toString() from Truck because Truck would inherit Vehicle's overriding toString() method.

Composition

Inheritance through class extension offers one approach to reusing classes. As you have learned, inheritance is concerned with extending a class with a new class, which is based upon an is-a relationship between them: a Truck is a Vehicle, for example.

Another approach to class reuse is *composition*, which is concerned with composing classes out of other classes based on a *has-a relationship* between them. For example, a Truck has an Engine, Wheels, and a SteeringWheel:

```
class Truck extends Vehicle
{
    private Engine engine;
    private Wheel[] wheels;
    private SteeringWheel steeringWheel;
}
```

This example demonstrates that composition and inheritance are not mutually exclusive. Although not shown, Truck inherits various members from its Vehicle superclass, in addition to providing its own engine, wheels, and steeringwheel instance fields.

The Trouble with Inheritance

Inheritance can be problematic because it breaks *encapsulation*, which, if you recall, combines fields, methods, and constructors into classes. In inheritance, a subclass relies on implementation details in its superclass. If the superclass's implementation details change, the subclass might break. This problem is especially serious when a developer doesn't have complete control over the superclass or when the superclass hasn't been designed and documented with extension in mind.

Composition provides a solution to this problem. This section presents an example that demonstrates the problem and then shows you how to solve it via composition.

Logging Appointments

To understand this problem, assume that you have purchased a library of classes that implement an appointment calendar. Although you don't have access to their source code, assume that Listing 7-21 describes the main ApptCal class.

Listing 7-21. ApptCal.java

```java
class ApptCal
{
   private final static int MAX_APPT = 1000;
   private Appointment[] appointments;
   private int size;

   ApptCal()
   {
      appointments = new Appointment[MAX_APPT];
      size = 0;
   }

   void addAppointment(Appointment appointment)
   {
      if (size == appointments.length)
         return; // array is full
      appointments[size++] = appointment;
   }
}
```

```
   void addAppointments(Appointment[] appointments)
   {
      for (int i = 0; i < appointments.length; i++)
         addAppointment(appointments[i]);
   }
}
```

ApptCal stores an array of appointments, with each appointment described by an Appointment object. For this discussion, the details of Appointment aren't important; it could be as trivial as an empty Appointment class – see Listing 7-22.

Listing 7-22. Appointment.java

```
class Appointment
{
}
```

Suppose you wanted to log each address to a file. Because a logging capability isn't provided, you extend ApptCal with Listing 7-23's LoggingApptCal class, which adds logging behavior in overriding addAppointment() and addAppointments() methods.

Listing 7-23. LoggingApptCal.java

```
class LoggingApptCal extends ApptCal
{
   LoggingApptCal()
   {
   }

   @Override
   void addAppointment(Appointment appointment)
   {
      Logger.log(appointment.toString());
      super.addAppointment(appointment);
   }
```

```
@Override
void addAppointments(Appointment[] appointments)
{
   for (int i = 0; i < appointments.length; i++)
      Logger.log(appointments[i].toString());
   super.addAppointments(appointments);
}
}
```

The LoggingApptCal class relies on a Logger class (see Listing 7-24) whose void log(String msg) class method logs a string to a file. An Appointment object is converted to a string via toString(), which is passed to log().

Listing 7-24. Logger.java

```
class Logger
{
   static void log(String msg)
   {
      System.out.println(msg);
   }
}
```

Although LoggingApptCal looks okay, it doesn't work as you might expect. Suppose you instantiated this class and added a few Appointment objects to the object via addAppointments(), which Listing 7-25's ApptCalDemo class accomplishes.

Listing 7-25. ApptCalDemo.java

```
class ApptCalDemo
{
   public static void main(String[] args)
   {
      Appointment[] appointments =
      {
         new Appointment(),
         new Appointment(),
         new Appointment()
      };
```

```
        LoggingApptCal lapptcal = new LoggingApptCal();
        lapptcal.addAppointments(appointments);
    }
}
```

Compile this code as follows:

```
    javac ApptCalDemo.java (or javac *.java)
```

Run the application as follows:

```
java ApptCalDemo
```

You should observe the following output (the hash codes might differ):

```
Appointment@5305068a
Appointment@279f2327
Appointment@2ff4acd0
Appointment@5305068a
Appointment@279f2327
Appointment@2ff4acd0
```

Six messages are output. Each of the expected three messages (one per `Address` object) is duplicated.

When `LoggingAB`'s `addAddresses()` method is called, it first calls `Logger.log()` for each `Address` object in the `addresses` array that is passed to `addAddresses()`. This method then calls AB's `addAddresses()` method via `super.addAddresses(addresses);`.

AB's `addAddresses()` method calls `LoggingAB`'s overriding `addAddress()` method, one for each `Address` object in its `addresses` array argument. The `addAddress()` method then executes `Logger.log(address.toString());`, to log its `address` argument's string representation, and you end up with three additional logged messages.

If you didn't override the `addAddresses()` method, this problem should go away. But in that case, the subclass would still be tied to an implementation detail: AB's `addAddresses()` method calls `addAddress()`.

It isn't a good idea to rely on an implementation detail when that detail isn't documented. (Recall that you don't have access to AB's source code.) When a detail isn't documented, it can change in a new version of the class.

Because a base class change can break a subclass, this problem is known as the *fragile base class problem*. A related cause of fragility (which also has to do with overriding methods) occurs when new methods are added to a superclass in a subsequent release.

For example, suppose a new version of the library introduces a `void addAddress(Address address, boolean unique)` method into the AB class. This method adds the address to the address book when `unique` is false. When `unique` is true, it adds the address only if it wasn't previously added.

Because this method was added after the `LoggingAB` class was created, `LoggingAB` doesn't override the new `addAddress()` method with a call to `Logger.log()`. As a result, `Address` objects passed to the new `addAddress()` method are not logged.

Here's another problem: you introduce a method into the subclass that is not also in the superclass. A new version of the superclass presents a new method that matches the subclass method signature and return type. Your subclass method now overrides the superclass method and probably doesn't fulfill the superclass method's contract.

Composed Objects and Forwarding to the Rescue

You can make all of these problems disappear in part by using a *composed object*, which is an object whose state refers to other objects. For example, a `Vehicle` object has `String` `make` and `model` fields that reference strings (which are objects in Java) that store a vehicle's make and model. We say that `Vehicle` is composed of these strings.

Declare a "`private ApptCal`" field in a new `LoggingApptCal` class, and have this field reference an instance of the former `ApptCal` superclass (`LoggingApptCal` will no longer extend `ApptCal`). This workaround forms a *has-a relationship* between the new class (`LoggingApptCal`) and former superclass (`ApptCal`), so your technique is known as *composition*.

Additionally, you can make each of the new class's object methods call the corresponding superclass method and return the called method's return value. You do this via the superclass object saved in the `private` field. This task is known as *forwarding*, and the new methods are known as *forwarding methods*.

Listing 7-26 presents an improved `LoggingApptCal` class that uses composition and forwarding to forever eliminate the fragile base class problem and the additional problem of unanticipated method overriding.

Listing 7-26. `LoggingApptCal.java`

```java
class LoggingApptCal
{
   private ApptCal apptcal; // Create a private field in new class.

   LoggingApptCal(ApptCal apptcal)
   {
      this.apptcal = apptcal;
   }

   void addAppointment(Appointment appointment)
   {
      Logger.log(appointment.toString());
      apptcal.addAppointment(appointment);
   }

   void addAppointments(Appointment[] appointments)
   {
      for (int i = 0; i < appointments.length; i++)
         Logger.log(appointments[i].toString());
      apptcal.addAppointments(appointments);
   }
}
```

In this example, the `LoggingApptCal` class doesn't depend upon the implementation details of the `ApptCal` class. You can add new methods to `ApptCal` without breaking `LoggingApptCal`.

Note   Listing 7-26's `LoggingApptCal` class is an example of a *wrapper class*, which is a class whose objects wrap other objects. Each `LoggingApptCal` object wraps an `ApptCal` object.

To use the new `LoggingApptCal` class, you must first instantiate `ApptCal` and pass the resulting object as an argument to `LoggingApptCal`'s constructor. The `LoggingApptCal` object wraps the `ApptCal` object, as follows:

```java
LoggingApptCal lapptcal = new LoggingApptCal(new ApptCal());
```

Compile and run this refactored application and you should observe output that's similar to the following:

```
Appointment@5305068a
Appointment@279f2327
Appointment@2ff4acd0
```

What's Next?

A developer can create a `Vehicle` object when it's better to create a more specific `Truck` object. Java provides an abstract class feature that can be used to prevent `Vehicle` from being instantiated. Chapter 8 introduces you to abstract classes. It also introduces you to the related interface concept, which is another form of abstraction.

CHAPTER 8

Changing Type via Polymorphism

Some real-world entities can change their forms. For example, water (on Earth as opposed to interstellar space) is naturally a liquid, but it changes to a solid when frozen, and it changes to a gas when heated to its boiling point. Insects such as butterflies that undergo metamorphosis are another example.

The ability to change form is known as *polymorphism* and is useful to model in a programming language. For example, code that draws arbitrary shapes can be expressed more concisely by introducing a single Shape class and its draw() method and by invoking that method for each Circle instance, Rectangle instance, and other Shape instance stored in an array. When Shape's draw() method is called for an array instance, it is the Circle's, Rectangle's, or other Shape instance's draw() method that gets called. We say that there are many forms of Shape's draw() method or that this method is polymorphic.

Java supports four kinds of polymorphism:

- Coercion: An operation serves multiple types through implicit type conversion. For example, division lets you divide an integer by another integer, or divide a floating-point value by another floating-point value. If one operand is an integer and the other operand is a floating-point value, the compiler coerces (implicitly converts) the integer to a floating-point value to prevent a type error. (There is no division operation that supports an integer operand and a floating-point operand.) Passing a subclass object reference to a method's superclass parameter is another example of coercion polymorphism. The compiler coerces the subclass type to the superclass type to restrict operations to those of the superclass.

© Jeff Friesen 2024
J. Friesen, *Learn Java Fundamentals*, https://doi.org/10.1007/979-8-8688-0351-2_8

- Overloading: The same operator symbol or method name can be used in different contexts. For example, + can be used to perform integer addition, floating-point addition, or string concatenation, depending on the types of its operands. Also, multiple methods having the same name can appear in a class (through declaration and/or inheritance).

- Parametric: In a class declaration, a field name can associate with different types, and a method name can associate with different parameter and return types. The field and method can then take on different types in each class instance. For example, a field might be of type Truck and a method might return a Truck reference in one class instance, and the same field might be of type Car and the same method might return a Car reference in another class instance. Java supports parametric polymorphism via generics, which I don't discuss in this book.

- Subtype: A type can serve as another type's subtype. When a subtype instance appears in a supertype context, executing a supertype operation on the subtype instance results in the subtype's version of that operation executing. For example, suppose that Circle is a subclass of Point and that both classes contain a draw() method. Assigning a Circle instance to a variable of type Point, and then calling the draw() method via this variable, results in Circle's draw() method being called. Subtype polymorphism partners with inheritance.

Many developers do not regard coercion and overloading as valid kinds of polymorphism. They see coercion and overloading as nothing more than type conversions and syntactic sugar. In contrast, parametric and subtype are regarded as valid kinds of polymorphism.

This chapter introduces you to subtype polymorphism through upcasting and late binding. We then move on to abstract classes and abstract methods, interfaces, downcasting and runtime type identification, and the additional topics of covariant return types and interface-based static methods.

Upcasting and Late Binding

Subtype polymorphism relies on upcasting and late binding. *Upcasting* is a form of casting where you cast up the inheritance hierarchy from a subtype to a supertype. No (*type*) operator is involved because the subtype is a specialization of the supertype. For example, Vehicle v = new Truck(); upcasts from Truck to Vehicle. This makes sense because a truck is a kind of vehicle.

After upcasting Truck to Vehicle, you cannot call Truck-specific methods, such as an isExtendedCab() method that returns an indication of whether the truck is a regular cab or an extended cab, because Truck-specific methods are not part of Vehicle's interface. Losing access to subtype features after narrowing a subclass to its superclass seems pointless but is necessary for achieving subtype polymorphism.

Suppose that Vehicle declares a drive() method, its Truck subclass overrides this method, Vehicle v = new Truck(); has just executed, and the next line specifies v.drive();. Which drive() method is called: Vehicle's drive() method or Truck's drive() method? The compiler doesn't know which drive() method to call. All it can do is verify that a method exists in the superclass and verify that the method call's arguments list and return type match the superclass's method declaration. However, the compiler also inserts an instruction into the compiled code that, at runtime, fetches and uses whatever reference is in v to call the correct drive() method. This task is known as *late binding*.

Note   Late binding is used for calls to non-final object methods. For all other method calls, the compiler knows which method to call. It inserts an instruction into the compiled code that calls the method associated with the variable's type (not its value). This task is known as *early binding*.

Abstract Classes and Abstract Methods

When designing class hierarchies, you'll find that classes nearer the top of these hierarchies are more generic than classes that are lower down. For example, a Vehicle superclass is more generic than a Truck subclass. Similarly, an Account superclass is more generic than a CheckingAccount subclass.

It doesn't make sense to create objects from a generic class. After all, what would an Account object describe apart from being an account? Is it a savings account or a checking account, or something else? Similarly, what kind of vehicle is represented by a Vehicle object (truck, plane, bicycle, and so on)? Rather than coding an empty drive() method in Vehicle (press the gas pedal in a truck, pedal a bicycle, and kick off and push forward on a skateboard), you can prevent this method from being called and this class from being instantiated by declaring both entities to be abstract.

Java's abstract reserved word lets you declare a class that cannot be instantiated. The compiler reports an error when you try to instantiate this class. The abstract reserved word is also used to declare a method without a body. The drive() method doesn't need a body because it is unable to drive an abstract vehicle. Listing 8-1 demonstrates.

Listing 8-1. Vehicle.java

```java
abstract class Vehicle
{
   private String make, model;
   private int year;

   Vehicle(String make, String model, int year)
   {
      this.make = make;
      this.model = model;
      this.year = year;
   }

   abstract void drive();

   String getMake()
   {
      return make;
   }

   String getModel()
   {
      return model;
   }
```

```java
  int getYear()
  {
    return year;
  }

  @Override
  public String toString()
  {
    return "Make: " + make + ", Model: " + model + ", Year: " + year;
  }
}
```

Listing 8-1 shows you that an abstract class can declare fields, constructors, and non-abstract methods in addition to (or even instead of) abstract methods.

Notice that Vehicle declares an abstract drive() method to describe how to drive the vehicle. For example, you press the gas pedal to drive a truck. Vehicle's subclasses would override drive() and provide an appropriate description. They would also inherit the methods, and their constructors would call Vehicle's constructor.

Caution   The compiler reports an error when you attempt to declare a class abstract and final. For example, the compiler complains about abstract final class Vehicle because an abstract class cannot be instantiated and a final class cannot be extended.

The compiler also reports an error when you declare a method abstract but don't declare its class abstract. Removing abstract from the Vehicle class's header in Listing 8-1 would result in an error. This would be an error because a non-abstract (concrete) class cannot be instantiated when it contains an abstract method.

Finally, when you extend an abstract class, the extending class must override all of the abstract methods, or else the extending class must itself be declared to be abstract; otherwise, the compiler will report an error.

Interfaces

An *interface* is a point where two entities meet and interact. For example, an electrical wall outlet is an interface between a power cable carrying electricity and an appliance cord that funnels that electricity to an appliance when the cord is plugged into the outlet.

From Java's perspective, an *interface* is the exposed part of a class (fields, constructors, and methods) or another reference type with which external code can interact. Consider Listing 8-2.

Listing 8-2. Stack.java

```java
class Stack
{
    private int[] stack;
    private int top;

    Stack(int size)
    {
        stack = new int[size];
        top = -1;
    }

    boolean isEmpty()
    {
        return top == -1;
    }

    void push(int item)
    {
        if (top == stack.length)
        {
            System.out.println("stack is full");
            return;
        }
        stack[++top] = item;
    }
```

```java
int pop()
{
   if (top == -1)
   {
      System.out.println("stack is empty");
      return -1;
   }
   return stack[top--];
}
}
```

Listing 8-2 presents a Stack class that implements a *stack*, a data structure where the last item stored is the first item retrieved. This data structure helps code remember things, like where it has been while traversing a maze as it looks for an exit.

You push an item (such as a 32-bit integer) on to the top of the stack and pop an item off of the top of the stack. It's also important to determine if the stack is empty because there is no way to know how many items have been pushed when popping them.

Stack's interface is its constructor and the isEmpty(), push(), and pop() method headers. The private stack and top fields along with the code in the constructor and methods form the implementation.

An implementation should be hidden from external code so that it can be changed to meet evolving requirements. When implementations are exposed, interdependencies between software components can arise. For example, method code may rely on external variables, and a class's users may become dependent on fields that should have been hidden. This *coupling* can lead to problems when implementations must evolve (perhaps exposed fields must be removed).

The concept of interface is so important that Java has codified this concept via the interface reserved word. Java developers use this feature to abstract class interfaces, thus *decoupling* classes from their users. By focusing on Java interfaces instead of classes, you can minimize the number of references to class names in your source code. This facilitates changing from one class to another (perhaps to improve performance) as your software matures. Here is an example:

```java
List countries = new ArrayList();
// Code to add countries to the countries list.
// ...
```

```
void print(List list)
{
    for (int i = 0; i < list.length(); i++)
        System.out.println(list.get(i));
}
```

This example declares and initializes a `countries` field that stores a list of string names. The example also declares a `print()` method for printing out this or any other list.

Assume that `List` is an interface describing a sequence of strings and that `ArrayList` is a class describing an array-based `List` implementation. A new `ArrayList` class object is obtained and assigned to `countries`.

When client code interacts with `countries`, it will invoke those methods that are declared by `List` and that are implemented by `ArrayList`. The client code will not interact directly with `ArrayList`. As a result, the client code will not break when a different implementation class, such as `LinkedList`, is required:

```
List countries = new LinkedList();
```

Note   `LinkedList` provides a `List` implementation that's based on a linked group of *nodes* (objects constructed from classes that declare reference fields named after them). For example: `class Node { String item; Node next; }`. In this example, Node declares a `next` field whose reference type is the name of the class in which it is declared. You can link a Node object to another Node object by assigning the Node object's reference to `next`.

Because `print()`'s parameter type is `List`, this method's implementation doesn't have to change. However, if the type had been `ArrayList`, the type would have to be changed to `LinkedList`. If both classes were to declare their own unique methods, you might need to significantly change `print()`'s implementation.

Decoupling `List` from `ArrayList` and `LinkedList` lets you write code that's immune to class-implementation changes. By using Java interfaces, you can avoid problems that could arise from relying on implementation classes. This decoupling is the main reason for using Java interfaces.

Interface Declaration

You declare an interface by adhering to a class-like syntax that consists of a header followed by a body. At minimum, the header consists of keyword `interface` followed by a name (a non-reserved identifier) that identifies the interface. The body starts with an open brace character ({) and ends with a close brace character (}). Between these delimiters are constant and method header declarations:

```
interface identifier
{
   // interface body
}
```

By convention, the first letter of an interface's name is uppercased, and subsequent letters are lowercased (e.g., `Listable`). If a name consists of multiple words, the first letter of each word is uppercased (such as `ListableAndIterable`). This naming convention is known as *camel casing*.

For example, Listing 8-3 presents a `Collection` interface that describes any grouping of objects, which is known as a *collection*.

Listing 8-3. `Collection.java`

```
interface Collection
{
   void add(String item);
   boolean contains(String item);
   int length();
}
```

The `add()` method adds strings to the collection. The `contains()` method returns true when its string argument is present in the collection; otherwise, it returns false. The `length()` method returns the number of strings stored in the list.

`Collection` identifies a reference type that describes a collection of strings but not how the collection is implemented. It leaves implementation details to classes that implement this interface.

Implementing Interfaces

A class implements an interface by appending Java's implements keyword followed
by a comma-separated list of interface names to the class header and by coding each
interface method in the class. Listing 8-4 presents an ArrayCollection class that
implements Listing 8-3's Collection interface.

Listing 8-4. ArrayCollection.java

```java
class ArrayCollection implements Collection
{
    private String[] items;
    private int length;

    ArrayCollection(int size)
    {
        items = new String[size];
        length = 0;
    }

    @Override
    public void add(String item)
    {
        if (length == items.length)
            resize(items.length * 2);
        items[length++] = item;
    }

    @Override
    public boolean contains(String item)
    {
        for (int i = 0; i < length; i++)
            if (item.equals(items[i]))
                return true;
        return false;
    }
```

```
@Override
public int length()
{
   return length;
}

void resize(int newSize)
{
   String[] items2 = new String[newSize];
   for (int i = 0; i < length; i++) // copy items to items2
       items2[i] = items[i];
   items = items2;
}
}
```

Listing 8-4 reveals ArrayCollection, which stores an array-based collection of strings in a private items array. The constructor creates this array with a size equal to the value in its size parameter. For brevity, I haven't bothered to do any error checking. I often avoid checking for errors in various listings, but error checking is still important.

After creating the array, the constructor initializes the length field to 0. This variable records the number of stored items. Although this initialization isn't necessary because object fields are zeroed when an object is constructed, it informs developers (who might not know this fact) that length starts at 0.

The add() method appends a string to the collection. It first makes sure the collection isn't full by comparing length to items.length (the array size). If they are equal, there is no more room to add an item, and resize() is called to double the array's size. The item is stored, the length is incremented because the array is larger, and true is returned.

The contains() method determines if its string argument is contained in the collection, implemented via an array. The method loops over the array, comparing each stored string with its string argument. If they are equal, true is returned; otherwise, false is returned.

The comparison is made via Object's equals() method. This method compares the object reference argument with the reference to the object on which equals() is called. If they match, equals() returns true; otherwise, equals() returns false.

The length() method returns the number of items stored in the array-based collection.

I've declared all three methods `public` because an `interface`'s methods are implicitly public.

Caution   When you implement an interface method (by overriding the interface's method header), remember that all of the methods whose headers are declared in the interface are implicitly declared `public`. If you forget to include `public` in the implemented method's declaration, the compiler will report an error informing you that you're attempting to assign weaker access to the implemented method.

The `resize()` method creates a new string array named `items2` sized to the value passed to its `newSize` parameter. It then copies `length` strings from `items` to `items2`. Copying begins at index 0. After `items2` is populated, its reference is assigned to `items` because `items2` was only a temporary placeholder.

Listing 8-5 presents a `LinkedCollection` class that implements Listing 8-3's `Collection` interface.

Listing 8-5. `LinkedCollection.java`

```java
class LinkedCollection implements Collection
{
    private Node top, last;
    private int length;

    LinkedCollection()
    {
        top = null;
        last = null;
        length = 0;
    }

    @Override
    public void add(String item)
    {
        Node node = new Node();
        node.item = item;
        node.next = null;
```

```java
        if (last != null)
            last.next = node;
        last = node;
        if (top == null)
            top = node;
        length++;
    }

    @Override
    public boolean contains(String item)
    {
        Node node = top;
        for (int i = 0; i < length; i++)
            if (item.equals(node.item))
                return true;
            else
                node = node.next;
        return false;
    }

    @Override
    public int length()
    {
        return length;
    }
}

class Node
{
    String item;
    Node next;
}
```

Listing 8-5 reveals LinkedCollection, which stores a collection of strings in a sequence of Node objects that are linked together. It presents a separate Node class consisting of an item field to record the string being stored and a next field to record a reference to the next Node object in the list.

The private `top` and `last` fields respectively identify the first and last nodes in the linked collection. (It's conventional to use a variable named `top` to identify the start of a linked list.) The `LinkedCollection()` constructor initializes these fields to null, signifying an empty collection.

The private `length` field identifies the number of stored nodes. This field exists for performance. If it didn't exist, you would have to scan the list to obtain the length. The `LinkedCollection()` constructor initializes this field to 0, although it doesn't have to because `length` defaults to 0.

The `add()` method first creates a `Node` object and populates its `item` field with the `String` reference stored in its `item` parameter. It then sets the `Node` object's `next` field to null to signify the end of the collection.

If `last` isn't null, there is already a last node in the collection. Therefore, `add()` appends this new node to the collection by first setting `last`'s `next` field to point to `node` (we want the last node to reference the new node being added to the collection). It then sets `last` to point to `node` because the new node is to be the last node in the collection.

The `add()` method now focuses on `top`. If `top` is null, the linked list is empty, and it points `top` to the node being added. The result is a single-node linked list.

Finally, `add()` increments `length` to signify that the list has grown by one node.

The `contains()` method determines if its string argument is contained in the collection, implemented via a linked list. This method is very similar to `ArrayList`'s `contains()` method except for traversing a linked list instead of an array.

The method loops over the array, comparing each stored string with its string argument. If they are equal, true is returned; otherwise, false is returned.

The `length()` method is simple: it returns the value of the `length` field.

An interface type's data values are the objects whose classes implement the interface and whose behaviors are those specified by the interface's method headers. This fact implies that you can assign an object's reference to a variable of the interface type, provided that the object's class implements the interface.

For example, if you have a variable of type `Collection` and assign to this variable a reference to an object created from a class that implements `Collection`, you can invoke only those methods described by `Collection`. You cannot invoke `resize()`, for instance. There is no point in declaring `resize()` in `Collection` because not every collection class (such as `LinkedList`) requires this capability and thus does not declare this method.

Listing 8-6 demonstrates the `Collection` interface along with the `ArrayCollection` and `LinkedCollection` classes.

Listing 8-6. `CollectionDemo.java`

```java
class CollectionDemo
{
   public static void main(String[] args)
   {
      String[] planetNames =
      {
         "Mercury", "Venus", "Earth", "Mars",
         "Jupiter", "Saturn", "Uranus", "Neptune"
      };

      Collection names = new ArrayCollection(5);
      for (int i = 0; i < planetNames.length; i++)
         names.add(planetNames[i]);
      System.out.println("Contains Mercury: " +
                         names.contains("Mercury"));
      System.out.println("Contains Pluto: " +
                         names.contains("Pluto"));
      System.out.println();

      names = new LinkedCollection();
      for (int i = 0; i < planetNames.length; i++)
         names.add(planetNames[i]);
      System.out.println("Contains Mercury: " +
                         names.contains("Mercury"));
      System.out.println("Contains Pluto: " +
                         names.contains("Pluto"));
   }
}
```

Because `ArrayCollection` and `LinkedCollection` implement `Collection`, `ArrayCollection` and `LinkedCollection` objects have `Collection` type in addition to their class types. Therefore, it's legal to store each object's reference in a variable (`names`) of type `Collection`, but only methods declared by `Collection` can be invoked.

Assuming that Listings 8-3 through 8-6 are located in the current directory, compile them via `javac *.java` or `javac CollectionDemo.java` (the Java compiler recursively compiles referenced source files). Assuming there are no compilation errors, execute the following command to run this application:

```
java CollectionDemo
```

You should observe the following output:

```
Contains Mercury: true
Contains Pluto: false

Contains Mercury: true
Contains Pluto: false
```

Implementing Multiple Interfaces

I previously mentioned that a class can implement multiple interfaces. Each interface's name is specified as part of a comma-separated list of names that follows the `implements` keyword. Listing 8-7 presents a simple example where class Z implements interfaces X and Y.

Listing 8-7. `Z.java` (demonstrating multiple interface implementation)

```
interface X
{
   // appropriate constants and/or method headers
}

interface Y
{
   // appropriate constants and/or method headers
}

class Z implements X, Y
{
   // override X's and Y's method headers
}
```

Beware of the potential for name collisions when implementing multiple interfaces. This occurs when the same constant name appears in each interface, possibly with different type and/or other information, and is accessed in the class. When a name collision occurs, the compiler will report an error, which is demonstrated in Listing 8-8.

Listing 8-8. Z.java (demonstrating constant collision)

```java
interface X
{
   int SOME_CONSTANT = 2;

   void some_method();
}

interface Y
{
   int SOME_CONSTANT = 3;

   int some_method(int i);
}

class Z implements X, Y
{
   int i = SOME_CONSTANT;

   @Override
   public void some_method()
   {
   }

   @Override
   public int some_method(int i)
   {
      return i;
   }
}
```

Class Z inherits two different constants named SOME_CONSTANT that are initialized to two different values. The Java compiler cannot determine which constant should be inherited by Z (the same problem would occur if each constant was assigned the same value) and reports the following error message:

```
Z.java:17: error: reference to SOME_CONSTANT is ambiguous
   int i = SOME_CONSTANT;
           ^
   both variable SOME_CONSTANT in X and variable SOME_CONSTANT in Y match
1 error
```

Extending Interfaces

A class that implements an interface reveals *interface inheritance*. The class inherits the interface's constants and method headers, which it overrides. For example, each of ArrayCollection and LinkedCollection inherits Collection's add(), contains(), and length() method headers.

Interface inheritance is also demonstrated when an interface extends another interface. Just as a subclass can extend a superclass via reserved word extends, you can use this reserved word to have a subinterface extend a superinterface. Listing 8-9 demonstrates.

Listing 8-9. List.java

```java
interface List extends Collection
{
   String get(int i);
}
```

The List interface extends Collection, inheriting its method headers. It also introduces a get() method that returns the string at the ith position in the list, or null when i is less than 0 or greater than or equal to list's length.

Listing 8-10 presents an ArrayList class that implements the List interface.

Listing 8-10. ArrayList.java

```java
class ArrayList implements List
{
   private String[] items;
   private int length;

   ArrayList(int size)
   {
      items = new String[size];
      length = 0;
   }

   @Override
   public void add(String item)
   {
      if (length == items.length)
         resize(items.length * 2);
      items[length++] = item;
   }

   @Override
   public boolean contains(String item)
   {
      for (int i = 0; i < length; i++)
         if (item.equals(items[i]))
             return true;
      return false;
   }

   @Override
   public int length()
   {
      return length;
   }
```

```java
    @Override
    public String get(int index)
    {
        if (index < 0 || index >= length)
            return null;
        return items[index];
    }

    void resize(int newSize)
    {
        String[] items2 = new String[newSize];
        for (int i = 0; i < length; i++) // copy items to items2
            items2[i] = items[i];
        items = items2;
    }
}
```

I previously described the add(), contains(), and length() methods that List inherits from Collection. I also described the resize() method.

List's get() method validates the argument passed to its index parameter: the argument must be greater than or equal to 0 and less than the length of the array that stores the list's strings. This method returns null when this is not the case; otherwise, it returns the string at that index.

Listing 8-11 presents a LinkedList class that implements the List interface.

Listing 8-11. LinkedList.java

```java
class LinkedList implements List
{
    private Node top, last;
    private int length;

    LinkedList()
    {
        top = null;
        last = null;
        length = 0;
    }
```

```java
@Override
public void add(String item)
{
    Node node = new Node();
    node.item = item;
    node.next = null;
    if (last != null)
        last.next = node;
    last = node;
    if (top == null)
        top = node;
    length++;
}

@Override
public boolean contains(String item)
{
    Node node = top;
    for (int i = 0; i < length; i++)
        if (item.equals(node.item))
            return true;
        else
            node = node.next;
    return false;
}

@Override
public int length()
{
    return length;
}

@Override
public String get(int index)
{
    if (index < 0 || index >= length)
        return null;
```

```java
      Node node = top;
      int count = 0;
      while (true)
      {
         if (count++ == index)
            break;
         node = node.next;
      }
      return node.item;
   }
}

class Node
{
   String item;
   Node next;
}
```

As with ArrayList, I previously described the add(), contains(), and length() methods that List inherits from Collection.

List's get() method first validates the argument passed to its index parameter: the argument must be greater than or equal to 0 and less than the length of the array that stores the list's strings. This method returns null when this is not the case; otherwise, it returns the string at that index.

The get() method then navigates through the linked list until it finds the node at the specified index value and returns the node's item.

The navigation logic might appear difficult to follow, but it isn't that hard. It starts by assigning top's value to the node local variable and then initializing a count local variable to 0. These variables control the navigation.

The navigation logic now enters an apparently infinite while loop. It first compares count with index, incrementing count to track the number of nodes that have been traversed. When count's value equals the value in index, exactly index nodes have been traversed and the loop is terminated; otherwise, node is made to point to the next node by assigning node.next's reference to node.

The loop will always terminate because get() first validates the index argument passed to index. When the loop terminates, get() returns node.item's string reference.

Finally, Listing 8-12 presents a ListDemo class that demonstrates Collection, List, ArrayList, and LinkedList.

Listing 8-12. ListDemo.java

```java
class ListDemo
{
   public static void main(String[] args)
   {
      String[] planetNames =
      {
         "Mercury", "Venus", "Earth", "Mars",
         "Jupiter", "Saturn", "Uranus", "Neptune"
      };
      List names = new ArrayList(5);
      for (int i = 0; i < planetNames.length; i++)
         names.add(planetNames[i]);
      print(names);
      names = new LinkedList();
      for (int i = 0; i < planetNames.length; i++)
         names.add(planetNames[i]);
      print(names);
   }

   static void addPlanetNames(List names)
   {
      names.add("Mercury");
      names.add("Venus");
      names.add("Earth");
      names.add("Mars");
      names.add("Jupiter");
      names.add("Saturn");
      names.add("Uranus");
      names.add("Neptune");
   }
```

```
static void print(List list)
{
    for (int i = 0; i < list.length(); i++)
        System.out.println(list.get(i));
    System.out.println();
}
}
```

Assuming that Listings 8-9 through 8-12 are located in the current directory, compile them via javac *.java or javac ListDemo.java (the Java compiler recursively compiles referenced source files). Assuming there are no compilation errors, execute the following command to run this application:

java ListDemo

You should observe the following output:

```
Mercury
Venus
Earth
Mars
Jupiter
Saturn
Uranus
Neptune

Mercury
Venus
Earth
Mars
Jupiter
Saturn
Uranus
Neptune
```

Extending Multiple Interfaces

As with interface implementation, you can extend multiple interfaces. Each interface's name is specified as part of a comma-separated list of names that follows the extends keyword. Listing 8-13 presents a simple example where interface Z extends interfaces X and Y.

Listing 8-13. Z.java demonstrating multiple interface extension

```
interface X
{
   // appropriate constants and/or method headers
}
interface Y
{
   // appropriate constants and/or method headers
}
interface Z extends X, Y
{
   // appropriate constants and/or method headers
}
```

Beware of the potential for name collisions when extending multiple interfaces. This occurs when the same constant name appears in each superinterface, possibly with different type and/or other information, and is accessed in the subinterface. When a name collision occurs, the compiler reports an error, which Listing 8-14 demonstrates.

Listing 8-14. Z.java (demonstrating colliding constants)

```
interface X
{
   int SOME_CONSTANT = 2;
   void some_method();
}
```

```
interface Y
{
   int SOME_CONSTANT = 3;
   int some_method(int x);
}

interface Z extends X, Y
{
   int SOME_CONSTANT2 = SOME_CONSTANT;
}
```

Here, interface Z inherits two different constants named SOME_CONSTANT that are initialized to two different values. The Java compiler cannot determine which constant should be inherited by Z (the same problem would occur if each constant was assigned the same value) and reports the following error message:

```
Z.java:15: error: reference to SOME_CONSTANT is ambiguous
   int SOME_CONSTANT2 = SOME_CONSTANT;
                        ^
  both variable SOME_CONSTANT in X and variable SOME_CONSTANT in Y match
1 error
```

Downcasting and RTTI

Moving up the class hierarchy, via upcasting, entails losing access to subtype features. For example, assigning a Truck object to Vehicle variable v means that you cannot use v to call Truck's isExtendedCab() method. However, it's possible to once again access Truck's isExtendedCab() method by performing an explicit cast operation like this one: Truck t = (Truck) v;.

This assignment is known as *downcasting* because you are casting down the inheritance hierarchy from a supertype to a subtype (from the Vehicle superclass to the Truck subclass). Although an upcast is always safe (the superclass's interface is a subset of the subclass's interface), a downcast isn't always safe. Listing 8-15 shows what kind of trouble could follow if you use downcasting incorrectly.

Listing 8-15. BadDowncast.java (demonstrating the problem with downcasting)

```java
class Vehicle
{
}

class Truck extends Vehicle
{
   private boolean isExtendedCab;

   boolean isExtendedCab()
   {
      return isExtendedCab;
   }
}
public class BadDowncast
{
   public static void main(String[] args)
   {
      Vehicle v = new Vehicle();
      Truck t = (Truck) v;
      System.out.println(t.isExtendedCab());
   }
}
```

Listing 8-15 presents a class hierarchy consisting of Vehicle and Truck, which extends Vehicle. Furthermore, Truck declares isExtendedCab(). A third class named BadDowncast provides a main() method that first instantiates Vehicle.

The main() method then tries to downcast this object to Truck and assign the result to variable t. The compiler will not complain because downcasting from a superclass to a subclass in the same type hierarchy is legal.

If the assignment was allowed, the application would crash when it tried to execute t.isExtendedCab(); because the Java Virtual Machine (JVM) would be attempting to call a nonexistent method: Vehicle doesn't declare isExtendedCab(). Fortunately, the JVM verifies that a cast is legal before performing a cast operation. Detecting that Vehicle doesn't declare isExtendedCab(), it would throw a ClassCastException object. (I'll discuss exceptions in Chapter 11.)

Compile Listing 8-15 as follows:

```
javac BadDowncast.java
```

Run the application as follows:

```
java BadDowncast
```

You should observe the following output:

```
Exception in thread "main" java.lang.ClassCastException: class Vehicle
cannot be cast to class Truck (Vehicle and Truck are in unnamed module of
loader 'app')
    at BadDowncast.main(BadDowncast.java:19)
```

Runtime Type Identification

The JVM's cast verification in Listing 8-15 illustrates *runtime type identification* (or RTTI for short). Cast verification performs RTTI by examining the type of the cast operator's operand to see whether the cast should be allowed or not. In this scenario, the cast should not be allowed.

Another form of RTTI involves the `instanceof` operator. This operator checks the left operand to see whether or not it's an instance of the right operand and returns true when this is the case. The following example introduces `instanceof` to Listing 8-15 to prevent the `ClassCastException`:

```
if (v instanceof Truck)
{
   Truck t = (Truck) v;
   System.out.println(t.isExtendedCab());
}
```

The `instanceof` operator detects that variable v's instance was not created from `Truck` and returns false to indicate this fact. As a result, the code that performs the illegal cast will not execute.

Because a subtype is a kind of supertype, `instanceof` will return true when its left operand is a subtype instance or a supertype instance of its right operand supertype. The following example demonstrates:

```
Vehicle v = new Truck();
Truck t = new Truck();
System.out.println(t instanceof Vehicle); // Output: true
System.out.println(v instanceof Vehicle); // Output: true
```

This example assumes the class structure shown in Listing 8-15 and instantiates Vehicle and Truck. The first System.out.println() method call outputs true because t's reference identifies an instance of a subclass of Vehicle; the second System.out.println() method call outputs true because v's reference identifies an instance of Vehicle.

Caution   Overusing instanceof can indicate poor software design. For example, suppose you decide to use multiple instanceof expressions to determine whether a vehicle object's type is Car, Truck, or another Vehicle subtype. When you introduce a new Vehicle subtype, you might forget to include an instanceof test to see if vehicle is an instance of that type, which would lead to a bug. Minimize your reliance on instanceof for special cases. Most of the time, you'll be better off using subtype polymorphism.

Additional Topics

In this section, I introduce you to a pair of additional topics related to this chapter's content. First, you explore covariant return types, which take advantage of subtype polymorphism to offer you a benefit. Next, you learn about interface-based static methods.

Covariant Return Types

When you override a method, and when the return type of the overriding method is allowed to be a subtype of the overridden method's return type, you end up with a *covariant return type*. A method's covariant return type can be replaced by a "narrower" (subclass) type when the method is overridden in a subclass.

I've created a small application that demonstrates this language feature. Check out Listing 8-16 for the source code.

223

Listing 8-16. OCRT.java

```java
// Observing Covariant Return Types

class ParentReturnType
{
    @Override
    public String toString()
    {
        return "parent class return type";
    }
}

class ChildReturnType extends ParentReturnType
{
    @Override
    public String toString()
    {
        return "child class return type";
    }
}

class ParentClass
{
    ParentReturnType createReturnType()
    {
        return new ParentReturnType();
    }
}

class ChildClass extends ParentClass
{
    // ChildClass overrides ParentClass's createReturnType() method.
    // Notice that the return type of ChildClass's createReturnType()
    // method has changed from ParentReturnType to ChildReturnType.
    // Without covariant return types, the return type would have to
    // be ParentReturnType.
```

```
    @Override
    ChildReturnType createReturnType()
    {
        return new ChildReturnType();
    }
}

class OCRT
{
    public static void main(String[] args)
    {
        ParentReturnType prt - new ParentClass().createReturnType();
        System.out.println(prt);

        // The following statement instantiates ChildClass and invokes its
        // createReturnType() method. The resulting ChildClass reference
        // that createReturnType() returns is assigned to crt. Without
        // covariant return types, you would have to explicitly cast the
        // new operator's returned object to ChildReturnType via the
        // (ChildClass) cast operator.

        ChildReturnType crt = new ChildClass().createReturnType();
        System.out.println(crt);
    }
}
```

Listing 8-16 declares ParentReturnType and ParentClass superclasses and ChildReturnType and ChildClass subclasses. Each of ParentClass and ChildClass declares a createReturnType() method. ParentClass's method has its return type set to ParentReturnType, whereas ChildClass's overriding method has its return type set to ChildReturnType, a subclass of ParentReturnType.

Covariant return types greatly reduce upcasting and downcasting. For example, ChildClass's createReturnType() method doesn't need to upcast its ChildReturnType instance to its ChildReturnType return type. Furthermore, this instance doesn't need to be downcast to ChildReturnType when assigning to variable crt.

Compile Listing 8-16 as follows:

```
javac OCRT.java
```

Run the resulting application as follows:

```
java OCRT
```

You should observe the following output:

```
parent class return type
child class return type
```

In the absence of covariant return types, you would end up with Listing 8-17.

Listing 8-17. OCRT.java (version 2)

```java
// Observing Covariant Return Types

class ParentReturnType
{
   @Override
   public String toString()
   {
      return "parent class return type";
   }
}

class ChildReturnType extends ParentReturnType
{
   @Override
   public String toString()
   {
      return "child class return type";
   }
}

class ParentClass
{
   ParentReturnType createReturnType()
   {
      return new ParentReturnType();
   }
}
```

226

```
class ChildClass extends ParentClass
{
   @Override
   ParentReturnType createReturnType()
   {
      return new ChildReturnType();
   }
}

class OCRT
{
   public static void main(String[] args)
   {
      ParentReturnType prt = new ParentClass().createReturnType();
      System.out.println(prt);
      ChildReturnType crt =
         (ChildReturnType) new ChildClass().createReturnType();
       System.out.println(crt);
   }
}
```

Listing 8-17 upcasts from ChildReturnType to ParentReturnType in ChildClass's createReturnType() method. Also, in the main() method, it uses the required (ChildReturnType) cast operator to downcast from ParentReturnType to ChildReturnType before the assignment to crt.

Interface-Based Static Methods

JDK 8 introduced programmers to interface-based static methods. Declaring static methods in interfaces lets you associate static methods with interfaces instead of associating them with utility classes. Doing this makes source code more readable and ensures that binary compatibility isn't broken.

To understand the usefulness of interface-based static methods, consider a Renderable interface with a void render(int color) method whose color parameter contains an integer color code. Because it's convenient to express this color as red, green, and blue components, suppose you add an rgb() static method that converts these components to an int. Check out Listing 8-18.

Listing 8-18. Renderable.java

```java
interface Renderable
{
    public void render(int color);

    public static int rgb(int r, int g, int b)
    {
        return r << 16 | g << 8 | b;
    }
}
```

You next declare a Circle class that describes a circle via integer-based center coordinates and a radius and that implements Renderable to render a circle. Listing 8-19 presents Circle's source code.

Listing 8-19. Circle.java

```java
class Circle implements Renderable
{
    private int x, y, r;

    Circle(int x, int y, int r)
    {
        this.x = x;
        this.y = y;
        this.r = r;
    }

    @Override
    public void render(int color)
    {
        System.out.println("Rendering circle(" + x + ", " + y + ", " + r + ")
        in color " + color);
    }
}
```

Finally, you declare a UseRenderable application class whose source code appears in Listing 8-20.

Listing 8-20. UseRenderable.java

```java
public class UseRenderable
{
    public static void main(String[] args)
    {
        Circle circle = new Circle(20, 30, 14);
        circle.render(Renderable.rgb(0x80, 0x60, 0x40));
    }
}
```

UseRenderable's main() method instantiates Circle and then calls the object's render() method to render the circle. Notice that the rgb() method call is prefixed by this static method's Renderable interface. You cannot prefix this method with the interface-implementing class (as in Circle.rgb(0x80, 0x60, 0x40)) because the static method belongs to Renderable.

Compile Listings 8-18, 8-19, and 8-20 as follows:

```
javac UseRenderable.java
```

The javac compiler tool recursively compiles the source files corresponding to the classes and interfaces that it encounters while compiling the source file specified as its command-line argument.

Run UseRenderable.class as follows:

```
java UseRenderable
```

You should observe the following output:

```
Rendering circle(20, 30, 14) in color 8413248
```

What's Next?

Java provides unusual language features for declaring classes in other classes and even blocks. Also, you can declare nameless classes. Chapter 9 introduces you to these strange features.

CHAPTER 9

Static, Non-static, Local, and Anonymous Classes

The classes that I've presented to this point are known as *top-level classes*. They don't belong to another class or structure. However, Java also lets you declare classes in other classes, *blocks* (groups of zero or more statements between { and } characters), and expression contexts.

Classes declared in other classes are known as *nested classes*. There are two kinds of nested classes: static classes and non-static classes. (Non-static classes are also known as *inner classes*).

Note   The Java Tutorials tutorial on nested classes (`http://docs.oracle.com/javase/tutorial/java/javaOO/nested.html`) presents three compelling reasons for using nested classes:

- **"It is a way of logically grouping classes that are only used in one place**: If a class is useful to only one other class, then it is logical to embed it in that class and keep the two together. Nesting such "helper classes" makes their package [see Chapter 10 for an introduction to packages] more streamlined.

- **It increases encapsulation**: Consider two top-level classes, A and B, where B needs access to members of A that would otherwise be declared `private`. By hiding class B within class A, A's members can be declared `private` and B can access them. In addition, B itself can be hidden from the outside world.

J. Friesen, *Learn Java Fundamentals*, https://doi.org/10.1007/979-8-8688-0351-2_9

- **It can lead to more readable and maintainable code**: Nesting small classes within top-level classes places the code closer to where it is used."

Classes declared in blocks are known as *local classes*. Classes declared in expression contexts are known as *anonymous classes*.

This chapter introduces you to static classes, inner classes, local classes, and anonymous classes.

Static Classes

Chapter 6 introduced you to static fields, static methods, static field initializers, and static initialization blocks. These entities differ from their non-static field, non-static method, non-static field initializer, and non-static initialization block counterparts in that they involve the static keyword.

You can declare these static members in a class. You can also declare classes marked with the static keyword in classes. Such a nested class is known as a *static class*. The following example clarifies this organization:

```
class C
{
   static int f; // field could be explicitly initialized

   static void m()
   {
      // method code
   }

   static // static initialization block
   {
      // initialization block code
   }
```

```
static class SC
{
   // members of static class
}
}
```

This example introduces top-level class C with static field f, static method m( ), a static initialization block, and static class SC. Notice that SC is a member of C in the same way that f, m( ), and the static initialization block are members of this class. They all belong to class C, which is an *enclosing class* – SC is an *enclosed class*.

A static class, like static methods and static fields, is associated with its enclosing class. And like static methods, a static class cannot directly access the enclosing class's non-static fields and invoke its non-static methods. It can access them only through an object reference. However, it can access the enclosing class's static fields and invoke its static methods.

Note   A static class interacts with the non-static members of its enclosing class (and other classes) just like any other top-level class. Essentially, a static class behaves as a top-level class that has been nested in another top-level class for packaging convenience.

As a member of the top-level class, a static class can be declared private, public, protected, or left package private (the default). In contrast, top-level classes can only be declared public or left package private. (Chapter 10 introduces you to packages.)

Listing 9-1 declares an EnclosingClass with an EnclosedClass that demonstrates access to the EnclosingClass's members.

Listing 9-1. EnclosingClass.java

```
class EnclosingClass
{
   private static String msg1;
   private static void enclosingMethod1()
   {
      System.out.println(msg1);
   }
```

```
private String msg2;
private void enclosingMethod2()
{
   System.out.println(msg2);
}

static class EnclosedClass
{
   static void enclosedMethod1()
   {
      msg1 = "called from EnclosedClass's enclosingMethod1() method";
      enclosingMethod1();
   }

   void enclosedMethod2()
   {
      System.out.println("unable to access msg2 or call
      enclosingMethod2()");
      // msg2 = "called from EnclosedClass's enclosingMethod2() method";
      // enclosingMethod2();
   }
}
}
```

Listing 9-1 declares a top-level class named EnclosingClass with static field msg1, static method enclosingMethod1(), non-static field msg2, non-static method enclosingMethod2(), and static class EnclosedClass. The enclosed class declares static method enclosedMethod1() and non-static method enclosedMethod2(). There are two items to note:

- enclosedMethod1() is able to access EnclosingClass's msg1 field and call its enclosingMethod1() method even though both have been declared private.

- enclosedMethod2() is unable to access EnclosingClass's msg2 field and call its enclosingMethod2() method because a non-static field and a non-static method in an enclosing class cannot be accessed from a static context.

Listing 9-2 presents the source code to an SCDemo application class that demonstrates how to invoke EnclosedClass's enclosedMethod1() static method. It also demonstrates how to instantiate EnclosedClass and invoke its enclosedMethod2() non-static method.

Listing 9-2. SCDemo.java

```java
class SCDemo
{
   public static void main(String[] args)
   {
      EnclosingClass.EnclosedClass.enclosedMethod1();
      EnclosingClass.EnclosedClass ec = new EnclosingClass.EnclosedClass();
      ec.enclosedMethod2();
   }
}
```

Listing 9-2's main() method first shows that you must prefix an enclosed class's name with the name of its enclosing class to invoke a static method. It then shows that you must prefix the name of the enclosed class with the name of its enclosing class when instantiating the enclosed class. You can then invoke the non-static method in the normal manner.

Compile both listings as follows:

```
javac *.java
```

Run the resulting application as follows:

```
java SCDemo
```

You should observe the following output:

```
called from EnclosedClass's enclosingMethod1() method
unable to access msg2 or call enclosingMethod2()
```

A More Practical Static Class Example

SCDemo gives you an opportunity to learn how to use static classes, but consider a more practical example. I've created a small Rectangle class (which is useful in a graphics context) that benefits from a pair of static classes. Listing 9-3 presents Rectangle's source code.

Listing 9-3. `Rectangle.java`

```java
abstract class Rectangle
{
    static class Float extends Rectangle
    {
        float x, y, w, h;

        Float()
        {
        }

        Float(float x, float y, float w, float h)
        {
            this.x = x;
            this.y = y;
            this.w = w;
            this.h = h;
        }

        @Override
        double getX()
        {
            return x;
        }

        @Override
        double getY()
        {
            return y;
        }

        @Override
        double getW()
        {
            return w;
        }
```

```java
    @Override
    double getH()
    {
        return h;
    }
}

static class Double extends Rectangle
{
    double x, y, w, h;

    Double()
    {
    }

    Double(double x, double y, double w, double h)
    {
        this.x = x;
        this.y = y;
        this.w = w;
        this.h = h;
    }

    @Override
    double getX()
    {
        return x;
    }

    @Override
    double getY()
    {
        return y;
    }
```

```
    @Override
    double getW()
    {
        return w;
    }

    @Override
    double getH()
    {
        return h;
    }
}

boolean contains(double x, double y)
{
    return (x >= getX() && x < getX() + getW() && y >= getY() && y < getY()
    + getH());
}

abstract double getX();

abstract double getY();

abstract double getW();

abstract double getH();
}
```

Rectangle describes a rectangular shape in terms of upper-left corner coordinates (x and y) and extents (width and height). This class is declared abstract because it declares four abstract methods: getX(), getY(), getW(), and getH(). Recall from Chapter 8 that it is an error to declare abstract methods in a non-abstract class.

Rectangle also declares a boolean contains(double x, double y) method that returns true when the point described by x and y lies inside the rectangle; otherwise, it returns false. The contains() method compares the arguments passed to itself with expressions formed by invoking Rectangle's abstract methods.

The most interesting part of Rectangle is its declaration of two static classes. These classes provide the fields needed to store a Rectangle object's location and extents.

The first static class is Float, and the second static class is Double. Each class declares x, y, w (width), and h (height) fields. Also, each class declares a no-argument constructor that initializes these fields to 0. This is followed by a constructor that explicitly initializes these fields to passed arguments.

Note   If a no-argument constructor is not declared, it will not be possible to invoke this constructor because the compiler will not generate the equivalent <init>() method – see Chapter 6 for a brief introduction to <init>().

Float and Double then declare getX(), getY(), getW(), and getH() methods that return the values of these fields. The only difference is that one set of fields and methods is of type float whereas the other set of fields and methods is of type double.

These methods are prefixed with the @Override annotation because Float and Double extend Rectangle and override their abstract getX(), getY(), getW(), and getH() counterparts, which Rectangle declares. (Except for a brief discussion of @ Override in Chapter 7, I don't discuss annotations in this book because I don't consider it to be a fundamental feature.)

You might be confused by this unusual organization. Perhaps the best way to understand it is to look at Listing 9-4, which presents the source code to a UseRect application that demonstrates Rectangle.

Listing 9-4. UseRect.java

```
class UseRect
{
   public static void main(String[] args)
   {
      System.out.println("Rectangle.Float Demo");
      System.out.println();

      Rectangle r = new Rectangle.Float(10.0f, 20.0f, 30f, 40f);
      System.out.println(r.getX());
      System.out.println(r.getY());
      System.out.println(r.getW());
      System.out.println(r.getH());
      System.out.println("contains(40.0, 45.0): " + r.contains(35.0, 40.0));
```

```
        System.out.println("contains(80.0, 45.0): " + r.contains(80.0, 40.0));
        System.out.println();

        System.out.println("Rectangle.Double Demo");
        System.out.println();
        r = new Rectangle.Double(15.0, 25.0, 35, 45);
        System.out.println(r.getX());
        System.out.println(r.getY());
        System.out.println(r.getW());
        System.out.println(r.getH());
        System.out.println("contains(40.0, 45.0): " + r.contains(40.0, 45.0));
        System.out.println("contains(80.0, 45.0): " + r.contains(80.0, 45.0));
    }
}
```

Notice the following statements:

```
Rectangle r = new Rectangle.Float(10.0f, 20.0f, 30f, 40f);
r = new Rectangle.Double(15.0, 25.0, 35, 45);
```

The first statement instantiates the Float class, and the second statement instantiates the Double class. The arguments passed to each class's constructor are stored in its x, y, w, and h fields. Because Float and Double extend Rectangle, the returned object is also of type Rectangle, and its reference can be assigned to Rectangle variable r.

Each of Float and Double extends Rectangle to provide floating-point and double-precision floating-point Rectangle implementations. Float exists to reduce memory consumption (you might have thousands or more of these objects when constructing a scene), and Double exists for when greater accuracy is required.

When a Rectangle method, such as getX(), is called, as in r.getX(), subtype polymorphism takes over. The upcasting and late binding mechanism (see Chapter 8) that Java uses to implement subtype polymorphism causes Float's getX() method (in the first statement) and Double's getX() method (in the second statement) to be called.

Compile Listings 9-3 and 9-4 as follows:

```
javac *.java
```

Run the application as follows:

```
java UseRect
```

You should observe the following output:

```
Rectangle.Float Demo

10.0
20.0
30.0
40.0
contains(40.0, 45.0): true
contains(80.0, 45.0): false

Rectangle.Double Demo

15.0
25.0
35.0
45.0
contains(40.0, 45.0): true
contains(80.0, 45.0): false
```

Inner Classes

Chapter 6 also introduced you to non-static fields, non-static methods, non-static field initializers, and non-static initialization blocks. These entities differ from their static field, static method, static field initializer, and static initialization block counterparts in that they don't involve the static keyword.

You can declare these non-static members in a class. You can also declare non-static classes (inner classes) in a class. The following example clarifies this organization:

```
class C
{
    int f; // field could be explicitly initialized

    void m()
    {
        // method code
    }
```

```
   // non-static initialization block
   {
      // initialization block code
   }

   class NSC
   {
      // members of non-static class
   }
}
```

This example introduces top-level class C with non-static field f, non-static method m(), a non-static initialization block (I could have shown a constructor instead), and inner class NSC. Notice that NSC is a member of C in the same way that f, m(), and the non-static initialization block are members of this class. They all belong to class C, which is an enclosing class – NSC is an enclosed class.

An inner class is a member of its enclosing class. Inner classes have access to other members of the enclosing class, even when they are declared private. In contrast, static classes do not have direct access to non-static members of the enclosing class.

As a member of the top-level class, an inner class can be declared private, public, protected, or left package private (the default). In contrast, top-level classes can only be declared public or left package private. (Chapter 10 introduces you to packages.)

Listing 9-5 declares EnclosingClass with EnclosedClass that demonstrates access to EnclosingClass's members.

Listing 9-5. EnclosingClass.java (version 2)

```
class EnclosingClass
{
   public final static double PI = 3.14159;

   public static double area(double radius)
   {
      return PI * radius * radius;
   }
```

```java
    private String msg;

    private void printMessage()
    {
        System.out.println(msg);
    }

    class EnclosedClass
    {
        void accessMembersOfEnclosingClass()
        {
            msg = "called from EnclosedClass's accessMembersOfEnclosingClass()
            " + "method";
            printMessage();
            System.out.println("PI = " + PI);
            System.out.println("area(10.0) = " + area(10.0));
        }
    }
}
```

Listing 9-5 declares a top-level class named EnclosingClass with static field PI, static method area(), non-static field msg, non-static method printMessage(), and non-static class EnclosedClass. Furthermore, EnclosedClass declares non-static method accessMembersOfEnclosingClass().

This method first assigns a string to msg. (Because the string is pretty long, I use the + operator to concatenate two smaller strings into the overall string.) Next, the method outputs msg. Moving on, accessMembersOfEnclosingClass() prints the value of PI and then (with 10.0 as the argument) invokes area() to calculate and return a circle's area. Again, I use + to join two strings into one string, which is then output.

Listing 9-6 presents the source code to an NSCDemo application class that demonstrates how to instantiate EnclosingClass and use this reference to instantiate EnclosedClass, which is used to call this class's accessMembersOfEnclosingClass() non-static method.

Listing 9-6. NSCDemo.java

```java
class NSCDemo
{
    public static void main(String[] args)
    {
        EnclosingClass ec = new EnclosingClass();
        ec.new EnclosedClass().accessMembersOfEnclosingClass();
    }
}
```

Listing 9-6's main() method first instantiates EnclosingClass and saves its reference in local variable ec. main() then uses this reference as a prefix to the new operator to instantiate NSClass, whose reference is subsequently used to call accessMembersOfEnclosingClass().

Note   Prefixing new with a reference to the enclosing class is rare. Instead, you will typically call an enclosed class's constructor from within a constructor or an instance method of its enclosing class.

Compile both listings as follows:

```
javac *.java
```

Run the resulting application as follows:

```
java NSCDemo
```

You should observe the following output:

```
called from EnclosedClass's accessMembersOfEnclosingClass() method
PI = 3.14159
area(10.0) = 314.159
```

Shadowing

When the declaration of a type (such as a member variable [field] or a parameter) in a specific block (such as an inner class or a method) has the same name as another type declaration in the enclosing block, the declaration *shadows* (hides) the declaration in

CHAPTER 9 STATIC, NON-STATIC, LOCAL, AND ANONYMOUS CLASSES

the enclosing block. In this context, you cannot refer to the shadowed declaration by its name only. Listing 9-7's ShadowDemo application provides a shadowing demonstration.

Listing 9-7. `ShadowDemo.java`

```java
class ShadowDemo
{
   String name = "Java";

   class EnclosedClass
   {
      String name = "More Java";

      void outputName(String name)
      {
         System.out.println("name = " + name);
         System.out.println("this.name = " + this.name);
         System.out.println("ShadowDemo.this.name = " +
         ShadowDemo.this.name);
      }
   }

   public static void main(String[] args)
   {
      ShadowDemo sd = new ShadowDemo();
      ShadowDemo.EnclosedClass ec = sd.new EnclosedClass();
      ec.outputName("Even more Java");
   }
}
```

`ShadowDemo.java` reveals three name variables: ShadowDemo's member variable, inner class EnclosedClass's member variable, and outputName()'s parameter. Parameter name shadows EnclosedClass's name variable. Consequently, when you use name in outputName(), you are referring to the name parameter. To refer to EnclosedClass's name variable, use keyword this to represent the enclosing block:

```java
System.out.println("this.x = " + this.x);
```

Refer to member variables that enclose larger blocks by the class name to which they belong. For example, the following statement accesses the member variable of the class ShadowDemo from the method outputName():

```
System.out.println("ShadowDemo.this.name = " + ShadowDemo.this.name);
```

Compile Listing 9-7 as follows:

```
javac ShadowDemo.java
```

Run the application as follows:

```
java ShadowDemo
```

You should observe the following output:

```
name = Even more Java
this.name = More Java
ShadowDemo.this.name = Java
```

Note   Refer to Chapter 6 for an introduction to shadowing.

A More Practical Inner Class Example

NSCDemo gives you an opportunity to learn how to use inner classes. Because it would be nice to learn how to use an inner class more practically, let's create a framework that lets you maintain a to-do list of items.

Each to-do item consists of a name and a description. Listing 9-8 presents a ToDo class that describes a to-do item in these terms.

Listing 9-8. ToDo.java

```
class ToDo
{
    private String name;
    private String desc;
```

```java
ToDo(String name, String desc)
{
   this.name = name;
   this.desc = desc;
}

String getName()
{
   return name;
}

String getDesc()
{
   return desc;
}

@Override
public String toString()
{
   return "Name = " + getName() + ", Desc = " + getDesc();
}
}
```

We'll next create a ToDoList class to store ToDo instances. ToDoList uses its ToDoArray non-static member class to store ToDo instances in a growable array. (It is growable because you don't know how many instances will be stored, and Java arrays have fixed lengths). See Listing 9-9.

Listing 9-9. ToDoList.java

```java
class ToDoList
{
   private ToDoArray toDoArray;
   private int index = 0;

   ToDoList()
   {
      toDoArray = new ToDoArray(2);
   }
```

```java
boolean hasMoreElements()
{
   return index < toDoArray.size();
}

ToDo nextElement()
{
   return toDoArray.get(index++);
}

void add(ToDo item)
{
   toDoArray.add(item);
}

private class ToDoArray
{
   private ToDo[] toDoArray;
   private int index = 0;

   ToDoArray(int initSize)
   {
      toDoArray = new ToDo[initSize];
   }

   void add(ToDo item)
   {
      if (index >= toDoArray.length)
      {
         ToDo[] temp = new ToDo[toDoArray.length * 2];
         for (int i = 0; i < toDoArray.length; i++)
            temp[i] = toDoArray[i];
         toDoArray = temp;
      }
      toDoArray[index++] = item;
   }
```

```
    ToDo get(int i)
    {
        return toDoArray[i];
    }

    int size()
    {
        return index;
    }
  }
}
```

As well as providing an add() method to store ToDo instances in the ToDoArray instance, ToDoList provides hasMoreElements() and nextElement() methods to iterate over and return the stored instances. Listing 9-10 demonstrates these methods.

Listing 9-10. ToDoList.java

```
class UseToDoList
{
    public static void main(String[] args)
    {
        ToDoList toDoList = new ToDoList();
        toDoList.add(new ToDo("#1", "Do laundry."));
        toDoList.add(new ToDo("#2", "Buy groceries."));
        toDoList.add(new ToDo("#3", "Vacuum apartment."));
        toDoList.add(new ToDo("#4", "Write report."));
        toDoList.add(new ToDo("#5", "Wash car."));

        while (toDoList.hasMoreElements())
            System.out.println(toDoList.nextElement());
    }
}
```

Assuming that the files described by Listings 9-8 through 9-10 are stored in the current directory, compile these files as follows:

```
javac UseToDoList.java
```

Run the resulting UseToDoList.class application class file as follows:

```
java UseToDoList
```

You should observe the following output:

```
Name = #1, Desc = Do laundry.
Name = #2, Desc = Buy groceries.
Name = #3, Desc = Vacuum apartment.
Name = #4, Desc = Write report.
Name = #5, Desc = Wash car.
```

Local Classes

It is often helpful to declare a class in a block such as a method body, or a *sub-block* (a block within a block). Such a class is known as a *local class* because (as with local variables) it is local to the block/sub-block in which it is declared.

Note   Local classes help improve code clarity. They do so because they are moved closer to where they are needed.

For example, you might declare a class that describes an *iterator* (an object that is used to traverse a container's objects) in a method that returns an instance of this class. Such classes are known as *local classes* because (as with local variables) they are local to the methods in which they are declared. Here is an example:

```
interface I
{
   // members
}

class C
{
   I m() // or even static I m()
   {
```

```
    class D implements I
    {
        // members
    }
    return new D();
  }
}
```

Top-level class C declares non-static method m(), which returns an instance of local class D, which is declared in this method. Notice that m()'s return type is interface I, which D implements. The interface is necessary because giving m() return type D would result in a compiler error – D isn't accessible outside of m()'s body.

Caution   The compiler will report an error when a local class declaration contains any of the access modifier keywords `private`, `public`, or `protected`, or the modifier keyword `static`.

A local class can be associated with an instance of its enclosing class, but only when used in a non-static context. Although a local class can be declared in a static context (such as a static method), it cannot declare any static members, which makes a local class similar to an inner class, which also cannot declare static members.

Note   You cannot declare an interface in a local block because interfaces are considered static and a local class cannot declare static members.

A local class can be declared anywhere that a local variable can be declared and has the same scope (essentially a block) as a local variable. It can access the surrounding scope's local variables and parameters (which are a kind of local variable).

Before JDK 8, these variables would have to be declared `final`. However, this is no long necessary because JDK 8 introduced the concept of *effectively final* (the compiler considers a variable that never changes `final` regardless of this keyword's presence or absence).

Note   Variables that are declared in a local class can *shadow* (mask or hide) same-named variables in the enclosing block.

When a local class accesses an enclosing block's local variable or parameter, it *captures* that local/parameter. Capturing a local variable or parameter implies making a copy of the local/parameter because an object created from the local class may outlive the current context in which the local/parameter is declared. Furthermore, the local/parameter must be declared final or (starting with JDK 8) be effectively final to prevent confusion about whether or not changes made to the local/parameter will be seen (because these changes won't be seen).

Consider Listing 9-11, which uses the final keyword. (This book's code archive contains a second version of EnclosingClass that doesn't use final. Pre-JDK 8 compilers will report an error when compiling that version of EnclosingClass.)

Listing 9-11. EnclosingClass.java

```java
class EnclosingClass
{
    void m(final int i)
    {
        final int j = i * 10;

        class LClass
        {
            int m = i;
            int n = j;
        }

        LClass lc = new LClass();
        System.out.println(lc.m);
        System.out.println(lc.n);
    }
}
```

Listing 9-11 declares EnclosingClass with non-static method m() declaring a local class named LClass.

LClass declares two non-static fields (m and n) that are initialized to the values of final parameter i and final local variable j when LClass is instantiated – see Listing 9-12 for the source code to an LCDemo application that demonstrates LClass.

Listing 9-12. LCDemo.java

```
class LCDemo
{
   public static void main(String[] args)
   {
      EnclosingClass ec = new EnclosingClass();
      ec.m(10);
   }
}
```

Listing 9-12's main() method first instantiates EnclosingClass. It then uses this object to invoke m(10). The called m() method multiplies this argument by 10; instantiates LClass, whose compiler-generated <init>() method (see Chapter 6 for a brief introduction to <init>()) assigns the argument and the argument multiplied by 10 to its pair of non-static fields (in lieu of using a constructor to perform this task); and outputs LClass's non-static field values.

Compile Listings 9-11 and 9-12 as follows:

```
javac *.java
```

When you compile a class whose method contains a local class, the compiler creates a class file for the local class whose name consists of its enclosing class's name, a dollar-sign character, a 1-based integer, and the local class's name. Following compilation, you'll discover EnclosingClass$1LClass.class and EnclosingClass.class, in addition to LCDemo.class.

COMPILER-GENERATED CLASS FILE NAMES FOR LOCAL CLASSES

When generating a name for a local class's class file, the compiler adds an integer to the generated name according to the pattern *enclosingClass*$(*integer*)*enclosedClass*. (The parentheses are not part of the final name.) If there are two local classes with the same name, the compiler increments the integer to avoid name conflicts. Consider the following example:

```
class EnclosingClass
{
    void m1()
    {
       class LClass
       {
       }
    }

    void m2()
    {
       class LClass
       {
       }
    }

    void m3()
    {
       class LClass2
       {
       }
    }
}
```

EnclosingClass declares three non-static methods that each declare a local class. The first two methods generate two different local classes with the same name. The compiler generates the following class files:

```
EnclosingClass$1LClass.class
EnclosingClass$1LClass2.class
EnclosingClass$2LClass.class
EnclosingClass.class
```

The compiler generates `EnclosingClass$1LClass.class` for `m1()`'s `LClass` local class, `EnclosingClass$1LClass2.class` for `m3()`'s `LClass2` local class, and `EnclosingClass$2LClass.class` for `m2()`'s `LClass` local class.

Run the application as follows:

```
java LCDemo
```

You should observe the following output:

```
10
100
```

A More Practical Local Class Example

`LCDemo` gives you an opportunity to learn how to use local classes. Because it would be nice to learn how to use a local class more practically, I've created a small `AddressBook` class that benefits from a local class. Before I present `AddressBook`, check out Listing 9-13's `Address` class on which `AddressBook` depends.

Listing 9-13. `Address.java`

```java
class Address
{
   private String street, city;

   Address(String street, String city)
   {
      this.street = street;
      this.city = city;
   }
```

```
String getStreet()
{
    return street;
}

String getCity()
{
    return city;
}

@Override
public String toString()
{
    return street + ": " + city;
}
}
```

Address records an address in terms of a street and a city. You can expand this class to include a province, a state, or a region; a country; and anything else that you desire.

Notice that I've overridden toString(), which Address inherits from Object. This method gives you a more readable representation of Address's contents than the default representation. (If you recall, the default representation is *class name@hexadecimal hashcode*.)

Now that Address is out of the way, let's explore AddressBook. Listing 9-14 presents this class's source code.

Listing 9-14. AddressBook.java

```
class AddressBook
{
    private Address[] addressList;
    private int index = 0;

    AddressBook(int size)
    {
        addressList = new Address[size];
    }
```

```
Iterator iterator()
{
   class LocalIterator implements Iterator
   {
      int index = 0;

      @Override
      public boolean hasMoreElements()
      {
         return index < addressList.length;
      }

      @Override
      public Object nextElement()
      {
         return addressList[index++];
      }
   }
   return new LocalIterator();
}

void add(Address address)
{
   addressList[index++] = address;
}
}
```

AddressBook first declares a pair of private fields: addressList and index, which is explicitly assigned 0 even though it is implicitly initialized to 0 when an AddressBook object is created. This is done to clarify to those not familiar with default initialization that the field is initialized to 0.

The addressList field references an array (created in the AddressBook(int size) constructor) of Address objects. The index field identifies the next location in which to insert an Address object into the addressList-referenced array.

The AddressBook(int size) constructor's size parameter receives an argument that specifies the desired number of elements to store in the array. Care should be taken to avoid trouble when this argument is less than 1. You are likely to run into a NegativeArraySizeException object being thrown and the program terminating if you specify a negative size. Alternatively, you are likely to run into an ArrayIndexOutOfBoundsException and the program terminating if you specify 0 for the size. After all, in this context, what is the point of creating an array with no elements? (Chapter 11 explores exceptions.)

The constructor executes addressList = new Address[size];, using the new operator to instantiate an Address array that can store size elements. A reference to this array is assigned to addressList.

The iterator() method that follows the constructor demonstrates a local class. Before we look at this class, consider that iterator()'s return type is set to Iterator, which is an interface whose contents are presented in Listing 9-15.

Listing 9-15. Iterator.java

```
interface Iterator
{
    boolean hasMoreElements();
    Object nextElement();
}
```

The Iterator interface describes what it means to be an *iterator*, which is an object that knows how to traverse stored *elements* (object values instead of primitive type-based values, in this case).

Iterator declares hasMoreElements() and nextElement() bodiless methods (their bodies are supplied by the class that implements Iterator):

- hasMoreElements() returns a Boolean true value when there are more elements to examine; otherwise, false is returned.

- nextElement() returns a reference to the next element to examine.

Let's return to the iterator() method, which does two things. First, it declares a local class named LocalIterator. Second, it instantiates this class and returns the resulting object's reference.

LocalIterator implements the Iterator interface that I presented earlier. It does so because iterator() will return an instance of the LocalIterator class and iterator()'s return type must agree with the type of the new LocalIterator() expression that appears in the return statement at the end of iterator().

LocalIterator declares an index field that tracks the next element to be returned from nextElement(). This field *shadows* (hides or masks) the index field in its AddressBook enclosing block.

We don't need to access AddressBook's index field because it serves a different purpose from LocalIterator's index field. The former index field tracks the location in the addressList-referenced array for inserting the next Address object via the add() method. The latter index field tracks the location in this array for returning the next Address object via the nextElement() method.

LocalIterator next overrides the hasMoreElements() and nextElement() methods that are declared by the Iterator interface. Notice the @Override annotation that prefixes each of these methods. This annotation indicates that overriding is occurring to prevent a problem when a method is accidentally overloaded instead of being overridden. See Chapter 7 to learn more about this dilemma and for a brief introduction to @Override.

The hasMoreElements() method compares index with addressList.length, returning true (via the return statement) when index is less than this other expression's value. Otherwise, hasMoreElements() returns false.

The nextElement() method presents a return statement that returns the next element from addressList, which it obtains by executing addressList[index++]. The index++ expression returns index's current value before incrementing index.

AddressBook's iterator() method is followed by an add() method whose address parameter contains a reference to an Address object. This method executes addressList[index++] = address;, storing address's reference in addressList at location index. Notice that index's value is incremented after the reference is stored.

Listing 9-16 presents the source code to a UseAB application class that demonstrates AddressBook along with its supporting Address class and Iterator interface.

Listing 9-16. UseAB.java

```java
class UseAB
{
   public static void main(String[] args)
   {
      AddressBook addressBook = new AddressBook(3);
      addressBook.add(new Address("100 Elm Street", "City #1"));
```

```
        addressBook.add(new Address("200 Bay Street", "City #2"));
        addressBook.add(new Address("300 Oak Street", "City #3"));
        Iterator iter = addressBook.iterator();
        while (iter.hasMoreElements())
            System.out.println(iter.nextElement());
    }
}
```

UseAB's main() method first instantiates AddressBook, passing 3 (the maximum number of addresses that can be stored) to AddressBook's constructor. A reference to the AddressBook object is assigned to the addressBook local variable.

The main() method next creates three Address objects and passes them to AddressBook's add() method. For each Address object, main() invokes AddressBook's constructor, passing street and city strings as arguments. The Address object's reference is passed as an argument to add().

The next task is to execute addressBook.iterator(), which returns an Iterator object (whose class implements the Iterator interface). The object's reference is assigned to local variable iter.

Finally, main() enters a while loop. This loop iterates for as long as iter.hasMoreElements() returns true. Each iteration invokes iter.nextElement() to return the next address element from the address book. This element is then output via System.out.println().

Compile Listings 9-13 through 9-16 as follows:

```
javac *.java
```

Run the UseAB application as follows:

```
java UseAB
```

You should observe the following output:

```
100 Elm Street: City #1
200 Bay Street: City #2
300 Oak Street: City #3
```

Anonymous Classes

You will encounter situations where it is helpful to declare a class in the context of an expression. For example, later in this chapter, I demonstrate an anonymous class based on an abstract Comparer class in a sorting context. Such a class is known as an *anonymous class* because it is not given a name.

Note   Anonymous classes help make your code even more compact than what a local class offers. They do so because they are moved even closer to where they are needed.

An anonymous class can be declared in a class-extension expression context as follows:

```
Superclass sc = new Superclass()
              {
                  // members
              };
```

In this example, an anonymous class extends Superclass (declared elsewhere), inheriting various methods and other members. Notice that the new operator is followed by the name of the superclass followed by a pair of brace characters.

The new operator instantiates the anonymous class and returns the resulting object's reference, which is assigned to sc.

Also, an anonymous class can be declared in an interface-implementation expression context as follows:

```
Interface i = new Interface()
             {
                 // members
             };
```

In this example, an anonymous class implements Interface (declared elsewhere), inheriting various method bodies. Notice that the new operator is followed by the name of the interface followed by a pair of brace characters.

The new operator instantiates the anonymous class and returns the resulting object's reference, which is assigned to i.

The anonymous class expression consists of four components:

- The new operator.

- The name of the class to extend or the interface to implement.

- Parentheses that surround optional constructor arguments. When implementing an interface, these parentheses are empty because interfaces don't have constructors.

- Brace characters that delimit the anonymous class body.

An anonymous class declaration must be part of a statement because it is an expression. In the first example, the anonymous class expression is part of the statement that instantiates SuperClass. Similarly, in the second example, the anonymous class expression is part of the statement that instantiates Interface.

INSTANCE INITIALIZATION BLOCKS AS CONSTRUCTORS

An anonymous class cannot have a constructor because a constructor must be named after the class and anonymous classes are unnamed. Instead, you can use an instance initialization block as a constructor.The following example demonstrates an instance initialization block in a class-extension context:

```
Superclass sc = new Superclass(10)
              {
                  {
                      // perform initialization tasks here
                  }

                  // additional members
              };
```

This example assumes that a class named Superclass exists and that it has declared a Superclass(int) constructor. The example executes as follows:

- Operator new allocates memory for and creates an object from an anonymous class that extends Superclass.

- Operator new invokes Superclass's constructor with argument 10. This is shown as Superclass(10).

- After the constructor executes, any code located in the anonymous class's instance initialization block (when present) executes.

The following example demonstrates an instance initialization block in an interface-extension context:

```
Interface i = new Interface()
          {
              {
                  // perform initialization tasks here
              }

              // additional members
          };
```

This example assumes that an interface named Interface exists. The example executes as follows:

- Operator new allocates memory for and creates an object from an anonymous class that implements Interface.

- Although it may appear otherwise, Interface() does not indicate a call to Interface's constructor because Interface does not have a constructor. Instead, any code located in the anonymous class's instance initialization block (when present) executes.

Before JDK 8, an anonymous class could access only those local variables that were declared final. When an anonymous class accesses an enclosing block's local variable or parameter, it *captures* that local or parameter. For example, suppose you have declared the following interface:

```
interface Foo
{
   void bar();
}
```

Note   There is an interesting history to the names foo (camel-cased to Foo –
see Chapter 6 for a definition of camel casing) and bar. Check out Wikipedia's
"Camel case" entry (http://en.wikipedia.org/wiki/Camel_case) to learn
about this history.

Now suppose you've populated a method with the following code fragment:

```
final int i;
Foo foo;

i = 42;
foo = new Foo()
     {
         @Override
         public void bar()
         {
             System.out.println(i);
         }
     };
foo.bar();
```

This fragment first declares local variables i and foo. Local i has been declared
final because it is going to be accessed from within an anonymous class. Because I'm
using JDK 21, I don't need to declare this local final. Instead, I could remove the final
keyword. However, if I was using a version of the JDK that pre-dates JDK 8, I would need
to use final.

I then initialize int variable i to 42. (If you are wondering why so many
programmers feature this number in their examples, there is an interesting history
behind it. According to Wikipedia's "Phrases from *The Hitchhiker's Guide to the Galaxy*"
entry (http://en.wikipedia.org/wiki/Phrases_from_The_Hitchhiker's_Guide_to_
the_Galaxy), 42 is the answer to the question about life, the universe, and everything
else – or is it?

Moving on, the code fragment declares an unnamed (anonymous) class that
implements the Foo interface. To implement this interface correctly, it must override
its bar() method. This is signified by the @Override annotation (see Chapter 7 to learn
about @Override.)

The code fragment instantiates the anonymous class that implements Foo and returns its reference, which is assigned to the previously declared foo variable. It then executes foo.bar().

Interface Foo's bar() method header is not explicitly declared public. Instead, it is implicitly declared public. This is why I declare it public when overriding the method header in the anonymous class.

The bar() method invokes System.out.println(), passing the captured i variable's value as println()'s argument.

Starting in JDK 8, an anonymous class can access local variables and parameters in the enclosing block that are effectively final. For example, in the previous sidebar, variable i was declared final. However, if I removed the final keyword, this variable would become effectively final because it never changes after it is initialized.

Note   If I changed System.out.println(i); to System.out. println(i++); (which post-increments variable i) in the previous example's bar() method, i would no longer be effectively final, which Java cannot allow. The JDK 21 compiler would report a "cannot assign a value to final variable i" error message.

Summarizing

As with local classes, anonymous classes can capture variables; they have the same access to local variables in the enclosing scope, be it a block that follows an if statement header, a method header, or a class header:

- An anonymous class can access the members of its enclosing class.

- An anonymous class cannot access local variables in its enclosing block that are not declared final or are effectively final.

- As with a nested class, a declaration of a variable in an anonymous class shadows any other declarations in the enclosing block that have the same name.

Anonymous classes also have the same restrictions as local classes with respect to their members:

- You cannot declare static initializers or member interfaces in an anonymous class.

- An anonymous class can have static members provided that they are constant variables.

You can declare the following language elements in anonymous classes:

- Fields

- Additional methods

- Instance initializers

- Local classes

Remember that you cannot declare constructors in an anonymous class.

A More Practical Anonymous Class Example

I've created a Sort application that provides a more practical demonstration of an anonymous class. This application's source code is spread across two source files: Sort. java and Comparer.java. Listing 9-17 presents Sort.java's source code.

Listing 9-17. Sort.java

```java
class Sort
{
   public static void main(String[] args)
   {
      System.out.println("Sort");
      System.out.println("----");
      System.out.println();

      int[] grades = new int[] { 96, 54, 71, 89, 63, 92 };
      outputArray("Unsorted array:", grades);
      sort(grades, new Comparer()
                  {
                     @Override
```

```java
                public int compare(int x, int y)
                {
                    return x - y;
                }
            });
    outputArray("Sorted array after ascending sort:", grades);
    System.out.println();

    int[] grades2 = new int[] { 79, 56, 100, 88 };
    outputArray("Unsorted array:", grades2);
    sort(grades2, new Comparer()
                {
                    @Override
                    public int compare(int x, int y)
                    {
                        return y - x;
                    }
                });
    outputArray("Sorted array after descending sort:", grades2);
}

static void outputArray(String msg, int[] x)
{
    System.out.println(msg);
    System.out.println();
    for (int i = 0; i < x.length; i++)
        System.out.print(x[i] + " ");
    System.out.println();
    System.out.println();
}

static void sort(int[] x, Comparer c)
{
    for (int pass = 0; pass < x.length - 1; pass++)
    {
        int min = pass;
```

```
        for (int i = pass + 1; i < x.length; i++)
           if (c.compare(x[i], x[min]) < 0)
              min = i;
        if (min != pass)
        {
           int temp = x[min];
           x[min] = x[pass];
           x[pass] = temp;
        }
      }
   }
}
```

Listing 9-17's `Sort` class declares `main()`, `outputArray()`, and `sort()` methods:

- `main()` is the entry point into this application. It first outputs a header. It then declares a 32-bit integer array of student grades (which are unsorted), outputs this array, sorts this array into ascending order, and outputs the sorted array. Continuing, it declares a second array of unsorted grades, outputs this array, sorts this array into descending order, and outputs the sorted array.

- `outputArray()` prints a message followed by the contents of a 32-bit integer array on the console.

- `sort()` organizes an integer array's elements in ascending or descending order, which is determined by a `Comparer` object that is passed as the second argument to the `sort()` method. It uses the Selection Sort algorithm to perform this organization.

Selection Sort is similar to Chapter 5's Bubble Sort algorithm in that they both use an outer loop to make multiple passes through an array. Each pass is associated with a pass index that identifies the next element to work with.

For Selection Sort, an inner loop selects the smallest element – the minimum. If the minimum element's index does not equal the pass index, a swap of the minimum and pass-numbered elements occurs. For Bubble Sort, an inner loop compares the inner loop–indexed element with the current pass-indexed element. If the inner loop–indexed element is smaller (ascending sort) or larger (descending sort) than the pass-indexed element, a swap occurs.

Selection Sort emphasizes reducing the number of swaps, and Bubble Sort emphasizes simplicity.

My discussion of the sort() method referred to a Comparer object. This object is created from an anonymous class that extends the abstract Comparer class. Listing 9-18 presents Comparer.java's source code.

Listing 9-18. Comparer.java

```
abstract class Comparer
{
   abstract int compare(int x, int y);
}
```

Comparer declares a single abstract int compare(int x, int y) method that compares the values in the x and y parameters, returning a negative result when one of these values is less than the other value, zero when these values are identical, and a positive result when one of these values is greater than the other value.

Refer back to the main() method and you'll encounter two occurrences of Comparer being subclassed by an anonymous class and then instantiated. I've excerpted the first instance as follows:

```
sort(grades, new Comparer()
            {
               @Override
               public int compare(int x, int y)
               {
                  return x - y;
               }
            });
```

The return x - y; statement subtracts the second parameter value from the first parameter value in order to perform an ascending sort. The second Comparer occurrence exchanges these parameters, resulting in a return y - x; statement that results in a descending sort.

Compile Listings 9-17 and 9-18 as follows:

```
javac *.java
```

Run the Sort application as follows:

```
java Sort
```

You should observe the following output:

```
Sort
----

Unsorted array:

96 54 71 89 63 92

Sorted array after ascending sort:

54 63 71 89 92 96

Unsorted array:

79 56 100 88

Sorted array after descending sort:

100 88 79 56
```

What's Next?

I've referred to packages in this and previous chapters. What is a package and how do you use it? You'll find out in the next chapter.

CHAPTER 10

Packages

Same-named reference types (e.g., two different Math classes) can cause name conflicts when you try to use them, but Java overcomes this problem with packages. This chapter introduces you to the package concept followed by the package and import statements. Finally, you learn about static imports, protected access, and JAR files.

What Are Packages?

Java developers group related classes and/or interfaces into *packages*, which are unique *namespaces* for storing reference types. Packages can store classes, interfaces, and *subpackages* (packages nested within other packages). Think of a package as a directory that stores files and subdirectories.

Note Packages make it easier to locate and use reference types, avoid name conflicts between same-named types, and control access to types.

A package has a name, which must be a non-reserved identifier, for example, java. The member selection operator (.) separates a package name from a subpackage name and separates a package or subpackage name from a type name. For example, the two . operators in java.lang.System separate package name java from the lang subpackage name and separate subpackage name lang from the System type name.

Note The System utility class provides several useful system-related constants and methods. We will look at its constants and some of its methods in Chapter 14.

Reference types (such as System) must be declared public to be accessible from outside their packages. The same applies to any constants, constructors, and methods that must be accessible. You'll see examples later in this chapter.

© Jeff Friesen 2024
J. Friesen, *Learn Java Fundamentals*, https://doi.org/10.1007/979-8-8688-0351-2_10

The Package Statement

Java provides the *package statement* for creating a package. This statement appears at the top of a source file and identifies the package to which the source file's types belong. It must conform to the following syntax:

`'package' identifier ('.' identifier)* ';'`

A `package` statement starts with reserved word `package` and continues with an *identifier*, which is optionally followed by a `.`-separated sequence of *identifiers*. A semicolon terminates this statement.

The first (leftmost) identifier names the package, and each subsequent identifier names a subpackage. For example, in `package x.y;`, all types declared in the source file belong to the y subpackage of the x package.

Note   By convention, a package/subpackage name is expressed in lowercase. When the name consists of multiple words, you might want to place an underscore between each word to improve readability.

A sequence of package names must be unique to avoid compilation problems. For example, suppose you create two different `report_generator` packages, and suppose that each package contains a `ReportGenerator` class with a different interface. When the Java compiler encounters, for example, `ReportGenerator rg = new ReportGenerator();` in the source code, it needs to verify that the `ReportGenerator()` constructor exists.

The compiler will search all accessible packages until it finds a `report_generator` package that contains a `ReportGenerator` class. If the found package contains the appropriate `ReportGenerator` class with a `ReportGenerator()` constructor, everything is fine. Otherwise, if the found `ReportGenerator` class doesn't have a `ReportGenerator()` constructor, the compiler reports an error.

This scenario illustrates the importance of choosing unique package name sequences. The convention in choosing a unique name sequence is to reverse your Internet domain name and use it as a prefix for the sequence. For example, I might choose `tech.javajeff` as my prefix if `javajeff.tech` was my domain name. I would then specify `tech.javajeff.report_generator.ReportGenerator` to access `ReportGenerator`.

Note   Domain name components are not always valid package names. One or more component names might start with a digit (`4seasons.com`), contain a hyphen (-) or other illegal character (`news-world.com`), or be one of Java's reserved words (`interface.com`). Convention dictates that you prefix the digit with an underscore (`com._4seasons`), replace the illegal character with an underscore (`com.news_world`), and suffix the reserved word with an underscore (`com.interface_`).

To avoid more problems with the `package` statement, there are a couple of rules that you need to follow:

- You can declare only one `package` statement in a source file.

- You cannot precede the `package` statement with anything apart from comments.

The first rule, which is a special case of the second rule, exists because it doesn't make sense to store a reference type in multiple packages. Although a package can store multiple types, a type can belong to only one package.

When a source file doesn't declare a `package` statement, the source file's types belong to the *unnamed package*. Nontrivial reference types are typically stored in their own packages and avoid the unnamed package.

Oracle's Java implementations map package and subpackage names to same-named directories (folders for you Macintosh folks). For example, an implementation would map `report_generator` to a directory named `report_generator`. In x.y, x would map to a directory named x and y would map to a y subdirectory of x. The compiler stores the class files that implement the package's types in the corresponding directory. Note that the unnamed package corresponds to the current directory.

The Import Statement

Imagine having to repeatedly specify `tech.javajeff.report_generator.ReportGenerator` for each occurrence of `ReportGenerator` in source code. Java provides a convenient alternative for omitting lengthy package details. This alternative is the `import` statement.

The *import statement* imports types from a package by telling the compiler where to look for *unqualified* (no package prefix) type names during compilation. It appears near the top of a source file and must conform to the following syntax:

```
'import' identifier ('.' identifier)]* '.' (typeName | '*') ';'
```

An `import` statement starts with reserved word `import` and continues with an *identifier*, which is optionally followed by a `.`-separated sequence of *identifiers*. A *typeName* or `*` (asterisk) follows, and a `;` (semicolon) terminates this statement.

The syntax reveals two forms of the `import` statement. First, you can import a single type name, which is identified via *typeName*. Second, you can import all types, which is identified via the `*`.

The `*` symbol is a *wildcard* that represents all unqualified type names. It tells the compiler to look for such names in the rightmost package of the `import` statement's package sequence, unless the type name is found in a previously searched package. Note that using the wildcard doesn't have a performance penalty or lead to code bloat. However, it can lead to name conflicts, which you will see.

For example, `import tech.javajeff.report_generator.ReportGenerator;` tells the compiler that an unqualified `ReportGenerator` class exists in the `tech.javajeff. report_generator` package. Similarly, `import tech.javajeff.report_generator.*;` tells the compiler to look in this package when it encounters a `ReportGenerator` name, a `Vehicle` name, or even an `Account` name.

Tip   When working on a multi-programmer project, avoid using the `*` wildcard so that other programmers can easily see which types are used in your source code.

You can run into name conflicts when using the wildcard version of the `import` statement because any unqualified type name matches the wildcard. For example, you have `math` and `statistics` packages that each contain a `Math` class, the source code begins with `import math.*;` and `import statistics.*;` statements, and it also contains an unqualified occurrence of `Math`. Because the compiler doesn't know if `Math` refers to `math`'s `Math` class or to `statistics`'s `Math` class, it reports an error. You can fix this problem by qualifying `Math` with the correct package name (`math.Math` or `statistics.Math`).

To avoid additional problems with the `import` statement, there are a couple of rules that you need to follow:

- Because Java is case sensitive, package and subpackage names specified in an `import` statement must be expressed in the same case as that used in the `package` statement.

- You cannot precede the `import` statement with anything apart from comments, a `package` statement, other `import` statements, and `static import` statements (which I introduce later in this chapter).

The compiler automatically imports types from the `java.lang` library package. As a result, you don't have to specify `import java.lang.System;` (import `java.lang`'s `System` class) or similar `import` statements in your source code.

Because Java implementations map package and subpackage names to same-named directories, an `import` statement is equivalent to loading a reference type's class file from the directory sequence corresponding to the package sequence.

Playing with Packages

A practical example will help you fully grasp the `package` and `import` statements. I'm demonstrating these statements in the context of a logging library that lets you log messages to the console, to a file, or to another destination.

Packaging a Logging Library

Suppose your application needs to log messages to the console, to a file, or to another destination. It can accomplish this task with the help of a logging library. My implementation of this library consists of an interface named `Logger`, an abstract class named `LoggerFactory`, and a pair of package-private classes named `Console` and `File`.

Listing 10-1 presents the `Logger` interface, which describes objects that log messages.

Listing 10-1. `Logger.java`

```
package logging;

public interface Logger
{
   boolean connect();
   boolean disconnect();
   boolean log(String msg);
}
```

Each of the `connect()`, `disconnect()`, and `log()` methods returns true on success and false on failure. (Chapter 11 presents a better technique for dealing with failure.) These methods are not declared `public` explicitly because an interface's methods are implicitly `public`.

Listing 10-2 presents the `LoggerFactory` abstract class.

Listing 10-2. `LoggerFactory.java`

```
package logging;

public abstract class LoggerFactory
{
   public final static int CONSOLE = 0;
   public final static int FILE = 1;

   public static Logger newLogger(int dstType, String... dstName)
   {
      switch (dstType)
      {
         case CONSOLE:
            return new Console(dstName.length == 0 ? null : dstName[0]);

         case FILE:
            return new File(dstName.length == 0 ? null : dstName[0]);
```

```
        default:
            return null;
      }
   }
}
```

Listing 10-2's LoggerFactory class is stored in file LoggerFactory.java. This listing begins with a package statement that identifies logging as the class's package.

LoggerFactory is declared public so that it can be referenced from outside of its package. Also, it is declared abstract so that it cannot be instantiated.

Caution   Only one public class or interface can appear in a source file. Furthermore, the source file must be named after the class or interface name. Failing to adhere to either requirement results in the compiler reporting an error.

---

newLogger() returns a Logger instance for logging messages to an appropriate destination. It uses the varargs feature (see Chapter 6) to optionally accept an extra String argument for those destination types that require the argument. For example, FILE requires a file name.

Listing 10-3 presents the package-private Console class – this class is not accessible beyond the classes in the logging package because reserved word class is not preceded by reserved word public.

Listing 10-3. Console.java

```
package logging;

class Console implements Logger
{
   private String dstName;

   Console(String dstName)
   {
      this.dstName = dstName;
   }
```

```
    @Override
    public boolean connect()
    {
        return true;
    }

    @Override

    public boolean disconnect()
    {
        return true;
    }

    @Override
    public boolean log(String msg)
    {
        System.out.println(msg);
        return true;
    }
}
```

Console's package-private constructor saves its argument, which most likely will be the null reference because there is no need for a String argument. Perhaps a future version of Console will use this argument to identify one of multiple console windows.

Listing 10-4 presents the package-private File class.

Listing 10-4. File.java

```
package logging;

class File implements Logger
{
    private String dstName;

    File(String dstName)
    {
        this.dstName = dstName;
    }
```

```java
@Override
public boolean connect()
{
   if (dstName == null)
      return false;
   System.out.println("opening file " + dstName);
   return true;
}

@Override
public boolean disconnect()
{
   if (dstName == null)
      return false;
   System.out.println("closing file " + dstName);
   return true;
}

@Override
public boolean log(String msg)
{
   if (dstName == null)
      return false;
   System.out.println("writing " + msg + " to file " + dstName);
   return true;
}
}
```

Unlike Console, File requires a non-null argument. Each method first verifies that this argument is not null. If the argument is null, the method returns false to signify failure.

Complete the following steps to build this library:

1. Select a suitable location in your file system as the current directory.

2. Create a logging subdirectory in the current directory.

3. Copy Listings 10-1 and 10-2 to files `Logger.java` and `LoggerFactory.java`, respectively; and store these files in the `logging` subdirectory.

4. Copy Listings 10-3 and 10-4 to files `Console.java` and `File.java`, respectively; and store these files in the `logging` subdirectory.

5. Assuming that the current directory contains the `logging` subdirectory, execute `javac logging/*.java` to compile the four source files in `logging`. If all goes well, you should discover `Logger.class`, `LoggerFactory.class`, `Console.class`, and `File.class` in the `logging` subdirectory. (Alternatively, for this example, you could switch to the `logging` subdirectory and execute `javac *.java`.)

Now that you've created the `logging` library, you'll want to use it. I'll present a small Java application that properly demonstrates this library in the next section.

Importing Types from the Logging Library

The logging library allows us to introduce portable logging code into an application. Apart from a call to `newLogger()`, this code will remain the same regardless of the logging destination. Listing 10-5 presents an application that tests this library.

Listing 10-5. `TestLogging.java`

```
import logging.Logger;
import logging.LoggerFactory;

class TestLogging
{
   public static void main(String[] args)
   {
      Logger logger = LoggerFactory.newLogger(LoggerFactory.CONSOLE);
      if (logger.connect())
      {
         logger.log("test message #1");
         logger.disconnect();
      }
```

```
   else
      System.out.println("cannot connect to console-based logger");

   logger = LoggerFactory.newLogger(LoggerFactory.FILE, "messages.txt");
   if (logger.connect())
   {
      logger.log("test message #2");
      logger.disconnect();
   }
   else
      System.out.println("cannot connect to file-based logger");

   logger = LoggerFactory.newLogger(LoggerFactory.FILE);
   if (logger.connect())
   {
      logger.log("test message #3");
      logger.disconnect();
   }
   else
      System.out.println("cannot connect to file-based logger");
   }
}
```

Listing 10-5 doesn't begin with a package statement because simple applications are typically not stored in packages. Instead, it begins with a pair of import statements for importing the logging library's Logger and LoggerFactory classes.

The main() method first invokes LoggerFactory's newLogger() method with the LoggerFactory.CONSOLE constant as this method's argument to create a logger that logs messages to the console. This method returns a Logger object (i.e., a logger created from a class – Console, in this case – that implements the Logger interface).

This method proceeds to connect to this logger by calling Logger's connect() method. If this method returns true, the method succeeded (it will succeed with a console but might not succeed when logging to a file), and main() proceeds to log a message by invoking Logger's log() method. It then disconnects from the logger by calling Logger's disconnect() method.

The main() method next repeats this process by creating a file-based logger that logs messages to a file named messages.txt.

This process is repeated a third time by attempting to create a file-based logger that logs messages to an unnamed file. Let's assume that a default name is used when no file name argument is passed to newLogger() – remember that newLogger() uses varargs to obtain the file name.

The newLogger() method is coded to not return a logger, but you could change it to choose a default file name. I wrote it this way to test the code when newLogger() fails to return a logger.

Copy Listing 10-5 to a file named TestLogging.java and place this file in the same directory as the logging directory that you previously created. Then, execute the following command to compile TestLogging.java (and the logging package's source files when not previously compiled):

```
javac TestLogging.java
```

Execute the following command to run TestLogging:

```
java TestLogging
```

You should observe the following output:

```
test message #1
opening file messages.txt
writing test message #2 to file messages.txt
closing file messages.txt
cannot connect to file-based logger
```

Suppose that TestLogging.java wasn't located in the same directory as logging. How would you compile this source file and run the resulting application? The answer is to use the class path.

The *class path* is a sequence of packages that the Java Virtual Machine (JVM) searches for reference types. It is specified via the -classpath (or -cp) option used to start the JVM or, when not present, the CLASSPATH environment variable.

Note   Whether you use the -classpath/-cp option or the CLASSPATH environment variable to specify a class path, there is a specific format that must be followed. Under Windows, this format is expressed as *path1*;*path2*;...., where *path1*, *path2*, and so on are the locations of package directories. Under Mac OS X, Unix, and Linux, this format changes to *path1*:*path2*:....

Suppose (on a Windows platform) that the logging library is stored in `C:\logging` and that `TestLogging.java` is stored in `C:\TestLogging`, which is the current directory. Specify the following commands to compile the source code and run the application:

```
javac -cp ../logging TestLogging.java
java -cp ../logging;. TestLogging
```

The period character after the `;` character in `../logging;.` represents the current directory. It must be specified so that the JVM can locate `TestLogging.class`.

Additional Topics

There are three additional topics to consider when working with packages: static imports, protected access, and JAR files.

Static Imports

Interfaces should only be used to declare types. They shouldn't be used to declare *constant interfaces*, which are interfaces that exist only to export constants. Listing 10-6's `Openable` constant interface provides an example.

Listing 10-6. `Openable.java`

```
package demo;

public interface Openable
{
   boolean OPEN = true;
   boolean CLOSED = false;
}
```

Programmers use constant interfaces to avoid having to prefix the constant's name with the name of its reference type (e.g., `Integer.MAX_VALUE`). For example, consider Listing 10-7's `Door` class, which implements the `Openable` interface so that the programmer is free to specify constants `OPEN` and `CLOSED` without having to include class prefixes (if they were declared in a class).

Listing 10-7. `Door.java`

```
package demo;

public class Door implements Openable
{
   private boolean state = CLOSED;

   public void status()
   {
      System.out.println("door is " + ((state == CLOSED) ? "CLOSED" : "OPEN"));
   }

   public void open()
   {
      state = OPEN;
   }

   public void close()
   {
      state = CLOSED;
   }
}
```

A constant interface provides constants that are to be used in a class's implementation. These constants are an implementation detail that you shouldn't leak into the class's exported interface because they could confuse the users of your class. Furthermore, in order to preserve binary compatibility, you're committed to support them even when they're no longer used by the class.

To satisfy the need for constant interfaces while avoiding the problems imposed by the use of these interfaces, JDK 5 introduced *static imports*. This language feature can be used to import a reference type's static members. It is implemented via the `import static` statement whose syntax appears as follows:

`'import' 'static'` *packagespec* `'.'` *typename* `'.'` `(` *staticmembername* `| '*' );`

This statement's placement of static after import distinguishes it from a regular import statement. Its syntax is similar to the regular import statement in terms of the standard period-separated list of package and subpackage names. Either a single static member name or all static member names (thanks to the asterisk) can be imported. Consider the following examples:

```
import static java.lang.Integer.*;          // Import all static members
                                            //    from Integer.
import static java.lang.Integer.MAX_VALUE; // Import the MAX_VALUE static
                                            //    constant only.
import static java.lang.Integer.max;        // Import the max() static
                                            //    method only.
```

Once imported, static members can be specified without having to prefix them with their type names. For example, after specifying either the first or third static import, you could specify max directly, as in int maxValue = max(10, 20);.

To fix Listing 10-7 so that it no longer relies on implements Openable, we can insert a static import, which Listing 10-8 demonstrates.

Listing 10-8. Door.java (version 2)

```java
package demo;

import static demo.Openable.*;

public class Door
{
   private boolean state = CLOSED;

   public void status()
   {
      System.out.println("door is " + ((state == CLOSED) ? "CLOSED" :
      "OPEN"));
   }

   public void open()
   {
      state = OPEN;
   }
```

```
    public void close()
    {
       state = CLOSED;
    }
}
```

Listing 10-8 begins with a `package demo;` statement because you cannot import static members from a type located in the unnamed package. This package name appears as part of the subsequent `import static demo.Openable.*;` static import.

There are two additional cautions in regard to static imports:

- When two static imports import the same named member, the compiler reports an error. For example, suppose package `math` contains a `Math` class that's identical to package `physics`'s `Math` class in that it implements the same E constant and logarithmic methods. When confronted by the following code fragment, the compiler reports errors because it cannot determine whether `math.Math`'s or `physics.Math`'s E constant is being accessed and `log()` method is being called:

```
import static math.Math.*;
import static physics.Math.*;

System.out.println(E);
System.out.println(log(2));
```

- Overuse of static imports can make your code unreadable and unmaintainable because it pollutes the code's namespace with all of the static members you import. Also, anyone reading your code could have a hard time finding out which type a static member comes from, especially when importing all static member names from a type.

Protected Access

Java provides the `protected` keyword for use in a package context. This keyword assigns the protected access level to a class member, such as a field or method. Declaring a class member `protected` makes the member accessible to all code in any class located in the same package and to subclasses regardless of their packages.

Class members are given protected access so that they can serve as hooks into a class's implementation. This lets programmers write efficient subclasses in an easier manner. I refer you to "Item 17: Design and document for inheritance or else prohibit it" in Joshua Bloch's book, *Effective Java, Second Edition* (`www.amazon.com/Effective-Java-2nd-Joshua-Bloch/dp/0321356683/`) for more information.

JAR Files

Distributing a package by specifying instructions for creating the necessary directory structure along with the package's class files (and instructions on which class files to store in which directories) is a tedious and error-prone task. Fortunately, JAR files offer a better alternative.

A *JAR (Java ARchive) file* is a Zip archive with a `.jar` file extension (instead of the `.zip` extension). It includes a special `META-INF` directory containing `manifest.mf` (a special file that stores information about the contents of the JAR file) and a hierarchical directory structure that organizes class files.

You use the JDK's `jar` tool to create and maintain a JAR file. You can also view the JAR file's table of contents. To show you how easy it is to use this tool, we'll create a `logging.jar` file that stores the contents of the `logging` package. We'll then access this JAR file when running `TestLogging.class`.

Note   If you try to run `jar` on Windows, you will probably discover an error message that `jar` cannot be found. This is due to JDK 21 storing only a few important executables in a special directory and setting the PATH environment variable to point to this directory during installation. For example, on the Windows 8.1 platform that I'm using to write this book, my `C:\Program Files\Common Files\Oracle\Java\javapath` path is added to PATH. The `javapath` directory contains `java.exe`, `javac.exe`, and a couple of other commonly run executables. To access `jar` (and any other JDK tools I might want to use), I need to add my `C:\Program Files\java\jdk-21\bin` directory to PATH. I can do this temporarily by specifying `set path=%path%;C:\Program Files\java\jdk-21\bin`. Alternatively, I can make this permanent by using the Windows Control Panel. You will want to do something equivalent on your platform.

Create `logging.jar` as follows:

1. Make sure that the current directory contains the previously created `logging` subdirectory and that `logging` contains `Logger.class`, `LoggerFactory.class`, `Console.class`, and `File.class`.

2. Execute the following command:

   `jar cf logging.jar logging\*.class`

The `c` option stands for "create new archive," and the `f` option stands for "specify archive file name."

You should now find a `logging.jar` file in the current directory. Prove to yourself that this file contains the four class files by executing the following command, where the `t` option stands for "list table of contents":

`jar tf logging.jar`

You can run `TestLogging.class` by adding `logging.jar` to its class path. For example, assuming that `logging.jar` is located in the same directory as `TestLogging.class`, you can run `TestLogging` under Windows via the following command:

`java -classpath logging.jar;. TestLogging`

For convenience, you could specify the shorter `-cp` instead of the longer `-classpath`.

What's Next?

Executing applications are prone to fail. Failure comes in different forms. Java classifies a failure as either an exception or an error. We'll review these failure categories and look at Java's language features for detecting failure and taking appropriate action to handle this failure in the next chapter.

Exceptions and Errors

In an ideal world, nothing bad ever happens when an application runs. For example, a file always exists when the application needs to open the file, the application is always able to connect to a remote computer, and the Java Virtual Machine (JVM) never runs out of memory when the application needs to instantiate objects.

In contrast, real-world applications occasionally attempt to open files that do not exist, attempt to connect to remote computers that are unable to communicate with them, and require more memory than the JVM can provide. Your goal is to write code that properly responds to these and other exceptional situations (exceptions).

This chapter introduces you to exceptions and errors (a relative of exceptions). After defining these terms, the chapter looks at representing exceptions and errors in source code. It then examines the topics of throwing and handling exceptions and concludes by discussing how to perform cleanup tasks before a method returns, whether or not an exception has been thrown.

You will discover two statements related to exceptions (try and try-with-resources):

- The try statement surrounds a block of code that can throw exceptions and errors. This statement's try block must be followed by a combination of catch blocks that handle these exceptions and/or a finally block for performing cleanup tasks.

- The try-with-resources statement is similar to the try statement but lets you automatically close any open resources when execution leaves the try block.

© Jeff Friesen 2024
J. Friesen, *Learn Java Fundamentals*, https://doi.org/10.1007/979-8-8688-0351-2_11

What Are Exceptions and Errors?

A Java program fails when its normal execution flow is interrupted by unexpected behavior. For example, the program attempts to open a file that doesn't exist or tries to divide an integer by 0. Maybe the program tries to create a very large array but there is insufficient free memory to accommodate the memory-allocation request.

Java categorizes a failure as either an exception or an error. An *exception* is a failure that occurs because something beyond the program's control (such as attempting to open a nonexistent file) has occurred or because of a bug in the code (division by 0 attempt). (In other words, it is a divergence from the normal flow of execution.) In the first case, there was no way to prevent the exception so the program would need to recover by taking corrective action. In the second case, the exception would not have happened if the program had been written correctly.

An *error* is a failure that is non-recoverable. Many errors involve the JVM, for example, running out of memory or attempting to load a corrupt class file. Some errors have nothing to do with the JVM, such as an input/output error or an assertion evaluating to false. (An *assertion* is a Boolean expression that must be true for execution to continue.)

Note   As a rule, don't handle an error because the JVM might not be able to recover from it. For example, once memory is exhausted, the JVM probably must be shut down. (An exception handler might try to release an object that's claiming a lot of memory, but that might not work.) Also, how would a program fix a corrupt class file?

Java classifies exceptions arising from external factors (such as a missing file) as *checked exceptions*. The Java compiler checks that such exceptions are either *handled* (corrected) where they occur or documented to be handled elsewhere.

Java classifies exceptions that arise from buggy code as *runtime exceptions*. These exceptions should be fixed by the programmer. Because the compiler doesn't check that runtime exceptions are handled or documented to be handled elsewhere, you can think of a runtime exception as an *unchecked exception*.

Exceptions are handled by *exception handlers*, which are sequences of code that respond to the exceptions and take appropriate action. An exception handler interrogates the context (e.g., reads values from variables that were in scope when the exception occurred) and uses what it learns to restore the Java program to a flow of normal behavior. For example, an exception handler might read a saved file name and prompt, via a dialog box, the user to replace the missing file, whose name is shown, and then close the dialog box.

Note   You might modify a program to handle a runtime exception, but it's better to fix the source code. Runtime exceptions often arise from passing invalid arguments to a library's methods; the buggy calling code should be fixed.

Representing Exceptions and Errors in Source Code

An exception is represented in source code as an error code or as an object. This section first reviews each kind of representation and explains why objects are superior. It then introduces Java's library of exception-oriented classes.

Error Codes vs. Objects

Programming languages such as C use integer-based *error codes* to represent failure and reasons for failure (exceptions). Here are a couple of examples:

```
FILE* fp = fopen("notes.txt", "rt");
if (fp == NULL)
{
   printf("unable to open file\n");
   // Terminate the program.
}
int handle = open("image.png", O_RDONLY);
if (handle == -1)
{
   printf("unable to open file\n");
   // Terminate the program.
}
```

C's `fopen()` (file open) function returns a non-null pointer (integer address) to a `FILE` structure on success or a null (0) pointer (represented by constant `NULL`) on failure. Similarly, C's `open()` function returns an integer other than -1 on success or -1 on failure.

There are some problems with error codes:

- Integers are meaningless; they don't describe the exceptions they represent. For example, what does -5 mean?

- It's awkward to associate context with an error code. For example, you might want to output the name of the file that couldn't be opened. Where are you going to store the file's name?

- Integers are arbitrary; their choice can lead to confusion when reading source code. For example, specifying `if (!chdir("C:\\windows"))` (! signifies NOT) instead of `if (chdir("C:\\windows"))` to test for failure is clearer. However, 0 was chosen to indicate success, and so `if (chdir("C:\\temp"))` must be specified to test for failure.

- Error codes are too easy to ignore, which can lead to buggy code. For example, the programmer could ignore the `if (fp == NULL)` check. By not testing for failure, the program behaves erratically when either function returns a failure indicator.

To overcome these problems, a new exception-handling approach was invented. This approach combines objects that describe exceptions with a mechanism based on throwing and catching these objects:

- An object can be created from a class with a meaningful name. For example, the `java.io` package's `FileNotFoundException` class is more meaningful than -5.

- Objects can store context in various fields. For example, you can store a message, the name of the file that could not be opened, the most recent position where a parse operation failed, and/or other items in an object's fields.

- You don't use `if` statements to test for failure. Instead, exception objects are thrown to a handler that's separate from the program code. As a result, the source code is easier to read and less prone to be buggy.

The Throwable Class Hierarchy

Java provides a hierarchy of classes in its reference types library that represent different kinds of exceptions. These classes are rooted in the java.lang package's Throwable class along with its Exception, RuntimeException, and Error subclasses. (Unless otherwise stated, all classes introduced in this chapter are located in java.lang.)

The Throwable Class

Throwable is the ultimate superclass where exceptions and errors are concerned. Only objects created from Throwable and its subclasses can be thrown (and subsequently caught). Such objects are known as *throwables*.

A Throwable object is associated with a detail message that describes an exception or error. Several constructors, including the pair described here, are provided to create a Throwable object with or without a detail message:

- Throwable(): Create a Throwable with no detail message. This constructor is appropriate for situations where there is no context. For example, you only want to know that a stack is empty or full.

- Throwable(String message): Create a Throwable with message as the detail message. This message can be output to the user and/ or logged.

Throwable provides the String getMessage() method to return the detail message. It also provides additional useful methods.

The Exception Class

Throwable has two direct subclasses. One of these subclasses is Exception, which describes an exception arising from an external factor (such as attempting to read from a nonexistent file). Exception declares the same constructors (with identical parameter lists) as Throwable; each constructor invokes its Throwable counterpart. Also, Exception inherits Throwable's methods. It declares no new methods.

Java provides many exception classes that directly subclass Exception. Here are three examples:

- IOException: Signals that some kind of I/O failure has occurred. This type is located in the java.io package.

- ParseException: Signals that a failure has occurred while parsing text. This type can be found in the java.text package.

- UnsupportedAudioFileException: Signals that an audio-oriented operation failed because a file did not contain valid data of a recognized file type or format. Check out the javax.sound.sampled package for this type.

Notice that each Exception subclass name ends with the word Exception. This convention makes it easy to identify the class's purpose.

You'll typically subclass Exception (or one of its subclasses) with your own exception classes (whose names should end with Exception). Here are a couple of custom subclass examples:

```
public class StackFullException extends Exception
{
}

public class EmptyCardReaderException extends Exception
{
    private String cardReaderName;

    public EmptyCardReaderException(String message, String cardReaderName)
    {
        super(message);
        this.cardReaderName = cardReaderName;
    }

    public String getCardReaderName()
    {
        return cardReaderName;
    }
}
```

The first example describes an exception class that doesn't require a detail message. Its default no-argument constructor invokes `Exception()`, which invokes `Throwable()`.

The second example describes an exception class whose constructor requires a detail message and the name of the empty card reader. The constructor uses `super(message);` to invoke `Exception(String message)`, which invokes `Throwable(String message)`.

Objects instantiated from `Exception` or one of its subclasses (except for `RuntimeException` or one of its subclasses) are checked exceptions.

The RuntimeException Class

`Exception` is directly subclassed by `RuntimeException`, which describes an exception most likely arising from poorly written code. `RuntimeException` declares the same constructors (with identical parameter lists) as `Exception`; each constructor invokes its `Exception` counterpart. Also, `RuntimeException` inherits `Throwable`'s methods. It declares no new methods.

Java provides many exception classes that directly subclass `RuntimeException`. Here are three examples:

- `ArithmeticException`: Signals an illegal arithmetic operation, such as attempting to divide an integer by 0

- `IllegalArgumentException`: Signals that an illegal or inappropriate argument has been passed to a method during a method call

- `NullPointerException`: Signals an attempt to invoke a method or access an object field via the null reference

Objects instantiated from `RuntimeException` or one of its subclasses are unchecked exceptions.

The Error Class

`Throwable`'s other direct subclass is `Error`, which describes a serious (even abnormal) problem (such as running out of memory, overflowing the JVM's stack, or attempting to load a class that cannot be found) that a reasonable application should not try to handle. Like `Exception`, `Error` declares identical constructors to `Throwable`, inherits `Throwable`'s methods, and doesn't declare any of its own methods.

You can identify `Error` subclasses from the convention that their class names end with `Error`. Examples include `OutOfMemoryError`, `LinkageError`, and `StackOverflowError`.

You shouldn't try to create your own `Error` subclasses and throw/handle `Error` subclass objects. For these reasons, I have nothing more to say about `Error` in this chapter.

Throwing Exceptions

A C library function notifies calling code of an exception by setting the global `errno` variable to an error code and returning a failure code. In contrast, a Java method throws an object. This section examines this throwing mechanism.

The Throw Statement

Java provides the `throw` statement to throw an object that describes an exception. Although you can use this statement to throw an error, that isn't normally done because a program cannot recover from running out of memory or another catastrophic event.

The `throw` statement has the following syntax:

```
throw throwable;
```

The object identified by `throwable` is an instance of `Throwable` or any of its subclasses. However, you usually only throw objects instantiated from subclasses of `Exception` or `RuntimeException`. Here are a couple of examples:

```
throw new ZipException("unable to read the next ZIP file entry" +
filename);
throw new ArrayIndexOutOfBoundsException("array index out of bounds");
```

The throwable is thrown from the current method to the JVM, which checks this method for a suitable handler. If not found, the JVM unwinds a data structure known as the *method-call stack*, looking for the closest calling method that can handle the exception described by the throwable. If it finds this method, it passes the throwable to the method's handler, whose code is executed to handle the exception. If no method is found to handle the exception, the JVM terminates with a suitable message.

You normally wouldn't throw an object from RuntimeException (which is too general to mean anything) or a subclass such as ArrayIndexOutOfBoundsException, which is thrown when you specify a negative array index or an index that is greater than or equal to an array's length. Instead, you would fix the code that gives rise to the exception. However, you might want to throw IllegalArgumentException when detecting an invalid argument in a library context:

```
static double sqrt(double n)
{
   if (n < 0)
      throw new IllegalArgumentException(n + " is negative");
   // ...
}
```

Assume that you are building a library based on a single Math class with a sqrt() method. Because you cannot calculate the square root of a negative number, you first check for this possibility and create/throw an IllegalArgumentException object describing this problem when a negative number is passed.

The Throws Clause

You need to inform the compiler when you throw a checked exception out of a method. Do this by appending a throws clause to the method's header. This clause has the following syntax:

```
'throws' checkedExceptionClassName (',' checkedExceptionClassName)*
```

A throws clause consists of keyword throws followed by a comma-separated list of the class names of checked exceptions thrown out of the method. Here is an example:

```
public static void main(String[] args) throws IOException
{
   FileInputStream fis = new FileInputStream("x.dat");
}
```

This example attempts to open a file named x.dat and return an input stream that lets us read bytes from the file. (I don't discuss files and streams beyond what I discuss in this chapter.) However, if the file doesn't exist or something else I/O related goes wrong, the FileInputStream() constructor will throw IOException or one of its subclasses (such as java.io.FileNotFoundException).

It's necessary to inform the compiler that an object from the checked IOException class (or subclass, which is also checked) is being thrown by attaching a throws IOException clause to the invoking main() method's header. After all, the exception isn't handled in this method. When the exception is thrown to the JVM, it will note this and (because there is no parent method of main()) terminate with a message.

There are a few rules that you need to keep in mind when working with throws clauses:

- If at all possible, don't include the names of unchecked exception classes (such as ArithmeticException) in a throws clause. These names don't need to be included because throws clauses are for checked exceptions only. Including unchecked class names only clutters the source code.

- You can append a throws clause to a constructor and throw a checked exception from the constructor when something goes wrong while the constructor is executing. The resulting object will not be created.

- If a superclass method declares a throws clause, the overriding subclass method doesn't have to declare a throws clause. However, if the subclass method declares a throws clause, the clause must not include the names of checked exception classes that are not also included in the superclass method's throws clause, unless they are the names of exception subclasses. For example, given superclass method void open(String name) throws IOException {}, the overriding subclass method could be declared as void open(String name) {}, void open(String name) throws IOException {}, or void open(String name) throws FileNotFoundException {}. However, you couldn't specify, in the subclass, void open(String name) throws ClassNotFoundException, because ClassNotFoundException doesn't appear in the superclass's throws clause.

- A checked exception class name doesn't need to appear in a `throws` clause when the name of its superclass appears. For example, you don't need to specify `throws FileNotFoundException, IOException`. Only `throws IOException` is necessary.

- The compiler reports an error when a method throws a checked exception and doesn't also handle the exception or list the exception in its `throws` clause.

- You can declare a checked exception class name in a method's `throws` clause without throwing an instance of this class from the method. (Perhaps the method has yet to be fully coded.) However, Java requires that you provide code to handle this exception, even though it isn't thrown.

There is one more rule to consider. Sometimes, a method throws many checked exceptions, and it's tempting to specify a `throws Exception` clause to save keystrokes. Although specifying only `Exception` saves time, it makes the source code less readable. Someone who is reading your code might have difficulty identifying all of the checked exceptions that are being passed on to the caller. I suggest following this practice for private throwaway code only.

The Try Statement

The `try` statement surrounds a block of code that can throw exceptions and errors. This statement's `try` block must be followed by a combination of `catch` blocks that handle these exceptions and/or a `finally` block for performing cleanup tasks.

The Try Block

A `try` block has the following syntax:

```
'try'
{
   // one or more statements that might throw exceptions
}
```

The statements in a `try` block serve a common purpose and might directly or indirectly throw an exception. Consider the following example:

```
FileInputStream fis = null;
FileOutputStream fos = null;
try
{
   fis = new FileInputStream(args[0]);
   fos = new FileOutputStream(args[1]);
   int c;
   while ((c = fis.read()) != -1)
      fos.write(c);
}
```

This example excerpts a larger `Copy` application (presented in its entirety later in this chapter) that copies a source file to a destination file. It uses the `java.io` package's `FileInputStream` and `FileOutputStream` classes (which I have yet to formally introduce) for this purpose. Think of `FileInputStream` as a way to read an input stream of bytes from a file and `FileOutputStream` as a way to write an output stream of bytes to a file.

The `FileInputStream(String filename)` constructor creates an input stream to the file identified by `file name`. This constructor throws `FileNotFoundException` when the file doesn't exist, refers to a directory, or another related problem occurs. The `FileOutputStream(String filename)` constructor creates an output stream to the file identified by `file name`. It throws `FileNotFoundException` when the file exists but refers to a directory, doesn't exist and cannot be created, or another related problem occurs.

`FileInputStream` declares an `int read()` method to read one byte and return it as a 32-bit integer. This method returns -1 on end-of-file. `FileOutputStream` provides a `void write(int b)` method to write the byte in the lower 8 bits of b. Either method throws `IOException` when something goes wrong.

The bulk of the example is a `while` loop that repeatedly reads the next byte from the input stream and writes that byte to the output stream, until `read()` signals end-of-file.

Catch Blocks

A try block is often followed by one or more catch blocks that are designed to handle different kinds of exceptions. A catch block has the following syntax:

```
'catch' '(' throwableType throwableObject ')'
'{'
   // one or more statements that handle an exception
'}'
```

The catch block is similar to a constructor in that it has a parameter list and no return type. However, this list consists of only one parameter, which is a *throwableType* (Throwable or one of its subclasses) followed by a *throwableObject* identifier for an object of that type.

When an exception occurs, a throwable is created and thrown to the JVM, which searches for the closest catch block whose parameter type directly matches or is the supertype of the throwable. When it finds this block, the JVM passes the throwable to the parameter and executes the catch block's statements, which can interrogate the passed throwable and otherwise handle the exception. Consider the following example:

```
catch (FileNotFoundException fnfe)
{
   System.out.println(fnfe.getMessage());
}
```

This example (which extends the previous try block example) describes a catch block that catches and handles throwables of type FileNotFoundException. Only throwables matching this type or a subtype are caught by this block.

Suppose the FileInputStream(String filename) constructor throws FileNotFoundException. The JVM checks the catch block following try to see if its parameter type matches the throwable type. Detecting a match, the JVM passes the throwable's reference to fnfe and transfers execution to the block. The block responds by invoking getMessage() to retrieve the exception's message, which it then outputs.

A `catch` block might be unable to fully handle an exception – perhaps it needs to access information provided by some ancestor method in the method-call stack. If it can partly handle the exception, the `catch` block should conclude by rethrowing the exception so that an ancestor handler can finish handling it. Another possibility is to log the exception (for later analysis) and then rethrow it, which is demonstrated here:

```
catch (FileNotFoundException fnfe)
{
   logger.log(fnfe);
   throw fnfe;
}
```

Multiple Catch Blocks

You can specify multiple `catch` blocks after a `try` block. For example, consider this larger excerpt from the aforementioned Copy application:

```
FileInputStream fis = null;
FileOutputStream fos = null;
try
{
   fis = new FileInputStream(args[0]);
   fos = new FileOutputStream(args[1]);
   int c;
   while ((c = fis.read()) != -1)
      fos.write(c);
}
catch (FileNotFoundException fnfe)
{
   System.out.println(fnfe.getMessage());
}
catch (IOException ioe)
{
   System.out.println("I/O error: " + ioe.getMessage());
}
```

The first `catch` block handles `FileNotFoundExceptions` thrown from either constructor. The second `catch` block handles `IOExceptions` thrown from the `read()` and `write()` methods.

When specifying multiple `catch` blocks, don't specify a `catch` block with a supertype before a `catch` block with a subtype. For example, don't place `catch (IOException ioe)` before `catch (FileNotFoundException fnfe)`. If you do, the compiler will report an error because `catch (IOException ioe)` would also handle `FileNotFoundExceptions`, and `catch (FileNotFoundException fnfe)` would never have a chance to execute.

Caution   Don't specify multiple `catch` blocks with the same throwable type. For example, don't specify two `catch (IOException ioe) {}` blocks. Otherwise, the compiler reports an error.

JDK 7 made it possible to catch multiple exceptions in a single `catch` block. You specify a vertical bar-separated list of exception types and then specify the parameter name, which is `final` (you cannot assign any values to the parameter in the `catch` block). Consider the following example, where ex might contain a `FileNotFoundException` reference or an `IOException` reference:

```
catch (FileNotFoundException | IOException ex)
```

The Finally Block

Whether or not an exception is handled, you may need to perform cleanup tasks, such as closing an open file. Java provides the `finally` block for this purpose.

The `finally` block consists of keyword `finally` followed by a brace-delimited sequence of statements to execute. This syntax is expressed as follows:

```
'finally'
'{'
   // one or more statements that perform cleanup tasks
'}'
```

The `finally` block may appear after the final `catch` block or after the `try` block.

Cleaning Up in a Try-Catch-Finally Context

When resources must be cleaned up and an exception isn't being thrown out of a method, a `finally` block is placed after the final `catch` block. This is demonstrated by Listing 11-1, which presents the first version of the Copy application.

Listing 11-1. `Copy.java`

```java
import java.io.*;

public class Copy
{
   public static void main(String[] args)
   {
     FileInputStream fis = null;
     FileOutputStream fos = null;
     try
     {
        fis = new FileInputStream(args[0]);
        fos = new FileOutputStream(args[1]);
        int c;
        while ((c = fis.read()) != -1)
           fos.write(c);
     }
     catch (FileNotFoundException fnfe)
     {
        System.out.println(fnfe.getMessage());
     }
     catch (IOException ioe)
     {
        System.out.println("I/O error: " + ioe.getMessage());
     }
     finally
     {
        if (fis != null)
           try
           {
```

```
            fis.close();
        }
        catch (IOException ioe)
        {
            // ignore exception
        }
    if (fos != null)
        try
        {
            fos.close();
        }
        catch (IOException ioe)
        {
            // ignore exception
        }
        }
    }
}
```

If the try block executes without an exception, execution passes to the `finally` block to close the file input/output streams. If an exception is thrown, the `finally` block executes after the appropriate catch block.

FileInputStream and FileOutputStream inherit a void close() method that throws IOException when the stream cannot be closed. For this reason, I've wrapped each of fis.close(); and fos.close(); in a try block. I've left the associated catch block empty to illustrate the common mistake of ignoring an exception.

An empty catch block that's invoked with the appropriate throwable has no way to report the exception. You might waste a lot of time tracking down the exception's cause, only to discover that you could have detected it sooner if the empty catch block had reported the exception, even if only in a log.

Compile Listing 11-1 as follows:

```
javac Copy.java
```

Run the application as follows:

```
java Copy Copy.java Copy.bak
```

If all goes well, you should discover a Copy.bak file in the current directory whose size and content match Copy.java's size and content.

Cleaning Up in a Try-Finally Context

When resources must be cleaned up and an exception is being thrown out of a method, a finally block is placed after the try block: there are no catch blocks. Consider Listing 11-2, which presents a second version of the Copy application.

Listing 11-2. Copy.java (version 2)

```java
import java.io.*;

public class Copy
{
   public static void main(String[] args)
   {
      if (args.length != 2)
      {
         System.out.println("usage: java Copy srcfile dstfile");
         return;
      }
      try
      {
         copy(args[0], args[1]);
      }
      catch (IOException ioe)
      {
         System.out.println("I/O error: " + ioe.getMessage());
      }
   }

   static void copy(String srcFile, String dstFile) throws IOException
   {
      FileInputStream fis = null;
      FileOutputStream fos = null;
```

```
    try
    {
        fis = new FileInputStream(srcFile);
        fos = new FileOutputStream(dstFile);
        int c;
        while ((c = fis.read()) != -1)
            fos.write(c);
    }
    finally
    {
        if (fis != null)
            try
            {
                fis.close();
            }
            catch (IOException ioe)
            {
                System.out.println(ioe.getMessage());
            }
        if (fos != null)
            try
            {
                fos.close();
            }
            catch (IOException ioe)
            {
                System.out.println(ioe.getMessage());
            }
    }
}
```

The file-copying logic has been moved into a copy() method. This method is designed to report an exception to the caller, but it first closes each open file.

This method's throws clause lists only IOException. It isn't necessary to include FileNotFoundException because FileNotFoundException subclasses IOException.

CHAPTER 11   EXCEPTIONS AND ERRORS

Once again, the `finally` clause presents a lot of code just to close two files. In the next section, I'll present the `try-with-resources` statement, which obviates the need to explicitly close these files.

Compile Listing 11-2 as follows:

```
javac Copy.java
```

Run the application as follows:

```
java Copy Copy.java Copy.bak
```

If all goes well, you should discover a `Copy.bak` file in the current directory whose size and content match `Copy.java`'s size and content.

The Try-with-resources Statement

I mentioned earlier that resources (actually, the system resources on which they depend) are released in a `finally` block. This can lead to tedious-to-write boilerplate, such as the previously shown file-closing code.

Not only does this boilerplate code add bulk to a class file, the tedium in writing it might lead to a bug, perhaps even failing to close a file. JDK 7 introduced `try-with-resources` to overcome this problem.

The `try-with-resources` statement is similar to the `try` statement but lets you automatically close any open resources when execution leaves the `try` block. Examples include open files, database connections, network sockets, and other resources that depend on related system resources (such as file handles). It has the following syntax:

```
'try' '(' resource acquisitions ')'
'{'
   // resource usage
'}'
```

The `try` keyword is parameterized by a semicolon-separated list of resource-acquisition statements, where each statement acquires a resource. Each acquired resource is available to the `try` block and is automatically closed when execution leaves this body. Unlike a regular `try` statement, `try-with-resources` doesn't require `catch` blocks and/or a `finally` block to follow `try()`, although they can be specified. Consider the following file-oriented example:

```
try (FileInputStream fis = new FileInputStream("notes.txt"))
{
   // Do something with fis and the underlying file resource.
}
```

In this example, an input stream to an underlying file resource (notes.txt) is acquired. The try block does something with this resource, and the stream (and file) is closed upon exit from the try block.

Listing 11-3 improves on Listing 11-2's Copy application by using try-with-resources to automatically close open files and eliminate this boilerplate.

Listing 11-3. Copy.java (version 3)

```java
import java.io.FileInputStream;
import java.io.FileNotFoundException;
import java.io.FileOutputStream;
import java.io.IOException;

public class Copy
{
   public static void main(String[] args)
   {
      if (args.length != 2)
      {
         System.err.println("usage: java Copy srcfile dstfile");
         return;
      }
      try
      {
         copy(args[0], args[1]);
      }
      catch (IOException ioe)
      {
         System.err.println("I/O error: " + ioe.getMessage());
      }
   }
```

```
static void copy(String srcFile, String dstFile) throws IOException
{
    try (FileInputStream fis = new FileInputStream(srcFile);
         FileOutputStream fos = new FileOutputStream(dstFile))
    {
        int c;
        while ((c = fis.read()) != -1)
            fos.write(c);
    }
}
}
```

The copy() method uses try-with-resources to manage source and destination file resources. The round bracketed code following try attempts to create file input and output streams to these files. Assuming success, its body executes, copying the source file to the destination file.

Whether an exception is thrown or not, try-with-resources ensures that both files are closed when execution leaves the try block. Because the boilerplate file-closing code that was shown earlier isn't needed, Listing 11-3's copy() method is much simpler and easier to read.

Compile Listing 11-3 as follows:

```
javac Copy.java
```

Run the application as follows:

```
java Copy Copy.java Copy.bak
```

If all goes well, you should discover a Copy.bak file in the current directory whose size and content match Copy.java's size and content.

What's Next?

So far, our focus has been mainly on language syntax. In the rest of this book, we will focus mainly on APIs from Java's reference types library. Chapter 12 begins by looking at Math and related classes.

CHAPTER 12

Math, BigDecimal, and BigInteger

Mathematics operations are an important part of computing. You learned about basic math operators (such as addition and multiplication) in Chapter 3. Java also provides a Math class in the java.lang package, along with BigDecimal and BigInteger classes in the java.math package. This chapter introduces you to these classes.

Math

The Math class augments the basic math operators with useful static constants and methods. This section presents these constants and explores a few of these methods.

Note You might be interested in the companion java.lang.StrictMath class. StrictMath appears to be identical to Math but more strictly defines various math operations so that they are 100% portable from platform to platform. Check out Math's JDK documentation to learn more about StrictMath.

Java also provides the strictfp (strict floating-point) keyword to serve as a modifier for classes and methods. It was introduced in Java version 1.2 to restrict floating-point calculations and ensure the same result on every platform. However, it is no longer being used (see http://en.wikipedia.org/wiki/Strictfp).

© Jeff Friesen 2024
J. Friesen, *Learn Java Fundamentals*, https://doi.org/10.1007/979-8-8688-0351-2_12

Math Constants

JDK 21's Math class declares three constants:

- E: The double value that is closer than any other to e, the base of the natural logarithms.

- PI: The double value that is closer than any other to pi (π), the ratio of the circumference of a circle to its diameter.

- TAU: The double value that is closer than any other to tau (τ), the ratio of the circumference of a circle to its radius.

The PI constant is useful in calculating a circle's circumference and area. Listing 12-1 presents a Circle application that does just this.

Listing 12-1. Circle.java

```java
public class Circle
{
   public static void main(String[] args)
   {
      if (args.length != 1)
      {
         System.out.println("usage: java Circle diameter");
         return;
      }
      double diameter = Double.parseDouble(args[0]);
      System.out.println("Diameter: " + diameter);
      System.out.println("Circle area: " + Math.PI * diameter);
      double radius = diameter / 2;
      System.out.println("Circle circumference: " +
                         Math.PI * radius * radius);
   }
}
```

Circle takes a single command-line argument, which identifies the diameter of a circle. I leverage the java.lang.Double class's parseDouble() method to parse the string-based diameter to a double. The rest of Circle is self-explanatory.

Note   Double is an example of a *wrapper class* because a Double object wraps itself around a double-precision floating-point value. Additional examples of wrapper classes include Long, Character, and Float.

Wrapper classes convert primitive type-based values into objects that can be stored in container objects, such as objects created from the container types (ArrayList, TreeSet, HashMap, and so on) in Java's Collections Framework. For brevity, I have little to say about wrapper classes and don't discuss Java's Collections Framework in this book.

Double and the other wrapper classes also contain useful utility methods. Double's parseDouble() method is one example.

Compile Listing 12-1 as follows:

```
javac Circle.java
```

Run the resulting Circle.class application as follows:

```
java Circle 10
```

You should observe the following output:

```
Diameter: 10.0
Circle area: 31.41592653589793
Circle circumference: 78.53981633974483
```

Trigonometric Methods

Math declares several methods for carrying out operations related to trigonometry. Consider the following overloaded trigonometric methods for obtaining the cosine, sine, and tangent of an angle:

- double cos(double a)

- double sin(double a)

- double tan(double a)

For each method, the angle passed to a must be expressed in radians.

I've created a Graph application that demonstrates cos() and sin(). Graph displays a graph of cosine and sine waves on the console. Listing 12-2 presents its source code.

Listing 12-2. Graph.java

```java
public class Graph
{
   final static int ROWS = 27; // Must be odd
   final static int COLS = 50;

   public static void main(String[] args)
   {
      char[][] screen = new char[ROWS][COLS];
      double scaleX = COLS / 360.0;

      // Draw sine and cosine waves in buffer.

      for (int degree = 0; degree < 360; degree++)
      {
         int row = ROWS / 2 +
         (int) Math.round(ROWS / 2 * Math.sin(Math.toRadians(degree)));
         int col = (int) (degree * scaleX);
         screen[row][col] = 'S';
         row = ROWS / 2 +
         (int) Math.round(ROWS / 2 * Math.cos(Math.toRadians(degree)));
         screen[row][col] = (screen[row][col] == 'S') ? '*' : 'C';
      }

      // Draw axes in buffer.

      for (int i = 0; i < COLS; i++)
         screen[ROWS / 2][i] = '-';
      for (int i = 0; i < ROWS; i++)
         screen[i][0] = '|';

      // Draw buffer on screen.

      for (int row = ROWS - 1; row >= 0; row--)
      {
         for (int col = 0; col < COLS; col++)
```

```
            System.out.print(screen[row][col]);
         System.out.println();
      }
   }
}
```

Listing 12-2's Graph class first introduces constants COLS and ROWS, which specify the dimensions of the table that I use as an offscreen buffer for storing the graph. ROWS must be assigned an odd number; otherwise, java.lang.ArrayIndexOutOfBoundsException is thrown. The exception occurs when one of the row calculations produces a value that equals ROWS: row can only take on a value from 0 through ROWS - 1. Also, the graph looks better with an odd number of rows.

Note   Graph demonstrates the value in using constants wherever possible. The source code is easier to maintain because you only need to change the constant's value in one place instead of having to change each corresponding value throughout the source code.

The main() method first creates screen, a two-dimensional array that serves as an offscreen buffer for storing the graph. The graph is drawn in the buffer, which is later copied to the console because it's impossible to position the cursor on the console.

The main() method next calculates a horizontal scale value for scaling each of the sine and cosine waves horizontally so that 360 horizontal positions representing degrees fit into the number of columns specified by NCOLS.

Next, main() enters a for loop that, for each of the sine and cosine waves, creates (row, column) coordinates for each degree value and assigns a value to the screen array at those coordinates. The character is C for the cosine wave, S for the sine wave, and * for where the waves intersect.

The row calculation invokes Math's double toRadians(double angdeg) method to convert its angle argument from degrees to radians, which the sin() and cos() methods require. The value that these methods return ranges from -1 through 1 and is then multiplied by ROWS / 2 to scale this value to half the number of rows in the screen array.

After rounding the result to the nearest long integer via Math's long round(double a) method, main() converts this long integer to an int via the (int) cast. The int value is added to ROWS / 2 to offset the row coordinate so that it is relative to the array's middle row. The column calculation is simpler, multiplying the degree value by the horizontal scale factor.

Lastly, the main() method dumps the screen array to the console via a pair of nested for loops. The outer for loop inverts the array vertically so that it appears right side up – row number 0 should be output last.

Compile Listing 12-2 as follows:

```
javac Graph.java
```

Run the resulting Graph.class application class file as follows:

```
java Graph
```

You should observe the output shown in Figure 12-1.

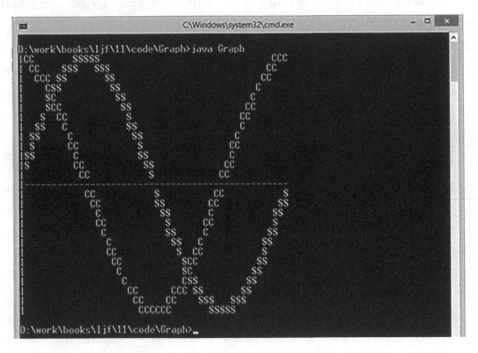

Figure 12-1. *The cosine and sine waves are 90 degrees out of phase with each other*

Random Number Generation

Math supports the generation of pseudorandom numbers via its double random() method. Each call to random() returns an algorithmically chosen double-precision floating-point number ranging from 0.0 to almost 1.0.

Note   Wikipedia's "Random number generator" topic (`http://en.wikipedia.org/wiki/Random_number_generation`) discusses random number generators and pseudorandom numbers in more detail. For convenience, I'll use the conventional term "random" in place of "pseudorandom."

Random number generation is important in computer games. For example, we can create a number-guessing game with `random()`. Check out Listing 12-3.

Listing 12-3. Guess.java

```java
import java.util.Scanner;

public class Guess
{
    public static void main(String[] args)
    {
        int answer = rnd(100) + 1;

        while (true)
        {
            System.out.print("Enter guess (1 - 100): ");

            int guess = new Scanner(System.in).nextInt();
            if (guess < answer)
            {
                System.out.println("Too low");
                continue;
            }
            else
            if (guess > answer)
            {
                System.out.println("Too high");
                continue;
            }
```

```
        else
        {
            System.out.println("Correct");
            break;
        }
    }
}

/*
    rnd() - Return random integer.

    Parameters:

    limit - Specifies the largest integer less 1 that
            may be returned. 0 is the smallest integer.

    Return:

    random integer from 0 through limit - 1.
*/

static int rnd(int limit)
{
    return (int) (Math.random() * limit);
}
}
```

Listing 12-3 presents the source code to a Guess application that generates a random integer between 1 and 100 and keeps prompting you to guess which integer has been generated. You are informed if you guess too low or too high. You are also informed if you are correct, and the program ends.

The following line will probably be confusing:

```
int guess = new Scanner(System.in).nextInt();
```

This line uses the java.util.Scanner class (from Java's reference types library) and its nextInt() method to obtain an integer from the user. The System.in argument specifies the console as the input source. (I won't discuss Scanner beyond this demonstration.)

Most important is the `rnd()` method and the `return (int) (Math.random() * limit);` statement. The `rnd()` method returns a randomly chosen integer ranging from 0 through `limit - 1`. For example, when passed `100`, `rnd()` returns a randomly chosen integer ranging from 0 through 99. This is why 1 is added to the result returned from `rnd()`.

The `return (int) (Math.random() * limit);` statement first obtains a random `double` from 0.0 to almost 1.0 via the `Math.random()` call and then multiplies this value by `limit`. The `(int)` cast chops off the fractional part as it casts from `double` to `int`. The resulting value is then returned to the caller via `return`.

Compile Listing 12-3 as follows:

```
javac Guess.java
```

Run the application as follows:

```
java Guess
```

Here is an example of one session with `Guess`:

```
Enter guess (1 - 100): 50
Too high
Enter guess (1 - 100): 25
Too high
Enter guess (1 - 100): 12
Too high
Enter guess (1 - 100): 6
Too high
Enter guess (1 - 100): 3
Correct
```

I used the Binary Search algorithm (see Chapter 5) to identify 3 as the correct number. In the guessing-game context, this algorithm works by selecting a value at the middle of the search space. If the guess is too high, the lower half of the search space is chosen for continuing the search. If the guess is too low, the higher half of the search space is chosen for continuing the search. This algorithm repeats in a recursive manner.

You can make this game much more interesting. For example, after the user guesses the correct number, the game could prompt the user to continue with another round (or not). After you learn more Java, you might add a timer facility so that the user must guess correctly within a time interval or lose the round (and not find out the number).

Math declares many additional methods. For example, the overloaded `abs()` methods let you obtain the absolute value of a number, the overloaded `max()` and `min()` methods let you obtain the maximum and minimum of two values, and `double sqrt(double a)` returns the square root of its argument. (The square root of a negative argument is NaN.)

BigDecimal

Many developers use the `double` and `float` types to represent monetary values. However, this approach is frowned upon. The problem is "`floats` and `doubles` cannot accurately represent the base 10 multiples that we use for money." I excerpted this answer from `http://stackoverflow.com/questions/3730019/why-not-use-double-or-float-to-represent-currency`, which goes on to develop the answer.

Developers also use the `int` and `long` types to represent monetary values that are expressed in pennies, but this approach is also problematic. In response to stackoverflow's "Why don't applications typically use `int` to internally represent currency values?" question (`http://stackoverflow.com/questions/5356123/why-dont-applications-typically-use-int-to-internally-represent-currency-values`), Matt explains:

"It does not make for simple coding. $1.10 translates to 110¢. Okay, but what about when you need to calculate tax (i.e., $1.10 * 4.225% -- Missouri's tax rate, which results in $0.046475)? To keep all money in whole numbers, you'd have to also convert the sales tax to a whole number (4225), which would require converting 110¢ further to 11000000. The math then can be 11000000 * 4225 / 100000 = 464750. This is a problem as now we have values in fractions of cents (11000000 and 464750, respectively). All this for the sake of storing money as whole numbers.

Therefore, it's easier to think and code in terms of the native currency. In the United States, this would be in dollars with the cents being a decimal fraction (i.e., $1.10). Coding such in terms of 110¢ isn't as natural. Using base-10 floating-point numbers (such as Java's `BigDecimal` and .NET's `Decimal`) is usually precise enough for currency values (compared to base-2 floating-point numbers like `Float` and `Double`)."

The `BigDecimal` class describes immutable, arbitrary precision signed decimal numbers. According to `BigDecimal`'s JDK documentation, "a `BigDecimal` consists of an arbitrary precision integer unscaled value and a 32-bit integer scale. If the scale is zero or positive, the scale is the number of digits to the right of the decimal point. If the scale is negative, the unscaled value of the number is multiplied by ten to the power of the negation of the scale. The value of the number represented by the BigDecimal [class] is therefore (unscaledValue × 10^{-scale})."

BigDecimal is ideal for performing calculations on money. Listing 12-4 presents the source code.

Listing 12-4. BDD.java

```java
// BigDecimal Demo

import java.math.BigDecimal;
import java.math.RoundingMode;

class BDD
{
   public static void main(String[] args)
   {
      BigDecimal purchaseAmount = new BigDecimal("586.32");
      BigDecimal pstRate = new BigDecimal("0.06");
      System.out.println("Purchase amount: " + purchaseAmount);
      System.out.println("PST rate: " + pstRate);

      // Calculate provincial sales tax on purchase.

      BigDecimal pst = purchaseAmount.multiply(pstRate);
      System.out.println("PST: " + pst);
      pst = pst.setScale(2, RoundingMode.HALF_UP);
      System.out.println("PST: " + pst);
   }
}
```

Listing 12-4 presents the source code to a simple application that demonstrates BigDecimal.

The main() method first invokes the BigDecimal(String val) constructor to construct a BigDecimal object representing a purchase amount of 586 dollars and 32 cents, followed by a BigDecimal object representing a provincial sales tax rate of 6% (I live in Canada).

This method then calls `System.out.println()` on each object to output its value (behind the scenes, `System.out.println()` invokes `BigDecimal`'s `toString()` method to convert the `BigDecimal` object to a string, which is then output).

At this point, `main()` invokes `BigDecimal`'s `BigDecimal multiply(BigDecimal multiplicand)` method to multiply the purchase amount by the PST rate. The returned `BigDecimal` object's reference is assigned to the `pst` local variable.

The returned `BigDecimal` object reveals four fraction digits for the cents. When dealing with money, we're accustomed to two fraction digits. We can achieve two fraction digits by invoking `BigDecimal`'s `BigDecimal setScale(int newScale, RoundingMode roundingMode)` method. The `main()` method invokes this method with 2 as the new scale (we want two fraction digits) and `RoundingMode.HALF_UP` as the rounding mode – half up is the rounding mode we learn in school.

Note   `RoundingMode` is an example of an *enum type*, which is a reference type consisting of named constants that are implemented as objects. I don't discuss enum types in this book because I don't consider it to be a fundamental feature.

Finally, `main()` outputs the rounded PST value.

Compile Listing 12-4 as follows:

```
javac BDD.java
```

Run the application as follows:

```
java BDD
```

You should observe the following output:

```
Purchase amount: 586.32
PST rate: 0.06
PST: 35.1792
PST: 35.18
```

BigInteger

The BigDecimal class uses the BigInteger class to represent the arbitrary precision integer unscaled value. As with BigDecimal, BigInteger objects are immutable – they cannot be changed. All operations behave as if BigIntegers were represented in two's-complement notation (like Java's primitive integer types).

BigInteger provides analogues to all of Java's primitive integer operators and all relevant methods from the Math class. Additionally, BigInteger provides operations for modular arithmetic, GCD (Greatest Common Divisor) calculation, primality testing, prime generation, bit manipulation, and a few other miscellaneous operations.

BigInteger is ideal for representing fantastically large integers such as what you find in astronomy, physics, and chemistry. For example, the *Avogadro constant* (the number of particles found in one mole of a substance) is $6.02214076 \times 10^{23}$. Also, the number of meters in 1,000,000 light years is $9.46052840500002 \times 10^{21}$. In contrast the largest positive integer that the long type can represent is just under 10^{19}.

I've created a simple application that demonstrates a portion of BigInteger. Listing 12-5 presents the source code.

Listing 12-5. BID.java

```
// BigInteger Demo

import java.math.BigInteger;

class BID
{
   public static void main(String[] args)
   {
      BigInteger bi1 = new BigInteger("100");
      BigInteger bi2 = new BigInteger("25");
      System.out.println("bi1 = " + bi1);
      System.out.println("bi2 = " + bi2);
      System.out.println("bi1 + bi2: " + bi1.add(bi2));
      System.out.println("bi1 - bi2: " + bi1.subtract(bi2));
      System.out.println("bi1 * bi2: " + bi1.multiply(bi2));
      System.out.println("bi1 / bi2: " + bi1.divide(bi2));
   }
}
```

Listing 12-5's main() method first invokes the BigInteger(String val) constructor to construct a pair of BigInteger objects. After outputting their values, it invokes BigInteger's BigInteger add(BigInteger val), BigInteger subtract(BigInteger val), BigInteger multiply(BigInteger val), and BigInteger divide(BigInteger val) methods to add val to the invoking BigInteger, to subtract val from the invoking BigInteger, to multiply the invoking BigInteger by val, and to divide the invoking BigInteger by val. In each case, a new BigInteger object is returned (as with BigDecimal objects, BigInteger objects cannot be changed – they are immutable). The results are output.

Compile Listing 12-5 as follows:

```
javac BID.java
```

Run the resulting application as follows:

```
java BID
```

You should observe the following output:

```
bi1 = 100
bi2 = 25
bi1 + bi2: 125
bi1 - bi2: 75
bi1 * bi2: 2500
bi1 / bi2: 4
```

What's Next?

Throughout this book, I've referred to strings and the java.lang.String class. Chapter 13 explores String as well as the related java.lang.StringBuffer class.

CHAPTER 13

String and StringBuffer

Chapter 1 briefly referred to the String type in the context of String[] args. This type showed up in subsequent chapters without a proper discussion. This chapter addresses this oversight by properly introducing you to String. It then introduces String's companion type: StringBuffer.

String

The java.lang.String class describes a *string*, which is a sequence of characters. You express a string literally by placing these characters between a pair of double quotes (e.g., "The quick brown fox jumps over the lazy dog.").

Creating Strings

String provides several constructors for creating a string. These constructors include String(char[] value), which creates a String object containing the characters in the value character array. The following code fragment demonstrates this constructor:

```
char[] c = new char[] { 'T', 'h', 'e', ' ', 'q', 'u', 'i', 'c', 'k', ' ',
                        'b', 'r', 'o', 'w', 'n', ' ', 'f', 'o', 'x', ' ',
                        'j', 'u', 'm', 'p', 's', ' ', 'o', 'v', 'e', 'r',
                        ' ', 't', 'h', 'e', ' ', 'l', 'a', 'z', 'y', ' ',
                        'd', 'o', 'g', '.' };
String s = new String(c); // Assign newly-created String object's
                             reference to s.
```

You might think that I should have used the String(String original) constructor, as in new String("The quick brown fox jumps over the lazy dog."). However, doing that would have been a mistake.

© Jeff Friesen 2024
J. Friesen, *Learn Java Fundamentals*, https://doi.org/10.1007/979-8-8688-0351-2_13

The argument passed to the constructor is another `String` object. When you invoke the constructor, you are making a copy of the argument – you now have a second `String` object.

Note   You might want to explore additional constructors for creating `String` objects. Check out the Java documentation for the JDK 21 reference types library's `String` class (http://docs.oracle.com/en/java/javase/20/docs/api/java.base/java/lang/String.html) to learn about these constructors as well as `String`'s methods.

It's much easier to create a `String` object by assigning a string literal to a `String` variable. The following example demonstrates:

```
String s = "The quick brown fox jumps over the lazy dog.";
```

This assignment takes advantage of *syntactic sugar* (syntax that makes the language sweeter to use) to create a `String` object more easily.

Comparing Strings

Another example of syntactic sugar that makes working with `String` much sweeter is string comparison via the == and != operators. For example, `System.out.println("abc" == "abc");` outputs `true` and `System.out.println("abc" != "Abc");` outputs `true`. This works because of interning, discussed later.

You cannot compare just any old strings. For example, you cannot compare a `String` object that is based on a string literal (again, check out my discussion on interning later in this chapter) with a `String` object that is based on a constructor. For example, `System.out.println("abc" == new String("abc"));` outputs `false`.

When it comes to `String` (and any type of object) comparisons, the == and != operators compare references. Because of interning where string literals are concerned, there is only a single `String` object. Comparing its reference with its reference produces a true result.

Comparison based on references results in a performance boost. It is faster to compare two objects via == and != than via an overloaded version of `java.lang.Object`'s `equals(Object obj)` method that compares their individual fields. (The `equals()` method defaults to using == for comparisons.)

`String`'s `equals(Object obj)` method compares this string to the specified object. The result is true if and only if the argument is not the null reference and is a `String` object that represents the same sequence of characters as this object. Otherwise, it returns false.

String also provides a boolean equalsIgnoreCase(String string) method that compares this string to the specified string. This method ignores case, which means that uppercase and lowercase letters are treated the same. For example, A and a are considered to be the same character for comparison purposes.

Note   Check out the documentation's coverage of the compareTo() and compareToIgnoreCase() methods, which also provide comparisons. Unlike equals() and equalsIgnoreCase(), they are designed for use in sorting applications.

Concatenating Strings

A third example of syntactic sugar is string concatenation via the + and += operators. In Chapter 3, I mentioned that + could be used to concatenate strings. However, I didn't mention that += could be used as well. I present an example of string concatenation via the + and += syntactic sugar:

```
String hello = "hello, ";
String world = "world";
String result = hello + world;
result += "!"; // equivalent to result = result + "!";
```

This example ends with result containing a reference to a String object containing hello, world!.

Exploring String Methods

String provides methods for performing operations on String objects. The following list samples these methods:

- char charAt(int index): Return the character at the specified index. The first character is located at index 0. If index is less than 0 or greater than or equal to the string's length, throw java.lang.IndexOutOfBoundsException.

- `int indexOf(String s)`: Return the position of the first occurrence of substring s in this string. Return -1 when not found.

- `int lastIndexOf(String s)`: Return the position of the last occurrence of substring s in this string. Return -1 when not found.

- `int length()`: Return the length of this string.

- `boolean endsWith(String suffix)`: Return true when this string ends with suffix; otherwise, return false.

- `String replace(char oldChar, char newChar)`: Return a new String object where all occurrences of oldChar have been replaced with newChar.

- `String replaceAll(String regex, String replacement)`: Return a new String object where each substring of this string that matches the regular expression identified by regex has been replaced with the replacement string. (Also known as a *regex* or *regexp*, a *regular expression* is a string-based pattern that represents the set of strings that match this pattern. I don't discuss regular expressions in this book because I don't consider them to be a fundamental feature.)

- `String replaceFirst(String regex, String replacement)`: Return a new String object where the first substring of this string that matches the regular expression identified by regex has been replaced with the replacement string.

- `boolean startsWith(String prefix)`: Return true when this string starts with prefix.

- `String toLowerCase()`: Return a new String object where all uppercase characters have been converted to lowercase.

- `String toUpperCase()`: Return a new String object where all lowercase characters have been converted to uppercase.

Listing 13-1 presents the source code to an SD (`String Demo`) application that demonstrates these methods.

Listing 13-1. `SD.java`

```java
public class SD
{
    public static void main(String[] args)
    {
        String s = "The quick brown fox jumped over the lazy dog.";
        for (int i = 0; i < s.length(); i++)
            System.out.print(s.charAt(i));
        System.out.println();
        System.out.println("Ends with 'dog.': " + s.endsWith("dog."));
        System.out.println("Ends with 'dog': " + s.endsWith("dog"));
        System.out.println("Starts with 'The': " + s.startsWith("The"));
        System.out.println("Starts with 'They': " + s.startsWith("They"));
        System.out.println("Index of 'he': " + s.indexOf("he"));
        System.out.println("Index of 'fix': " + s.indexOf("fix"));
        System.out.println("Last index of 'he': " + s.lastIndexOf("he"));
        System.out.println("Last index of 'fix': " + s.lastIndexOf("fix"));
        System.out.println("Replace spaces with dashes: " + s.replace(' ', '-'));
        String rep = "a";
        System.out.println("Replace all occurrences of 'the' (regardless of " +
                           "case) with " +
                           "'" + rep + "'" +
                           " (first '" + rep + "'" +
                           " is capitalized): " +
                           s.replaceAll("(?i)the", rep)
                            .replaceFirst("^[a-z]", rep.toUpperCase()));
        System.out.println("Lowercase: " + s.toLowerCase());
        System.out.println("Uppercase: " + s.toUpperCase());
    }
}
```

Compile Listing 13-1 as follows:

```
javac SD.java
```

Run the resulting SD.class application class file as follows:

```
java SD
```

You should observe the following output:

```
The quick brown fox jumped over the lazy dog.
Ends with 'dog.': true
Ends with 'dog': false
Starts with 'The': true
Starts with 'They': false
Index of 'he': 1
Index of 'fix': -1
Last index of 'he': 33
Last index of 'fix': -1
Replace spaces with dashes: The-quick-brown-fox-jumped-over-the-lazy-dog.
Replace all occurrences of 'the' (regardless of case) with 'a' (first 'a'
is capitalized): A quick brown fox jumped over a lazy dog.
Lowercase: the quick brown fox jumped over the lazy dog.
Uppercase: THE QUICK BROWN FOX JUMPED OVER THE LAZY DOG.
```

The s.replaceAll("(?i)the", rep).replaceFirst("^[a-z]", rep.toUpperCase()) expression deserves some explanation. For convenience, let's reduce the expression to *a.b.c*, where *a* represents s, *b* represents replaceAll("(?i)the", rep), and *c* represents replaceFirst("^[a-z]", rep.toUpperCase().

The member selection operator (.) has left-to-right associativity (see Chapter 3 for an introduction to associativity), which means that the expression evaluates as $(a.b).c$. Therefore, the compiler generates bytecode that first evaluates s.replaceAll("(?i) the", rep), which invokes the replaceAll() method on the String object reference stored in s.

The first argument passed to `replaceAll()` is `"(?i)the"`. The `(?i)` portion of this string enables case-insensitive matching. Following the `(?i)` noncapturing group (see `docs.oracle.com/javase/tutorial/essential/regex/groups.html`) is literal text sequence the. This sequence is searched for regardless of case (e.g., the, The, tHe, and so on would all match). The `replaceAll()` method returns a new `String` object with each case-insensitive occurrence of the replaced by the string represented by `rep`.

The bytecode next evaluates `replaceFirst("^[a-z]", rep.toUpperCase())` on the returned `String` object. The `"^[a-z]"` argument passed to `replaceFirst()` identifies the lowercase letter at the beginning of the string, and the `rep.toUpperCase()` argument converts the replacement character in `rep` to uppercase. The `replaceFirst()` method uses these arguments to replace the first letter in "a quick brown fox..." with A.

The string resulting from `replaceFirst()` is passed to `System.out.println()`, which outputs the string to the console.

Immutability and Interning

Three of the previously listed methods have `String` as their return type: `replace()`, `toLowerCase()`, and `toUpperCase()`. They appear to modify the current `String` object and return its reference, but this isn't the case. Instead, they create a new `String` object, extract the character array from the current `String` object, modify the contents of this array, then invoke the new `String` object's `String(char[] value)` constructor with the modified character array as its argument, and finally return a reference to the new `String` object.

Why do `replace()`, `toLowerCase()`, and `toUpperCase()` behave this way? `String` objects are *immutable* – they cannot be changed. When you invoke a method that appears to change the character array in the `String` object on which the method is invoked (also known as this `String` object), a new `String` object is created and populated with the modified character array, and its reference is returned.

Why are `String` objects immutable? There are several benefits, such as caching.

Java objects including constructor-created `String` objects are stored in a region of memory known as the *heap*. `String` objects that are based on string literals are stored in a special heap memory area known as the *string pool*. This caching process, known as *interning*, lets the Java Virtual Machine (JVM) optimize the amount of allocated memory by storing one copy of each literal string-based object in the pool.

Note   Some sources state that only string literals are stored in the string pool. I might be wrong that it is `String` objects containing the character sequences identified by these literals that are stored. Regardless, the point is the same. Strings are stored in the string pool.

Because of the close relationship between string literals and `String` objects, you can invoke `String` methods on a string literal. For example, you can specify `"abc".length()` to return the length of string `"abc"` or `"abc".charAt(1)` to return character b from `"abc"`.

Consider the following example:

```
static string FILENAME = "report.txt";
File file;
if ((file = open("report.txt", "r")) != null)
    processReport(file);
else
    error("unable to open file " + FILENAME);
```

This example first introduces a constant named `FILENAME` that stores the name of a file, which happens to be `report.txt`. It then presents a local variable named `file` (of some type named `File`). Moving on, the example attempts to open the file by calling an `open()` method with the name of the file and `r` (indicating that the file is to be read as opposed to being written or read and written).

If `open()` succeeds, it returns a reference to a `File` object, which is assigned to `file`; otherwise, it returns `null` to signify failure.

Assuming success, `open()` invokes the `processReport()` method with `file`'s value passed to this method as its only argument. If `open()` fails to open the file, it invokes the `error()` method with a message consisting of a string expression (string literal `"unable to open file "` followed by + [string concatenation operator] followed by the `FILENAME` constant).

There is a coding mistake in the example. The mistake is that a second copy of the `"report.txt"` string literal is present. The idea of using a `FILENAME` constant is to have the file name in one place so that it can be changed easily in one place. Without the constant, the programmer might forget to change all occurrences of the file name – it is a potential *bug* (defect) in the program.

The JVM ensures that there is only a single `"report.txt"`-based `String` object in the string pool. As a result, a potentially significant amount of heap memory is saved.

When you create a `String` object via a `String` constructor, this object is not interned. For example, if the string pool contains a `String` object containing `report.txt`, and you invoke `String s = new String("report.txt");`, a new `String` object containing `report.txt` in its internal character array will be created on the heap – the JVM will not place a reference to the string pool's `report.txt` `String` object in variable s.

However, if you would prefer to use the `String` object stored in the string pool, you can explicitly request this by invoking `String`'s `String intern()` method on this `String` object. Here is how you would do this:

```
String s = new String("report.txt").intern();
```

Now the reference assigned to s is the reference from the string pool.

Word Counting

To give you a more practical example of the `String` class, I've created a WC (Word Count) application that counts *words* (sequences of uppercase/lowercase alphabetic characters) read from the console. Listing 13-2 presents WC's source code.

Listing 13-2. `WC.java`

```java
public class WC
{
   public static void main(String[] args) throws java.io.IOException
   {
      int ch, nwords = 0;
      boolean isWord = false;

      while ((ch = System.in.read()) != -1)
      {
         if (!isalpha(ch))
            isWord = false;
         else
         if (!isWord)
         {
            isWord = true;
```

```
            ++nwords;
         }
      }
      System.out.println("Number of words: " + nwords);
   }

   static boolean isalpha(int ch)
   {
      return ((ch >= 'A' && ch <= 'Z') || (ch >= 'a' && ch <= 'z'));
   }
}
```

WC's `main()` method first introduces local variables ch (the next character read from the console), nwords (a count of words read from the console), and isWord (a Boolean flag – true when the start of a new word has been detected; otherwise, false). The nwords variable is initialized to 0, and isWord is initialized to false.

The `main()` method now enters a while loop, repeatedly invoking System.in.read() to read a character from the console, which is assigned to local variable ch. This method returns -1 when there is nothing left to read. (I'll properly introduce System.in.read() in Chapter 14.)

Each loop iteration invokes the `isalpha()` helper method to test the character in ch. If this character is alphabetic, true is returned; otherwise, false is returned.

Note   I've coded `isAlpha()` to assume English text. In an application designed to include a non-English audience, I would use the `java.lang.Character` class's `isAlpha()` method. However, I prefer to leave a discussion of Character to a different book.

If false is returned, the character in ch is not an alphabetic character, and false is assigned to isWord, which means that we are not in a word. Otherwise, an alphabetic character has been detected and the statement following else is executed.

The statement consists of a chained-if statement, which starts with if (!isWord). If isWord contains false, we execute the contents of the following block, which assigns true to isWord and increments nwords – main() has detected another word.

Once the while loop finishes, main() outputs the word count.

Compile Listing 13-2 as follows:

```
javac WC.java
```

Run the resulting application as follows:

```
java WC <WC.java
```

If you have never worked at the command line, the < symbol might look strange. Although I'll discuss working with the console more formally in Chapter 14, < is a redirection symbol for obtaining input from the file whose name follows < (WC.java, in this case) instead of from the console's keyboard (which is the default input source).

Assuming that WC.java hasn't been modified, you should observe the following output:

```
Number of words: 56
```

StringBuffer

The java.lang.StringBuffer class describes a *mutable* (changeable) sequence of characters. StringBuffer is similar to the String class, but unlike with a String object, a StringBuffer object's contents can be modified following the object's creation.

Like String, StringBuffer stores characters in an internal array. Unlike String, which cannot resize its array to make it larger, StringBuffer has this capability.

StringBuffer uses the concept of *capacity*, which is the maximum number of characters that can be stored before the internal array must be replaced with a larger array. When the length of the character sequence to be stored in the array exceeds the capacity, a new internal array is allocated and populated with the character sequence.

Creating String Buffers

StringBuffer provides several constructors for creating a string buffer. These constructors include the following trio:

- StringBuffer(): Construct a string buffer with no characters in it and an initial capacity of 16 characters.

- StringBuffer(int capacity): Construct a string buffer with no characters in it and an initial capacity set to the value passed to capacity.

- `StringBuffer(String s)`: Construct a string buffer initialized to the contents of the string whose reference is passed to s.

Be careful with `StringBuffer(int capacity)`. If you pass a negative integer to this constructor, it will throw a `java.lang.NegativeArraySizeException` object.

Note   You might want to explore additional constructors for creating `StringBuffer` objects. Check out the Java documentation for the JDK 21 reference types library's `StringBuffer` class (`http://docs.oracle.com/en/java/javase/21/docs/api/java.base/java/lang/StringBuffer.html`) to learn about these constructors as well as `StringBuffer`'s methods.

Exploring StringBuffer Methods

`StringBuffer` provides various methods, including the `append()` and `insert()` methods that are overloaded to accept any type of data (such as `int`, `char`, or `double`).

Each `append()` and `insert()` method first converts its data item to a string and then appends the string's characters to or inserts the string's characters into the string buffer. Each `append()` method always adds these characters at the end of the buffer; each `insert()` method adds the characters at a specified position.

A few additional methods are presented as follows:

- `int capacity()`: Return this string buffer's current capacity.

- `char charAt(int index)`: Return the `char` value from this string buffer at the specified `index`. An `IndexOutOfBoundsException` object is thrown when `index` is negative or greater than or equal to `length()`'s return value.

- `StringBuffer delete(int start, int end)`: Remove from this string buffer the characters from `start` to end - 1 (or the end of the string buffer when end is greater than or equal to the string buffer's length). No changes are made when `start` and end contain the same value. This method throws `java.lang.StringIndexOutOfBoundsException` when `start` is negative, greater than `length()`, or greater than end.

- `int indexOf(String s)`: Return the index of the first occurrence of substring `s` in this string buffer. Return -1 when there is no occurrence.

- `int lastIndexOf(String s)`: Return the index of the last occurrence of substring `s` in this string buffer. Return -1 when there is no occurrence.

- `int length()`: Return the length (number of stored characters) of this string buffer.

- `StringBuffer reverse()`: Replace this string buffer's character sequence with the reverse of this sequence. For example, if this string buffer contains ABC, replace it with CBA.

- `void setCharAt(int index, char ch)`: Set the character at the specified `index` to `ch`. Throw `IndexOutOfBoundsException` when `index` is negative or is greater than or equal to `length()`'s return value.

- `void setLength(int newLength)`: Set the length of this string buffer's character sequence. The sequence is changed to a new character sequence whose length is specified by `newLength`.

- `String substring(int start, int end)`: Return a new `String` object that contains a subsequence of the characters currently contained in this character sequence. The subsequence begins at `start` and continues to end - 1. This method throws `IndexOutOfBoundsException` when `start` or `end` is negative, end is greater than `length()`, or `start` is greater than `end`.

- `void trimToSize()`: Attempt to reduce the storage used for the character sequence. If the internal array is larger than necessary to hold its current sequence of characters, it may be resized to become more space efficient. Calling this method may, but is not required to, affect the value returned by a subsequent call to the `capacity()` method.

Listing 13-3 presents the source code to an SBD (`StringBuffer` Demo) application that demonstrates these methods.

Listing 13-3. SBD.java

```java
public class SBD
{
    public static void main(String[] args)
    {
        StringBuffer sb = new StringBuffer();

        System.out.println("Initial capacity: " + sb.capacity());
        System.out.println("Initial length: " + sb.length());

        System.out.println("Appending 'The quick brown fox jumped over " +
                           "the lazy dog.'");
        sb.append("The quick brown fox jumped over the lazy dog.");
        System.out.println("Capacity: " + sb.capacity());
        System.out.println("Length: " + sb.length());
        System.out.println("Current contents of string buffer (between [
        and ]):");
        System.out.print("[");
        for (int i = 0; i < sb.length(); i++)
            System.out.print(sb.charAt(i));
        System.out.println("]");

        System.out.println("Deleting characters from 3 through 8");
        sb.delete(3, 9);
        printSB(sb);

        System.out.println("Inserting 'quick ' at position 4");
        sb.insert(4, "quick ");
        printSB(sb);

        System.out.println("Index of 'dog': " + sb.indexOf("dog"));
        System.out.println("Index of 'dig': " + sb.indexOf("dig"));
        System.out.println("Last index of 'he': " + sb.lastIndexOf("he"));
        System.out.println("Last index of 'fix': " + sb.lastIndexOf("fix"));
        System.out.println("Reversing string buffer");
        sb.reverse();
        printSB(sb);
```

```
        System.out.println("Reversing string buffer");
        sb.reverse();
        printSB(sb);

        System.out.println("Changing length to 48");
        sb.setLength(48);
        printCapLenCon(sb);

        System.out.println("Extracting substring from 5 through 9");
        System.out.println("[" + sb.substring(5, 10) + "]");

        System.out.println("Trimming string buffer");
        sb.trimToSize();
        printCapLenCon(sb);

        System.out.println("Changing length to 15");
        sb.setLength(15);
        printCapLenCon(sb);
    }
    static void printCapLenCon(StringBuffer sb)
    {
        System.out.println("Capacity: " + sb.capacity());
        System.out.println("Length: " + sb.length());
        printSB(sb);
    }

    static void printSB(StringBuffer sb)
    {
        System.out.println("Current contents of string buffer:");
        System.out.print("[");
        System.out.print(sb);
        System.out.println("]");
    }
}
```

Compile Listing 13-3 as follows:

```
javac SBD.java
```

Run the resulting SBD.class application class file as follows:

```
java SBD
```

You should observe the following output:

```
Initial capacity: 16
Initial length: 0
Appending 'The quick brown fox jumped over the lazy dog.'
Capacity: 45
Length: 45
Current contents of string buffer (between [ and ]):
[The quick brown fox jumped over the lazy dog.]
Deleting characters from 3 through 8
Current contents of string buffer:
[The brown fox jumped over the lazy dog.]
Inserting 'quick ' at position 4
Current contents of string buffer:
[The quick brown fox jumped over the lazy dog.]
Index of 'dog': 41
Index of 'dig': -1
Last index of 'he': 33
Last index of 'fix': -1
Reversing string buffer
Current contents of string buffer:
[.god yzal eht revo depmuj xof nworb kciuq ehT]
Reversing string buffer
Current contents of string buffer:
[The quick brown fox jumped over the lazy dog.]
Changing length to 48
Capacity: 92
Length: 48
Current contents of string buffer:
[The quick brown fox jumped over the lazy dog.   ]
Extracting substring from 5 through 9
[uick ]
Trimming string buffer
```

```
Capacity: 48
Length: 48
Current contents of string buffer:
[The quick brown fox jumped over the lazy dog.    ]
Changing length to 15
Capacity: 48
Length: 15
Current contents of string buffer:
[The quick brown]
```

Text Reversal

To give you a more practical example of the StringBuffer class, I've created a TR (Text Reversal) application that reverses the sequence of words passed as arguments. Listing 13-4 presents TR's source code.

Listing 13-4. TR.java

```java
public class TR
{
   public static void main(String[] args)
   {
      if (args.length == 0)
      {
         System.out.println("usage: java TR sequence of words");
         return;
      }

      StringBuffer sb = new StringBuffer();
      for (int i = 0 ; i < args.length; i++)
         sb.append(args[i] + " ");

      System.out.println("Text: " + sb.toString());
      System.out.println("Reversed text: " + sb.reverse().toString());
   }
}
```

The main() method first verifies that at least one command-line argument has been specified. If not, a usage message is output.

Continuing, main() creates a StringBuffer object and then enters a for loop to append each command-line argument to the string buffer. It performs the append operation by invoking StringBuffer's append(String s) method, passing expression args[i] +" " to append().

Finally, main() outputs the text stored in the string buffer and, after invoking StringBuffer's reverse() method on the string buffer's contents, outputs the reversed string. In either case, StringBuffer's inherited (from Object) toString() method converts the string buffer's contents to a string.

Compile Listing 13-4 as follows:

```
javac TR.java
```

Run the resulting application as follows:

```
java TR The quick brown fox
```

You should observe the following output:

```
Text: The quick brown fox
Reversed text:  xof nworb kciuq ehT
```

What's Next?

Throughout this book, I've referred to the java.lang.System class in contexts such as System.out.println() and System.in.read(). Chapter 14 takes you on a tour of System where you learn about in, out, and much more.

CHAPTER 14

System

The java.lang.System class provides access to system-level capabilities such as array copying and virtual machine shutdown. This chapter introduces you to seven capabilities.

Note System is an example of a utility class because all of its methods and fields are declared `static`.

Array Copying

Chapter 5 introduced you to arrays. You learned that arrays have fixed sizes and also learned that to resize an array, you have to create a new array of the desired size, then copy the elements from the current array to the new array, and finally destroy the current array. (I'll talk about array destruction later in this chapter when I discuss garbage collection.)

Let's focus on resizing an array. Here is one way to accomplish this task:

```
int[] src = new int[] { 20, 30, 50 };
int[] dest = new int[10];
for (int i = 0; i < src.length; i++)
   dest[i] = src[i];
```

This code fragment first creates and initializes an src array of 32-bit integers. This array consists of three elements: 20, 30, and 50.

The fragment then creates a dest array of ints. This array consists of 10 elements that are each initialized (behind the scenes) to 0.

© Jeff Friesen 2024
J. Friesen, *Learn Java Fundamentals*, https://doi.org/10.1007/979-8-8688-0351-2_14

Finally, the fragment enters a for loop. This loop's header creates local variable i and initializes it to 0. It then compares i to src.length (the length of the src array). If i is less than src.length, the loop continues and the dest[i] = src[i]; assignment statement executes, copying src[i]'s integer to the equivalent dest[i] location. The end result for dest is 20, 30, 50, 0, 0, 0, 0, 0, 0, 0.

There is a faster way to perform an array copy: System's arraycopy() method. Here is the method's signature:

```
void arraycopy(Object src, int srcPos, Object dest, int destPos, int length)
```

The arraycopy() method copies the number of elements specified by length from the src array starting at zero-based offset srcPos into the dest array starting at zero-based offset destPos. This method throws java.lang.NullPointerException when src or dest contains the null reference, java.lang.ArrayIndexOutOfBoundsException when copying causes access to data outside array bounds, and java.lang. ArrayStoreException when an element in the src array could not be stored to the dest array because of a type mismatch.

Caution   It's easy to misspell arraycopy(). You might type an uppercase C instead of a lowercase c, which would ultimately result in a compiler error.

I've created an ArrayResize application that demonstrates traditional and arraycopy() techniques for copying an array. Listing 14-1 presents its source code.

Listing 14-1. ArrayResize.java

```
public class ArrayResize
{
   public static void main(String[] args)
   {
      int[] src = new int[] { 20, 30, 50 };
      int[] dest = new int[10];
      for (int i = 0; i < src.length; i++)
         dest[i] = src[i];
      dump(dest);
      int[] dest2 = new int[10];
      System.arraycopy(src, 0, dest2, 0, src.length);
```

```
    dump(dest2);
  }

  static void dump(int[] array)
  {
    for (int i = 0; i < array.length; i++)
      System.out.print(array[i] + " ");
    System.out.println();
  }
}
```

The source code presents main() and dump() utility methods. The main() method runs the application, and dump() is a helper method that exists to support main().

After creating src and dest, and after copying src to dest in the traditional manner, main() dumps dest to the console. It then creates dest2, a second destination array.

Continuing, main() executes System.arraycopy(src, 0, dest2, 0, src. length);. The first argument is a reference to the source array (src), and the third argument is a reference to the destination array (dest).

A 0 is passed as the second and fourth arguments. The first 0 is the starting index in src from where an int value is read. The second 0 is the starting index in dest to where the int value is written.

The final argument is the number of elements in the source array to be copied. This argument is obtained by executing src.length. If you recall, . is the member selection operator. It is accessing the read-only length member of the src array. Note that length is the only member of an array object.

Compile Listing 14-1 as follows:

```
javac ArrayResize.java
```

Run the resulting application as follows:

```
java ArrayResize
```

You should observe the following output:

```
20 30 50 0 0 0 0 0 0 0
20 30 50 0 0 0 0 0 0 0
```

The first line is the output from dest. The second line is the output from dest2.

Current Time and Nano Time

The `long` `currentTimeMillis()` method returns the current system time in milliseconds since January 1, 1970 00:00:00 UTC.

Note   UTC stands for Coordinated Universal Time (`http://en.wikipedia.org/wiki/Coordinated_Universal_Time`). Perhaps you were expecting the acronym to read CUT, but UTC is actually a compromise between CUT and the French version, TUC, which stands for Temps Universel Coordonné. Check out `www.space.com/what-is-utc.html` to learn more about UTC.

Perhaps you are curious about the January 1, 1970 00:00:00 portion of the previous date and time. Why does `currentTimeMillis()` return the time relative to that value? `http://kb.narrative.io/what-is-unix-time`, January 1st, 1970 at 00:00:00 UTC is referred to as the *Unix epoch*. Early Unix engineers picked that date arbitrarily because they needed to set a uniform date for the start of time, and New Year's Day, 1970, seemed most convenient.

By itself, the value returned from `currentTimeMillis()` is meaningless. Fortunately, you can convert the resulting long integer to a human-readable string by passing it to a `java.util.Date` constructor as follows:

```
String date = new Date(System.currentTimeMillis()).toString();
```

ABOUT THE DATE CLASS

JDK 1.0 (the first release of the Java Development Kit) introduced the `Date` class as a way to represent dates and times in a platform-independent manner. Problems with this class (including poor API design) led to JDK 8's introduction of the Date and Time API, which replaces `Date`. For this reason, much of `Date` has been deprecated. (I don't discuss Date and Time in this book because it's an advanced feature.)

One method that was not deprecated is `Date`'s `toString()` method, which returns a string representation of a `currentTimeMillis()` value. This representation adheres to the following format:

dow mon dd hh:mm:ss zzz yyyy

where

- **dow** is the day of the week (Sun, Mon, Tue, Wed, Thu, Fri, Sat).

- **mon** is the month (Jan, Feb, Mar, Apr, May, Jun, Jul, Aug, Sep, Oct, Nov, Dec).

- **dd** is the day of the month (01 through 31), as two decimal digits.

- **hh** is the hour of the day (00 through 23), as two decimal digits.

- **mm** is the minute within the hour (00 through 59), as two decimal digits.

- **ss** is the second within the minute (00 through 61), as two decimal digits.

- **zzz** is the time zone (and may reflect daylight saving time). Standard time zone abbreviations include those recognized by Date's parse(String s) method. If time zone information is not available, then **zzz** is empty: it consists of no characters.

- **yyyy** is the year, as four decimal digits.

I was curious about why the **ss** field's allowance of 60 and 61 and asked ChatGPT 3.5 about this anomaly: "Why does java.util.Date's toString method appear to allow 60 or 61 for a seconds value?" ChatGPT replied as follows:

"In Java, the java.util.Date class does not explicitly prevent you from setting a seconds value of 60 or 61. This behavior is a consequence of how java.util.Date is implemented.

java.util.Date represents a point in time as the number of milliseconds since the "epoch" (January 1, 1970, 00:00:00 GMT). It does not have separate fields for seconds, minutes, etc. When you set a value higher than 59 for seconds, Java automatically adjusts the minute and second components accordingly.

For example, if you set the seconds to 60, it will increment the minute by 1 and set the seconds to 0. Similarly, if you set the seconds to 61, it will increment the minute by 1 and set the seconds to 1.

This behavior is related to how leap seconds are handled. Leap seconds are added or subtracted from the Coordinated Universal Time (UTC) to account for irregularities in the Earth's rotation. In cases where a leap second is added, the seconds value in the java.util. Date object may momentarily reach 60 or 61.

However, it's important to note that not all Java platforms may handle leap seconds in the same way, and the behavior can depend on the underlying operating system and Java Virtual Machine (JVM) implementation.

For precise date and time handling, especially if you're working with scenarios that involve leap seconds, it's recommended to use the newer date and time API introduced in Java 8, which is part of the java.time package. Classes like LocalDateTime in java.time operate on a simplified model that does not have the same leap second behavior."

I can vouch for the correctness of this answer.

The long nanoTime() method returns the value of the JVM's high-resolution time source, which happens to be the most precise system timer. The value that this method returns represents the number of nanoseconds that have elapsed since some fixed but arbitrary origin time (perhaps in the future, so values may be negative). The same origin is used by all invocations of this method in an instance of a JVM; other virtual machine instances are likely to use a different origin.

Listing 14-2. TimeDemo.java

```java
public class TimeDemo
{
   public static void main(String[] args)
   {
      System.out.println("Number of milliseconds since midnight,
      January 1, " +
                      "1970 UTC: " +
                      System.currentTimeMillis());
      System.out.println("Number of milliseconds since midnight,
      January 1, " +
                      "1970 UTC in human-readable format: " +
                      new java.util.Date(System.currentTimeMillis()));
      System.out.println("Number of nanoseconds since some arbitrary
      origin " +
                      "time: " + System.nanoTime());
```

```
// Calculate how much time (in nanoseconds) it takes to calculate and
// output all of a circle's sine values in increments of 0.1 radians 100
// times:

long start = System.nanoTime();
for (int i = 0; i < 100; i++)
    for (double angle = 0; angle < Math.PI * 2; angle += 0.1)
        System.out.println(Math.sin(angle));
long end = System.nanoTime();
System.out.println("Elapsed time (in nanoseconds): " + (end - start + 1));
System.out.println("Elapsed time (in seconds): " +
                        ((end - start + 1) / (1000 * 1000 * 1000)));
    }
}
```

Listing 14-2's main() method first obtains and outputs the current time in milliseconds. It then obtains the current time in milliseconds, converts this time to a Date object, invokes the Date object's toString() method (behind the scenes) to convert this object to a string representation of the current time, concatenates this string to the string literal that is the left operand of the + operator – polymorphism makes this operator perform integer addition, floating-point addition, or string concatenation based on the types of its operands – and outputs the concatenated string via System.out. println().

The main() method next invokes System.nanoTime() to return the elapsed time in nanoseconds, which is output.

Finally, main() calculates how much time (in nanoseconds) it takes to calculate and output all of a circle's sine values in increments of 0.1 radians. It does so 100 times.

This calculation first obtains a start time, then performs the code to compute and output these sine values, and finally obtains an end time following the calculate/output logic. The start time is subtracted from the end time, and 1 is added to the result to obtain the elapsed time in nanoseconds. (Dividing the number of nanoseconds by one billion [1000 * 1000 * 1000] converts the value to number of seconds.)

Note   You'll often use logic like this when determining the frame rate in an animation (possibly a game). Check out Wikipedia's "Frame rate" topic (`http://en.wikipedia.org/wiki/Frame_rate`) to learn about frame rate.

Compile Listing 14-2 as follows:

```
javac TimeDemo.java
```

Run the application as follows:

```
java TimeDemo
```

You should observe output (abbreviated by omitting most of the sine values) that's similar to what is shown here – the time values will differ:

```
Number of milliseconds since midnight, January 1, 1970 UTC: 1695386074105
Number of milliseconds since midnight, January 1, 1970 UTC in human-
readable format: Fri Sep 22 07:34:34 CDT 2023
Number of nanoseconds since some arbitrary origin time: 423955941265551
0.0
0.09983341664682815
0.19866933079506122
0.2955202066613396
0.3894183423086505
0.479425538604203
...
-0.5506855425976414
-0.4646021794137613
-0.37387666483024096
-0.27941549819893097
-0.18216250427210112
-0.0830894028175026
Elapsed time (in nanoseconds): 189494701
Elapsed time (in seconds): 0
```

It looks like almost no time (in nanoseconds) or no time (in seconds) has passed. This isn't the case because I redirected the program's output to a file, which resulted in 0 seconds. Had I not performed this redirection, I would have seen (on my platform) an elapsed time of one or two seconds.

Garbage Collection

The void gc() method tells the JVM to expend effort toward recycling unused objects (including array objects) in order to make the memory they currently occupy available for reuse. When control returns from the method call, the JVM has made its best effort to reclaim space from all unused objects.

There is no guarantee that the JVM's effort will recycle any specific number of unused objects, reclaim any particular amount of space, or complete at any specific time (if at all) before the method returns (or ever).

Listing 14-3 presents the source code to an application that demonstrates gc().

Listing 14-3. GCDemo.java

```java
public class GCDemo
{
   public final static int MAXMB = 50;
   public final static int MAXTRIES = 1000;

   public static void main(String[] args)
   {
      class LargeObject
      {
         private byte[] memory = new byte[MAXMB * 1024 *1024]; // convert 50
                                                               // megabytes to
                                                               // bytes

         @Override
         public void finalize()
         {
            System.out.println("Large object has been finalized.");
         }
      }
```

```
LargeObject lo = new LargeObject();

// Prove that there is no garbage collection of lo-referenced LargeObject
// at this point.

System.out.println("Performing garbage collection before
assigning " +
                   "null to lo.");

for (int i = 0; i < MAXTRIES; i++)
   System.gc();

// Assign null to lo to disconnect object from variable and make it
// available for garbage collection.

System.out.println("Assigning null to lo.");

lo = null;

// Prove that there is garbage collection of lo-referenced LargeObject
// at this point. (You might have to assign a larger value to MAXTRIES
// to see this proof.)

System.out.println("Performing garbage collection after assigning " +
                   "null to lo.");

for (int i = 0; i < MAXTRIES; i++)
   System.gc();
   }
}
```

Listing 14-3's GCDemo class first declares a pair of constants that declares the maximum number of megabytes (MAXMB) and maximum number of tries (MAXTRIES). I'll introduce these constants later in this tour.

GCDemo next declares a LargeObject inner class. It is useful to make LargeObject an inner class because of its close relationship to GCDemo.

LargeObject declares a memory field and initializes it to a byte array whose size is MAXMB megabytes. It's useful to use a constant here in case I want to change the size later and don't want to waste time trying to track the place in the source code where 50 appears.

LargeObject also overrides the finalize() method that it inherits from Object. This method is invoked before the memory belonging to an object instantiated from LargeObject is reclaimed.

The finalize() method invokes System.out.println() with a message to alert the user that the object is just about dead.

At this point, GCDemo instantiates LargeObject and assigns its reference to local variable lo. It then outputs a message and makes MAXTRIES attempts to call the garbage collector via System.gc();. You won't see a message about the large object being finalized.

Another message is output about null being assigned to lo, and then this assignment takes place.

Finally, GCDemo outputs its final message (apart from the message output by LargeObject's finalize() method) and then makes MAXTRIES attempts to call the garbage collector. This time, you should see a message about the large object being finalized (you might have to increase the value assigned to MAXTRIES).

Compile GCDemo.java as follows:

```
javac GCDemo.java
```

Ignore the following compiler warning:

```
GCDemo.java:15: warning: [removal] finalize() in Object has been deprecated
and marked for removal
        public void finalize()
            ^
1 warning
```

Run the resulting application as follows:

```
java GCDemo
```

You should observe the following output:

```
Performing garbage collection before assigning null to lo.
Assigning null to lo.
Performing garbage collection after assigning null to lo.
Large object has been finalized.
```

Don't be surprised if you have to wait a while after the first "Performing" message is output and after the "Large object has been finalized." message. (It may take time before the garbage collector runs.)

Line Separator

The String lineSeparator() method returns the system-dependent line separator string. It always returns the same value, which is the initial value of the system property line.separator. (I explore system properties later in this chapter.)

On Linux/Unix operating systems, this method returns \n. On Microsoft Windows operating systems, it returns \r\n.

Tip   Use the string returned from lineSeparator() instead of hard-coding \r and/or \n in your source code to keep your application portable between Linux/Unix and Windows.

Listing 14-4 presents the source code to an application that obtains the line separator and prints it in decimal notation.

Listing 14-4. ShowLineSeparator.java

```java
public class ShowLineSeparator
{
    public static void main(String[] args)
    {
        String lineSeparator = System.lineSeparator();
        System.out.print("Line separator: ");
```

```
    for (int i = 0; i < lineSeparator.length(); i++)
       System.out.print((int) lineSeparator.charAt(i) + " ");
    System.out.println();
  }
}
```

ShowLineSeparator's main() method first invokes System.lineSeparator() to obtain the line separator string. It stores this string's reference in the lineSeparator local variable.

Next, main() outputs a label for the line separator string and then enters a for loop. This loop iterates over the length of the string, outputting a decimal integer for each string character.

The evaluation order for expression (int) lineSeparator.charAt(i) + " " is ((int) lineSeparator.charAt(i)) + " ". In other words, lineSeparator.charAt(i) is called to return a character, which is then cast to an integer. The integer is converted to a string via the string concatenation operator (+), and a space character is appended to this string.

Compile Listing 14-4 as follows:

```
javac ShowLineSeparator.java
```

Run the resulting application as follows:

```
java ShowLineSeparator
```

I observe the following output on my Windows platform:

```
Line separator: 13 10
```

Standard I/O

Standard I/O is a communications framework that connects a running program to its source of input via a byte stream (or channel, if you prefer). It also connects the program to its normal output and error output destinations.

Note   System declares in, out, and err class fields that connect a program to its input source, output destination, and error destination. The in field is of type java.io.InputStream; the out and err fields are of type java.io.PrintStream.

I won't be discussing InputStream and PrintStream in this book beyond what I present in this section. Instead, I refer you to my *Java I/O, NIO and NIO.2* book where I discuss these and other I/O-related types in more detail. (See www.amazon.ca/Java-NIO-NIO-2-JEFF-FRIESEN/dp/1484215664/ to obtain this book.)

I hope to update *Java I/O, NIO and NIO.2* and rename it to *Learn Java I/O, NIO and NIO.2* to make it part of a "Learn Java …" series.

Standard Input

A running program receives its input from *standard input*, which is an operating system mechanism that abstracts the input source. This mechanism defaults to a console's keyboard but can be *redirected* to a file or other output device.

Consider Chapter 13's WC application. It calls System.in.read() to read bytes from standard input. These bytes could come from the keyboard, a file, or some other source. The program doesn't know or care about the source. It just "sees" a stream of bytes and performs some action on them.

Note   Various character-encoding standards are used to encode characters. For example, ASCII (American Standard Code for Information Interchange – see http://en.wikipedia.org/wiki/ASCII) was the dominant character-encoding standard before Unicode (see en.wikipedia.org/wiki/Unicode) emerged.

ASCII uses seven bits of an 8-bit byte to encode a character. In contrast, Unicode originally used two bytes to encode a character (which is why Java's char type occupies 16 bits) but now uses up to four bytes. The java.lang.Character class compensates. (Check out http://docs.oracle.com/en/java/javase/21/docs/api/java.base/java/lang/Character.html for more information on Character.)

System.in refers to System's in class field, which is of type InputStream.

InputStream provides an int read() method that reads a byte from an input source and returns the byte as a 32-bit integer (int). It returns -1 when the end of the byte stream is reached. It throws java.io.IOException when an I/O error (such as an attempt to read from a file source that has been closed) occurs.

Suppose you run the WC application as follows:

```
java WC
```

In this execution, WC's input (via System.in.read() method calls) comes from the keyboard.

Standard I/O lets you redirect standard input from the console keyboard default to a file or another input source. To achieve this with WC, you would specify the < symbol followed by the name of the input source, as follows:

```
java WC <words.txt
```

Here, the input is coming from a file named words.txt.

Note   System provides the void setIn(InputStream in) method to redirect standard input to another stream. For example, System.setIn(new FileInputStream("words.txt")); is the equivalent of <words.txt.

The java.io.FileInputStream class lets you obtain input from a file. I don't discuss this class in this book.

Standard Output

A running program sends its non-error output to *standard output*, which is an operating system mechanism that abstracts the non-error output destination (also known as a *sink*). This mechanism defaults to a console's screen but can be redirected to a file or other output device.

Consider Chapter 13's WC application. It calls System.out.println() to write a string to standard output. This string is sent to a file or some other sink. The program doesn't know or care about the sink.

System.out refers to System's out class field, which is of type PrintStream.

PrintStream provides assorted print() and println() methods to write various types of data to a sink. For example, print(double d) writes a double-precision floating-point value, whereas println(String s) writes a string.

Note   The difference between print() and println() is that println() writes a newline character (expressed literally as \n) after writing its argument. The newline character causes the *cursor* (a movable indicator where input is entered or where output is sent) to be positioned at the start of the next input or output line. It is written as a platform-specific byte sequence, which is 13 followed by 10 on a Windows platform or 10 on a Unix/Linux platform.

You can write a blank line to separate lines of output by calling the System.out.println() method that takes no arguments. This method outputs the line separator that I mentioned earlier in this chapter.

Suppose you run the WC application as follows:

```
java WC
```

In this execution, WC's output is sent to the screen (via System.out.println() method calls).

Standard I/O lets you redirect standard output from the console screen default to a file or another output sink. To achieve this with WC, you would specify the > symbol followed by the name of the output sink, as follows:

```
java WC >stats.txt
```

Here, the output is going to a file named stats.txt.

Note   System provides the void setOut(PrintStream out) method to redirect standard output to another stream. For example, System.setOut(new FileOutputStream("stats.txt")); is the equivalent of >stats.txt.

The java.io.FileOutputStream class lets you send output to a file. I don't discuss this class in this book.

Formatted Output

The PrintStream class also provides the PrintStream printf(String format, Object... args) method to achieve formatted output.

Note JDK 5 introduced the printf() method, which is patterned after the C language's printf() function. Check out http://en.wikipedia.org/wiki/Printf to learn more about this function.

The printf() method's implementation works with the java.util.Formatter class (also introduced by JDK 5) to achieve formatted output. For this reason, printf() is an example of a *convenience method*.

The format argument identifies a format string that consists of literal text and format specifiers. Each format specifier begins with the % symbol and ends with a conversion letter. For example, %d indicates that a decimal integer is required. Also, %s indicates that a string is needed.

Note For more information about the format string and format specifiers, check out JDK 21's API documentation on the Formatter class (http://docs. oracle.com/en/java/javase/21/docs/api/java.base/java/util/Formatter.html).

The args argument is a varargs list of arguments. Each argument's type must be compatible with its matching format specifier.

Listing 14-5's FormattedOutputDemo application demonstrates formatted output.

Listing 14-5. FormattedOutputDemo.java

```java
public class FormattedOutputDemo
{
   public static void main(String[] args)
   {
      int i = 10;
```

```
        System.out.printf("i = [%d]%n", i);
        System.out.printf("i = [%5d]%n", i);
        System.out.printf("i = [%05d]%n", i);
        System.out.printf("i = [%-5d]%n", i);

        String s = "hello, world";

        System.out.printf("s = [%s]%n", s);
        System.out.printf("s = [%30s]%n", s);
    }
}
```

FormattedOutputDemo's main() method first declares local int variable i and initializes it to 10. It then executes System.out.printf() four times to demonstrate four ways to format this integer:

- System.out.printf("i = [%d]%n", i);: default format

- System.out.printf("i = [%5d]%n", i);: format in a five-character field with leading spaces

- System.out.printf("i = [%05d]%n", i);: format in a five-character field with leading zeroes

- System.out.printf("i = [%-5d]%n", i);: left format in a five-character field

In each case, the format string ends with %n. This format specifier indicates that a newline character is to be output.

main() next declares local String variable s and initializes it to "hello, world". It then executes System.out.printf() two times to demonstrate two ways to format this string:

- System.out.printf("s = [%s]%n", s);: default format

- System.out.printf("s = [%30s]%n", s);: format in a 30-character field with leading spaces

Compile Listing 14-5 as follows:

```
javac FormattedOutputDemo.java
```

Run the application as follows:

```
java FormattedOutputDemo
```

You should discover the following output:

```
i = [10]
i = [    10]
i = [00010]
i = [10    ]
s = [hello, world]
s = [                    hello, world]
```

Standard Error

A running program sends its error output to *standard error*, which is an operating system mechanism that abstracts the error output destination. This mechanism defaults to a console's screen but can be redirected to a file or another output device.

Consider Chapter 13's TR application. It calls `System.out.println()` to write a usage error message to standard output. Instead, it would be more appropriate to write this message to standard error in order to improve the organization of the program's output.

Note   Standard output lets you send non-error output to one destination, and standard error lets you send error output to another destination. This segregation helps you organize your output so you can focus on error messages without being sidetracked by non-error output.

`System.err` refers to `System`'s `err` class field, which is of type `PrintStream`. You can use `PrintStream`'s `print()` and `println()` methods to write various types of error-oriented data to a sink.

Suppose you create a new version of TR that replaces the following code fragment:

```
if (args.length == 0)
{
   System.out.println("usage: java TR sequence of words");
   return;
}
```

with:

```
if (args.length == 0)
{
    System.err.println("usage: java TR sequence of words");
    return;
}
```

I've bolded out and err so you can see what needs to change.

Compile and run TR as you did in Chapter 13. When you don't specify any command-line arguments, you'll notice the following error message:

```
usage: java TR sequence of words
```

If you try to redirect it to a file via the following command line:

```
java TR >out
```

you'll notice that out is empty.

However, if you try to redirect the error message to a file via the following command line:

```
java TR 2>out
```

you'll discover that the error message appears in the file.

The number 2 in 2>out identifies the standard error stream.

Note   System provides the void setErr(PrintStream out) method to redirect standard error output to another stream. For example, System. setErr(new FileOutputStream("out")); is the equivalent of 2>out.

System Properties

A *system property* is a key-value pair that provides current information about some aspect of the JVM's runtime environment. Several System methods and the java.util. Properties class facilitate working with system properties. Here are the methods that System provides:

- `String clearProperty(String key)`: Remove the system property identified by the specified key.

- `static Properties getProperties()`: Return the current set of system properties. If there is no current set of system properties, a set of system properties is first created and initialized.

- `static String getProperty(String key)`: Get the system property identified by the specified key.

- `static String getProperty(String key, String defaultValue)`: Get the system property identified by the specified key. If the system property isn't present, the string referenced by `defaultValue` is returned.

- `static void setProperties(Properties props)`: Set the system properties to the contents of `props`.

- `static String setProperty(String key, String value)`: Set the system property identified by the specified key to value. `System.setProperty()` only sets properties for the current runtime. Once the program exits, the properties are no longer set. If you need to persist properties across sessions, consider using properties-based configuration files (discussed shortly) or another form of persistent storage.

Caution   Regarding `setProperty()` **and** `setProperties()`, **changing a standard system property may have unpredictable results unless otherwise specified**. Property values may be cached during initialization or on first use. Setting a standard property after initialization using `getProperties()`, `setProperties(Properties)`, `setProperty(String, String)`, or `clearProperty(String)` may not have the desired effect.

Setting system properties can be useful in various configurations, but it's important to use them responsibly and ensure that they don't interfere with the JVM's or application's normal operation.

Listing 14-6's `PropertiesDemo` application demonstrates all of these methods.

Listing 14-6. `PropertiesDemo.java`

```java
import java.util.Properties;

public class PropertiesDemo
{
   public static void main(String[] args)
   {
      // Demonstrating setProperty(), getProperty(), and clearProperty().

      System.setProperty("temp.location", "C:\\temp");
      showProperty("Temporary Location before clear", "temp.location");
      System.clearProperty("temp.location");
      showProperty("Temporary Location after clear", "temp.location");

      // Demonstrating getProperties() and Properties.

      Properties properties = System.getProperties();
      showProperty("Java Version", properties.getProperty("java.version"));
      showProperty("OS Name", properties.getProperty("os.name"));
      showProperty("User's Home Directory", properties.getProperty("user.home"));
      System.out.println();
      properties.list(System.out);

      // More demonstrations of getProperty().

      showProperty("Java Version", "java.version");
      showProperty("OS Name", "os.name");
      showProperty("Java Class Path", "java.class.path");
      showProperty("Line Separator", "line.separator");
      showProperty("User's Account Name", "user.name");
      showProperty("User's Home Directory", "user.home");

      // Demonstrating setProperty().

      System.setProperty("someprop", "somevalue");
      showProperty("Some Property", "someprop");
```

```
    // Demonstrating setProperties().

    Properties newProperties = new Properties();
    newProperties.setProperty("someprop1", "somevalue1");
    newProperties.setProperty("someprop2", "somevalue2");
    System.setProperties(newProperties);
    showProperty("Some Property 1", "someprop1");
    showProperty("Some Property 2", "someprop2");
  }

  static void showProperty(String msg, String propertyName)
  {
    System.out.printf("%s: %s%n", msg, System.getProperty(propertyName));
  }
}
```

This listing should be fairly easy to follow. I created a showProperty() helper method to facilitate outputting a message and a property value.

Compile Listing 14-6 as follows:

```
javac PropertiesDemo.java
```

Run the resulting application as follows:

```
java PropertiesDemo
```

You should observe output that is similar to the following output:

```
Temporary Location before clear: C:\temp
Temporary Location after clear: null
Java Version: null
OS Name: null
User's Home Directory: null

-- listing properties --
java.specification.version=21
sun.cpu.isalist=amd64
sun.jnu.encoding=Cp1252
java.class.path=.
java.vm.vendor=Oracle Corporation
```

```
sun.arch.data.model=64
user.variant=
java.vendor.url=https://java.oracle.com/
java.vm.specification.version=21
os.name=Windows 8.1
sun.java.launcher=SUN_STANDARD
user.country=CA
sun.boot.library.path=C:\Program Files\Java\jdk-21\bin
sun.java.command=PropertiesDemo
jdk.debug=release
sun.cpu.endian=little
user.home=C:\Users\jeffrey
user.language=en
java.specification.vendor=Oracle Corporation
java.version.date=2023-10-17
java.home=C:\Program Files\Java\jdk-21
file.separator=\
java.vm.compressedOopsMode=Zero based
line.separator=

java.vm.specification.vendor=Oracle Corporation
java.specification.name=Java Platform API Specification
user.script=
sun.management.compiler=HotSpot 64-Bit Tiered Compilers
java.runtime.version=21.0.1+12-LTS-29
user.name=jeffrey
stdout.encoding=Cp1252
path.separator=;
os.version=6.3
java.runtime.name=Java(TM) SE Runtime Environment
file.encoding=UTF-8
java.vm.name=Java HotSpot(TM) 64-Bit Server VM
java.vendor.url.bug=https://bugreport.java.com/bugreport/
java.io.tmpdir=C:\Users\jeffrey\AppData\Local\Temp\
java.version=21.0.1
user.dir=D:\WRK\BOOKS\LJF\14\code\PropertiesDemo
```

```
os.arch=amd64
java.vm.specification.name=Java Virtual Machine Specification
sun.os.patch.level=
native.encoding=Cp1252
java.library.path=C:\Program Files\Java\jdk-21\bin;C:\W...
java.vm.info=mixed mode, sharing
stderr.encoding=cp850
java.vendor=Oracle Corporation
java.vm.version=21.0.1+12-LTS-29
sun.io.unicode.encoding=UnicodeLittle
java.class.version=65.0
Java Version: 21.0.1
OS Name: Windows 8.1
Java Class Path: .
Line Separator:

User's Account Name: jeffrey
User's Home Directory: C:\Users\jeffrey
Some Property: somevalue
Some Property 1: somevalue1
Some Property 2: somevalue2
```

The Properties Class

Java provides the Properties class to facilitate the management of an application's configuration data. It provides a simple way to manage key-value pairs, which makes it useful for maintaining application settings (such as a window's location and size – I don't discuss windows and other user interface concepts in this book), database connections (I don't discuss databases either), and other configurable items.

Understanding Properties

The Properties class extends the java.util.Hashtable class (I briefly mentioned hash tables, which are also known as hash maps, in Chapter 7), which supports key-value pair-based storage. However, Properties introduces some specific features tailored for managing configuration data.

Data Storage and Retrieval

Developers benefit from the simplicity of the Properties class. Data can be easily stored and retrieved using familiar syntax. Listing 14-6 provided an example. The following code fragment provides another:

```
Properties dbms = new Properties();

dbms.setProperty("database.url", "jdbc:mysql://localhost:3306/mydatabase");
dbms.setProperty("database.username", "myusername");
dbms.setProperty("database.password", "mypassword");

String url = dbms.getProperty("database.url");
String username = dbms.getProperty("database.username");
String password = dbms.getProperty("database.password");
```

This code fragment first instantiates Properties. In contrast, Listing 14-6 obtained a Properties object by calling System's getProperties() method.

The Properties object's reference is assigned to the dbms variable. (The name dbms is an acronym for database management system.) This reference is then used in three setProperty() calls to set three database-prefixed properties and three getProperty() calls to retrieve the property values, which are stored in other variables.

Properties Loading and Saving

The Properties class can also load a list of properties from and store a list of properties to files, which allows configuration data to be persisted. The following methods are used to accomplish these tasks:

- void load(Reader reader): Read a *property list* (a list of key/value pairs) from the input character stream (in a simple line-oriented format) to this Properties object.

- void store(Writer writer, String comments): Write the property: list in this Properties object to the output character stream in a format suitable for using the load(Reader) method.

Both methods refer to a character stream, which is similar to the byte stream discussed earlier but streams 16-bit characters instead of 8-bit bytes.

These methods are useful for scenarios where settings need to be modified without altering the source code. Consider the following code fragment:

```java
try (FileInputStream fis = new FileInputStream("config.properties"))
{
    dbms.load(fis);
}
catch (IOException ioe)
{
   ioe.printStackTrace();
}

try (FileOutputStream output = new FileOutputStream("config.properties"))
{
   dbms.store(output, "Updated Database Configuration");
}
catch (IOException ioe)
{
   ioe.printStackTrace();
}
```

This code fragment uses a pair of try-with-resources statements to handle IOExceptions, which can be thrown from the load() and store() methods.

These statements first create FileInputStream and FileOutputStream for connecting to a file named config.properties. The dbms-related properties list will be loaded from and stored to this file.

Note   I don't discuss FileInputStream and FileOutputStream any further in this book. You'll find complete coverage in my book, *Java I/O, NIO and NIO.2* (see www.amazon.ca/Java-NIO-NIO-2-JEFF-FRIESEN/dp/1484215664/ for more information about this book and to order a copy).

Virtual Machine Shutdown

System provides the void exit(int status) method to initiate the JVM's shutdown sequence. The argument passed to status is a code that provides information about the shutdown to a script (such as a Windows batch file) that can take appropriate action based on the code. By convention, a nonzero status code indicates abnormal termination.

SHUTDOWN SEQUENCE

The JVM initiates the *shutdown sequence* in response to one of several events, including when the System.exit() method is called for the first time.

At the beginning of the shutdown sequence, any registered shutdown hooks are started in an unspecified order. (See the java.lang.Runtime class for more information.)

The shutdown sequence finishes when all shutdown hooks have terminated. At this point, the JVM terminates.

Although I've previously used return to return execution from an application's main() method when the wrong number of command-line arguments is passed, I could use exit() when I need to pass a code to the caller. Here is an example:

```
public static void main(String[] args)
{
   if (args.length != 1)
   {
      System.err.println("usage: java SomeApp argument");
//      return;
      System.exit(1); // Indicate abnormal termination: wrong number of
                         arguments
   }
}
```

It's a good idea to use constants instead of hard-coding integer values such as 1. This is especially true when your application has multiple exit points (for different reasons). For example, I could declare the following constant:

```
public static final BAD_NUM_OF_ARGS = 1;
```

and later pass this constant to `exit()`, as follows:

```
System.exit(BAD_NUM_OF_ARGS);
```

The argument passed to `status` is a code that provides information about the shutdown to a script (such as a Windows batch file) that can take appropriate action based on the code. By convention, a nonzero status code indicates abnormal termination.

What's Next?

This concludes my book. I hope you enjoyed it. If you would like me to create a series of "Learn Java ..." books, let Apress (`www.apress.com`) know.

Check out the pair of appendixes that follow for quick references on reserved words (A) and operators (B). All the best in your Java career.

APPENDIX A

Reserved Words Quick Reference

Almost any valid identifier can be used to name a language feature. However, some identifiers are reserved for special use by Java. These reserved identifiers are known as *reserved words*. Figure A-1 reveals Java's 53 reserved words.

abstract	assert	boolean	break
byte	case	catch	char
class	const	continue	default
do	double	else	enum
extends	false	final	finally
float	for	goto	if
implements	import	instanceof	int
interface	long	native	new
null	package	private	protected
public	return	short	static
strictfp	super	switch	synchronized
this	throw	throws	transient
true	try	void	volatile
while			

Figure A-1. *The identifiers that Java reserves*

JDK 9 added a single underscore character (_) to Java's list of reserved words. It's an error to use a single underscore to name anything. However, it's okay to use multiple underscores (although you probably shouldn't).

Note   Most of Java's reserved words are also known as *keywords*. The three exceptions are `false`, `null`, and `true`. They are examples of *literals* (values expressed verbatim).

Also, `const` and `goto` are reserved by Java but are not used.

© Jeff Friesen 2024
J. Friesen, *Learn Java Fundamentals*, https://doi.org/10.1007/979-8-8688-0351-2

APPENDIX B

Operators Quick Reference

Table B-1 presents all of Java's operators in terms of their symbols, descriptions, precedences, and associativity.

Table B-1. *Java's Operators Grouped by Precedence*

Operator	Type	Precedence	Associativity
( )	Parentheses	15	Left to right
[ ]	Array index		
.	Member selection		
++	Unary post-increment	14	Right to left
--	Unary post-decrement		
++	Unary pre-increment	13	Right to left
--	Unary pre-decrement		
+	Unary plus		
-	Unary minus		
!	Unary logical negation		
~	Unary bitwise complement		
(*type*)	Unary type cast		
*	Multiplication	12	Left to right
/	Division		
%	Modulus		
+	Addition	11	Left to right
+	String concatenation		
-	Subtraction		

(*continued*)

© Jeff Friesen 2024
J. Friesen, *Learn Java Fundamentals*, https://doi.org/10.1007/979-8-8688-0351-2

Table B-1. (*continued*)

Operator	Type	Precedence	Associativity
<<	Bitwise left shift	10	Left to right
>>	Bitwise right shift with sign extension		
>>>	Bitwise right shift with zero extension		
<	Relational less than	9	Left to right
<=	Relational less than or equal to		
>	Relational greater than		
>=	Relational greater than or equal to		
instanceof	Relational type comparison for objects		
==	Is equal to	8	Left to right
!=	Is not equal to		
&	Bitwise AND	7	Left to right
^	Bitwise exclusive OR	6	Left to right
|	Bitwise inclusive OR	5	Left to right
&&	Logical AND	4	Left to right
||	Logical OR	3	Left to right
?:	Conditional	2	Right to left
=	Assignment	1	Right to left
+=	Addition assignment	1	Right to left
-=	Subtraction assignment	1	Right to left
*=	Multiplication assignment	1	Right to left
/=	Division assignment	1	Right to left
%=	Modulus assignment	1	Right to left
&=	Bitwise AND assignment	1	Right to left
^=	Bitwise exclusive OR assignment	1	Right to left
|=	Bitwise inclusive OR assignment	1	Right to left
<<=	Bitwise left shift assignment	1	Right to left
>>=	Bitwise signed right shift with sign extension assignment	1	Right to left
>>>=	Bitwise unsigned right shift with zero extension assignment	1	Right to left
		1	Right to left

Each row identifies one or more operators. These operators share the same *precedence*, which determines the grouping of operands with operators and decides how an expression will evaluate.

Operators with higher priority are evaluated first. The Precedence column reveals a number ranging from 1 through 15 that specifies the precedence of all operators in the intersecting table row. The higher this number, the higher the precedence. For example, multiplication's precedence (12) is greater than addition's precedence (11) because multiplication is performed before addition.

When generating bytecode for an expression that involves operators having the same precedence, the compiler has to determine which operator's bytecode to generate first. To accomplish this task, the compiler takes into account *associativity*, which determines how an expression is evaluated when it contains two or more operators with the same precedence.

For example, suppose the expression is 4 / 2 * 3. Because / and * have the same precedence, the compiler notes that the associativity is from left to right and generates bytecode to evaluate the expression as if it was (4 / 2) * 3. The result is 6.

Consider the expression x <<= x >>= 1. (Assume that x has been initialized to 5.) Because <<= and >>= have the same precedence, the compiler notes that the associativity is right to left and generates bytecode to evaluate the expression as if it was x <<= (x >>= 1). The result is 20.

Index

© Jeff Friesen 2024
J. Friesen, *Learn Java Fundamentals*, https://doi.org/10.1007/979-8-8688-0351-2

Printed in the United States
by Baker & Taylor Publisher Services